Anonymous

Donors

THE
MISSISSIPPI
RIVER
IN MAPS & VIEWS

St Paul, Minn.

THE MISSISSIPPI RIVER
IN MAPS & VIEWS

From Lake Itasca to the Gulf of Mexico

ROBERT A. HOLLAND

RIZZOLI
NEW YORK

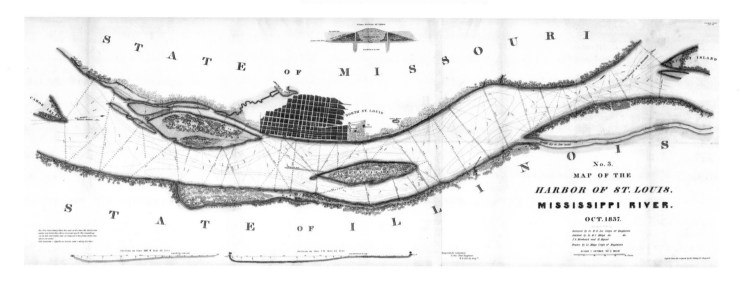

First published in the United States of America in 2008 by
RIZZOLI INTERNATIONAL PUBLICATIONS, INC.
300 Park Avenue South, New York, NY 10010
www.rizzoliusa.com

ISBN-13: 978-0-8478-3071-8
Library of Congress Control Number: 2008922996

Page 2: View of St. Paul, Minnesota (p. 216)
Page 4: No. 3 Map of the Harbor of St. Louis, Mississippi River, Oct. 1837 (p. 182)
Pages 6–7, 8–9, 10–11: Ribbon Map of the Father of Waters (p. 176)
Page 13: Fort Snelling (p. 134)

Designed by Aldo Sampieri

Distributed to the U.S. Trade by Random House, New York
Printed and bound in China

2008 2009 2010 2011 2012/ 10 9 8 7 6 5 4 3 2 1

CONTENTS

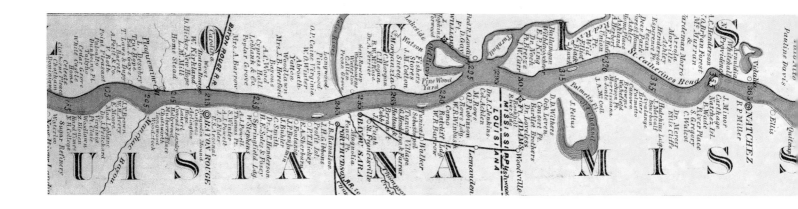

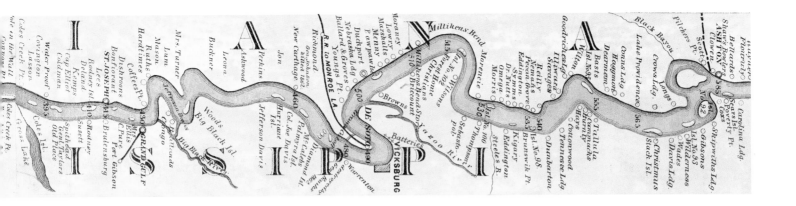

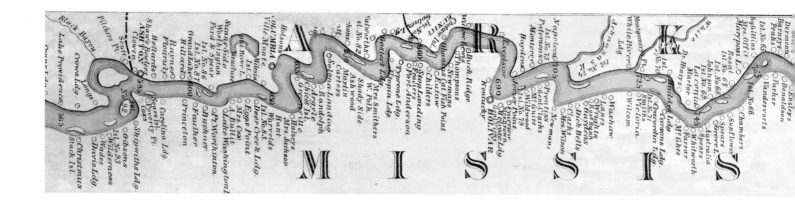

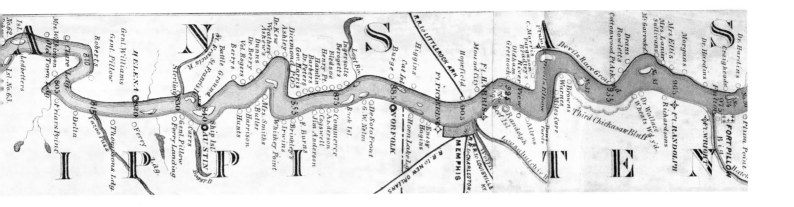

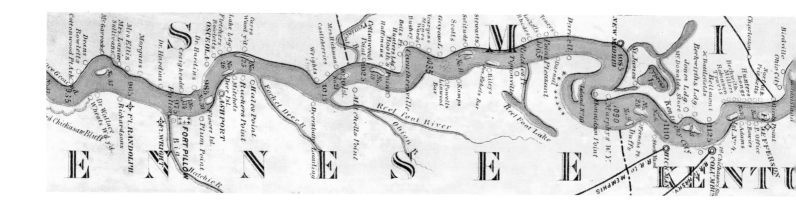

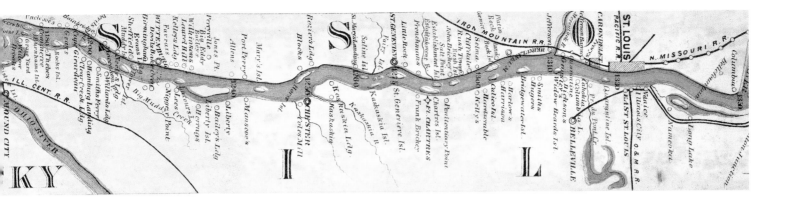

PREFACE

The term "Mississippi" comes from a word in the American Indian language of the Ojibwa that means "Great River." Coursing from Lake Itasca in northern Minnesota to the Gulf of Mexico, the Mississippi has played a prominent role in American history, commerce, agriculture, art, and literature. In the words of Mark Twain, it "is not a commonplace river, but on the contrary is in all ways remarkable."

This book conveys some of the history of the Great River in a novel way—through the use of maps. It begins with maps that illustrate the European discovery and exploration of the Mississippi and the subsequent colonization of the Great River's valley. Next are maps that attempt to fix two aspects of the geography of the Mississippi—the mouth of the Great River and its relation to the Gulf Coast, and the location of the river's source. In 1803 the Louisiana Purchase more than doubled the size of the United States, placing the Mississippi at the young country's western frontier. Cartographic depictions of the Purchase were soon to appear, several of which are included in a chapter of maps that documents the early efforts of the United States to explore and settle this newly acquired territory. Militarily, the Mississippi River has been the key to the control of the interior of the vast continent of North America, a reality clearly represented by the maps of several North American conflicts illustrated here. The chapter entitled "Commerce on the River" is comprised of charts that depict a time when the Mississippi was the country's main commercial thoroughfare. The Mississippi remains, of course, one of the world's most important commercial waterways; it is also one of the world's most intensely regulated rivers. Here the term "regulated" applies to rivers that are dammed and constrained, and efforts to maintain a navigable commercial channel in the Mississippi and to protect its valley from flooding are the subject of the chapter titled "Taming the Great River." The last chapter in this book contains a number of nineteenth-century views that artistically record the settlement of the banks of the Mississippi.

I have profited greatly from discussions with others concerning the structure and content of this work, and in particular I would like to acknowledge the help of George and Mary Ritzlin, Art Holzheimer, and Jerry Danzer. I would like to also thank my editor at Rizzoli, Douglas Curran, and the designer for Rizzoli, Aldo Sampieri, for their work on this project. My wife, Lori, provided invaluable editorial assistance. I should also acknowledge two works that I relied heavily upon in the production of this work: The Historic Collection of New Orleans's magnificent volume, *Charting Louisiana*, and John Reps' book of panoramic views entitled *Cities of the Mississippi*. Some of the people who have been instrumental in the acquisition of the images in this book include Carley Robison, Ruth Anderson, Bob Augustyn, Harry Newman, Yvonne Crumpler, Sally Stassi, John Magill, Lesley Martin, John Alderson, Helen Long, Melinda Shelton, Virginia Cooper, Steve Nielsen, Tom Brittnacher, Steve Zuppa, Thomas Lanham, Alain Morgat, Guilhem Laurent, Esperanza Adrados Villar, Andrew Knight, David Taylor, and Mark Lewis. Many of the maps presented here can be studied in more detail on-line, particularly those from the David Rumsey Collection and from the Library of Congress Collections.

CHAPTER 1

THE GREAT RIVER—EARLY MAPS OF DISCOVERY

Spanish Contact with the Mississippi

Although Hernando de Soto is popularly credited with the discovery of the Mississippi River in 1541, the Spanish had earlier contact with the Great River. In 1519, Alonso Álvarez de Pineda led an expedition in search of a strait connecting the Caribbean Sea to the Pacific Ocean. Álvarez de Pineda's voyage resulted in a crude sketch map that accurately outlined the Gulf of Mexico, demonstrating conclusively that there was no such passage. The Pineda chart properly situates Cuba and the Yucatán Peninsula, was the first dated map to name Florida, and depicts the mouth of a mighty river roughly at the present mouth of the Mississippi. The river was given the name Río del Espíritu Santo (River of the Holy Spirit) because it was on or about the feast day of Espíritu Santo (Pentecost) when Álvarez de Pineda chronicled its discharge.

The first map shown here accompanied a Latin translation of Hernán Cortés's second letter to the King of Spain, and hence is known as the Cortés Map. The earliest printed map to show the Gulf of Mexico, the Cortés Map was based on the Pineda chart and on the Álvarez de Pineda expedition's rutter—a written log of sailing directions and observations that would supply many of the names and coastal features to appear on maps for the next generation. Alongside this map of the gulf, which is oriented with the south at its top, is a fanciful plan of the Aztec capital Tenochtitlán (before Cortés orchestrated its destruction).

In some respects, the Cortés Map is less precise than the Pineda chart: the Yucatán Peninsula, for example, is shown as an island and the outline of Florida is not as well defined. In general, however, the conformity of the map to the actual coastline is admirable. The Río del Espíritu Santo is depicted with a large bay to the east of its entrance, and it is the sixth river east of the Río Pánuco, rather than the fifth as portrayed on the Pineda chart. This places the river over one hundred miles east of the Mississippi Delta, and with its twin forks some scholars have suggested that Río del Espíritu Santo signifies the Tombigbee and Alabama rivers emerging into Mobile Bay.

If so, the Cortés Map might illustrate an early confusion of the Mississippi River and Mobile Bay, both large sources of inland water that were evident from the sea. There is no scholarly consensus, however, as to which river the Espíritu Santo represents in early Spanish cartographic representations of the gulf. As noted above, some thinkers argue that it empties into Mobile Bay; others maintain that it empties into Galveston Bay, still others identify it as the Sabine River, and there are those who contend that it is the Mississippi. These matters aside, the Cortés Map would serve as a prototype for a long series of maps that portray a large river (usually labeled the Espíritu Santo) with its entrance bay at the center of the north side of the Gulf of Mexico and due north of the west coast of the Yucatán Peninsula.

Another early Spanish expedition that made contact with the Mississippi was led by Pánfilo de Narváez. With the permission of the Spanish crown, Narváez set out to explore and conquer the Spanish province from the Río de las Palmas (the Rio Grande) to Cape Florida. Putting ashore on the west coast of Florida in 1528, Narváez marched his soldiers up the Gulf Coast, reconnoitering and living off the land. After becoming separated from its transport ships, the expedition built barges near the shore of Apalachee Bay and put out to sea in an attempt to reach Mexico. They unsuccessfully attempted to enter the Mississippi, and the barges eventually became separated by currents and storms. Only four men survived the voyage, including Álvar Núñex Cabeza de Vaca, whose account of riches and maize in Florida piqued the interest of Hernando de Soto.

De Soto already had experience as a conquistador in the New World, serving both in Central America and in the Spanish conquest of Peru. In 1537 he was given the title of Governor of Cuba by the Spanish crown, and he set his sights on the North American mainland. Using Cuba as his supply base, his brutal plan was to proceed inland from the west coast of Florida, moving from local Indian chiefdom to chiefdom, taking chiefs hostage while he explored and lived off the land in search of gold, silver, and jewels.

De Soto landed near Tampa Bay in 1539, and after wintering at Anhaica Apalachee near modern-day Tallahassee, set out a three-year march that would take him halfway across the continent. Traveling on foot and by horseback, he and his men ventured north into the mountains of North Carolina before turning south into central Alabama. There they were attacked by the Tuscaloosa Indians at the battle of Mabila (near modern Montgomery), and de Soto lost many of his men. From Mabila, the party traveled northwest and wintered at Chicasa, located in northeastern Mississippi. Again facing attack, they moved on to Quizquiz (south of present-day Memphis), which the expedition's chronicler Luys Hernández de Biedma wrote, "was near the river of Espíritu Santo." Crossing the great river, the expedition journeyed through Arkansas and eastern Texas before returning to the Mississippi, where de Soto died on May 21, 1542. Instead of burial, de Soto's comrades cast his weighted body into the river that he discovered so that the surrounding Indians, whom de Soto had maltreated and intimidated, would not learn of his death. After searching for an overland route to Mexico, the remnants of de Soto's party subsequently made their way there by traveling down the Mississippi to the Gulf of Mexico under the direction of de Soto's successor as commander of the expedition, Luís de Moscoso.

Although they had not found material wealth, the surviving members of de Soto's expedition did return to Spain with valuable firsthand information of the land they traversed. Much of this information was included in Gacilaso de la Vega's *La Florida del Inca*, a 1605 publication that recounted the de Soto expedition. The expedition's observations of the region's terrain and inhabitants also appeared on the De Soto Map, a pen-and-ink sketch map drawn around 1544 and usually ascribed to the Spanish royal cartographer Alonso de Santa Cruz. Shown here, this map was very widely reproduced and was the first map to record de Soto's expedition across the Gulf's coastal plain; in fact,

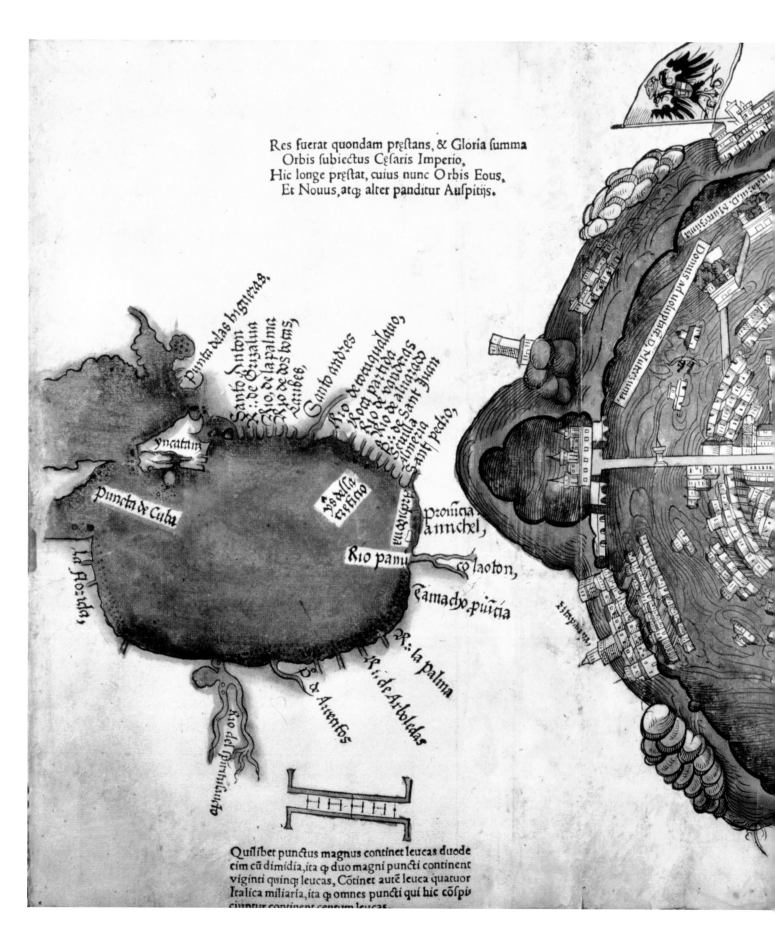

Res fuerat quondam prestans, & Gloria summa
Orbis subiectus Cesaris Imperio,
Hic longe prestat, cuius nunc Orbis Eous,
Et Nouus, atq; alter panditur Auspitijs.

Punta delas higueras,
Santo Anton
R. de Grizalua
Rio de la palma
Rio de dos bocas
Lacubes,
Santo andres
Rio de touqualquo
Boca partida
Rio de vandeas
Rio de almarias
Scitilla; de Sant Juan
Almeria
Sant pedro,

Yucatan

Puncta de Cuba

Ysdela cretino

La florida,

prouicia
annchel,

Rio panu

co laoton,

Tamacho puicia

R.: la Palma

B. de Arboledas

R: de Arboledas

B. de Arentos

Rio del spirihilauto

Quilibet punctus magnus continet leucas duode
cim cū dimidia, ita q; duo magni puncti continent
viginti quinq; leucas, Cōtinet autē leuca quatuor
Italica miliaria, ita q; omnes puncti qui hic cōspi-
ciuntur continent centum leucas.

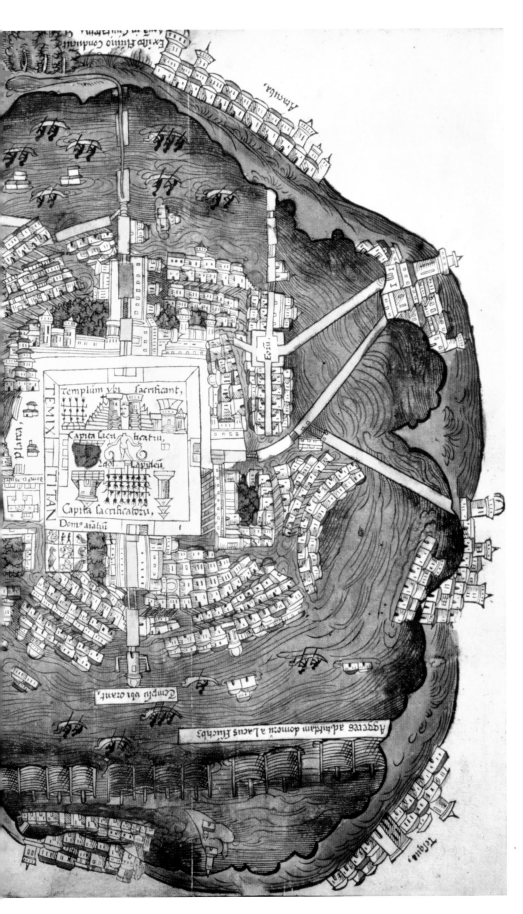

Title: [Map of the Northern Gulf of Mexico Coast]
Date Issued: 1524
Cartographer: Friedrich Peypus
Published: *Praeclara Ferdinãdi Cortesii de Nova Maris Oceani Hyspania narratio* (Nuremberg, Germany)
Woodcut, 12 x 18.1 inches
Newberry Library, VAULT folio Ayer 655.51 C8 1524 d, opposite signature A

it was the first map to depict the interior portion of southeastern North America. The most important features of this map are the detailed delineation of interior rivers that flow from a ring of mountains to the north (the Appalachians incorrectly oriented) and the site of various American Indian communities (especially on the map's western half). Much of this information was derived by the de Soto expedition from American Indian informants. Notable too is the Río del Espíritu Santo, which is now located well to the west of the center of the Gulf Coast, and is by far the largest of the rivers depicted, eventually curving away very far to the east. Although Moscoso had led the remnant of de Soto's force through the Mississippi's delta, there is no representation of the lower river on this map. The De Soto Map, with its network of rivers and a barrier of mountains to the north, as well as its placement of the mouth of the Espíritu Santo, would serve as a cartographic standard for 130 years. Entrenched in this tradition, rightly or wrongly, was the Biedma-Moscoso identification of the Mississippi River as the Río del Espíritu Santo.

The most disseminated map to follow the de Soto pattern was *La Florida*, the third map presented here. This map was published in the *Additamentum III* to the 1584 edition of Abraham Ortelius's *Theatrum Orbis Terrarum*, and is attributed to Gerónimo de

Title: *Mapa del Golfo y costa de la Nueva España desde el Río de Panuco hasta el Cabo de Santa Elena & De los Papeles que Traxeron*
Date Issued: 1544
Cartographer: Alonso de Santa Cruz
Published: Manuscript
Pen and ink, 7.9 x 10.6 inches
Archivo General de Indias, MP, Mexico, 1

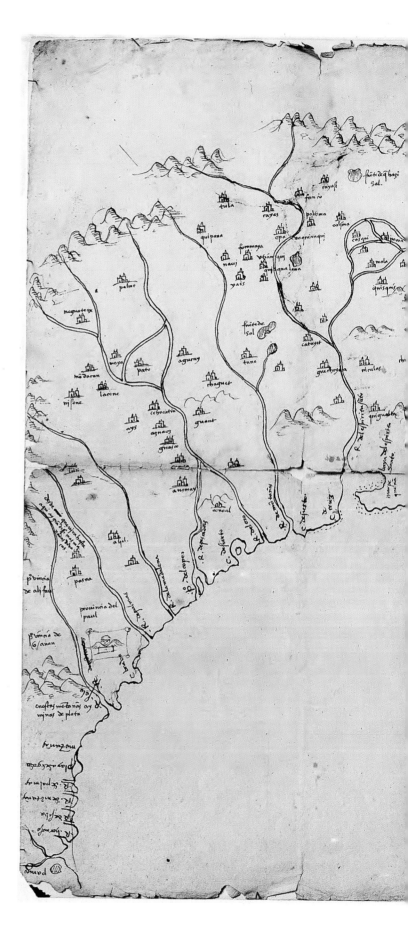

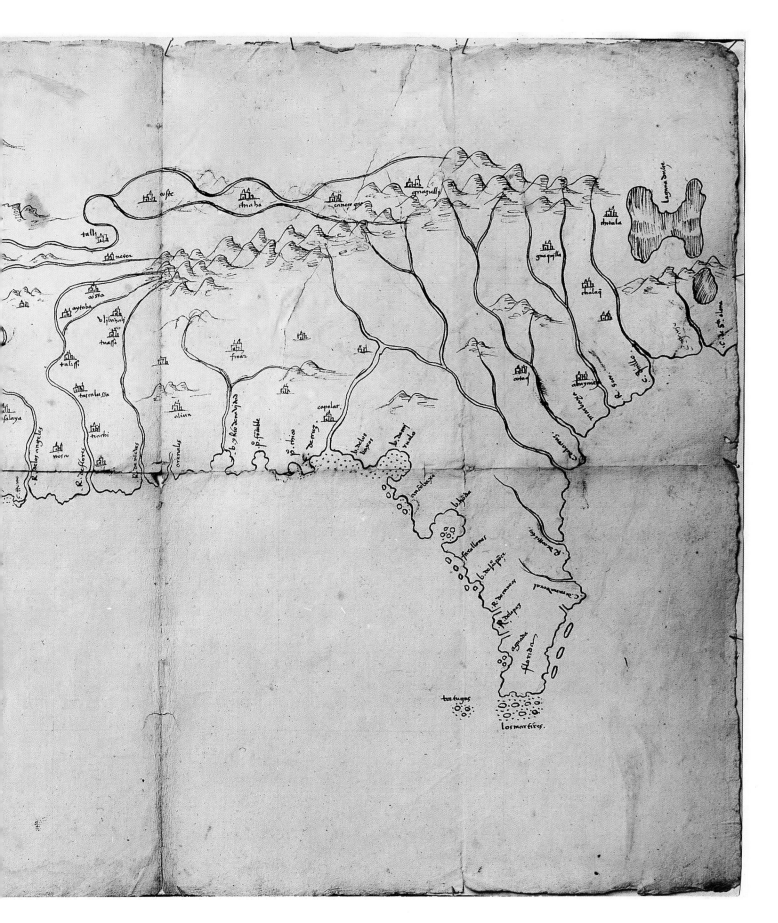

coste
ynaha
caneso qui
gnazully
dntala

talli
laguna dulce

neter

ausia
graprilla

aytaba
cholaq

bjibahali
tnassi

taliffi
finar
tasralussa

aliun
cotay

alaya
tiarbi
capalar
abaymad

nosso
demay

avendly
Rio dembiha
po table
p thos

b.dbaymeda
ancolaya
vitipa

facellones
b.nelipfe

R.derenas
R.deloses

laguna honda
tortugas
losmartires.

19

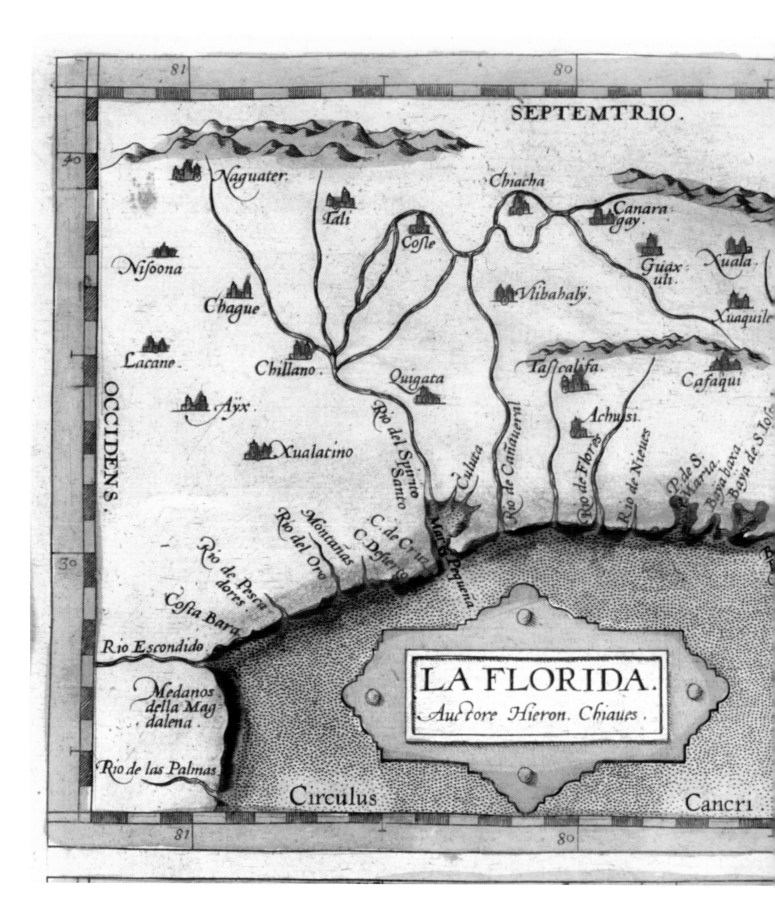

SEPTEMTRIO.

OCCIDENS.

Naguater.

Tali

Chiacha

Cofte

Canaragay.

Nifoona

Vlibahaly.

Guaxuli.

Xuala

Chague

Xuaquile

Tafcalifa.

Cafaqui

Lacane.

Chillano.

Quigata

Achufi.

Ayx.

Rio del Spirito Santo

Culuca

Rio de Cañaueral

Rio de Flores

Rio de Nieues

P. de S. Marria

Baya baxa

Baya de S. Iof

Xualatino

Montañas

C. de Cruz

C. Dfuergo

Rio del Oro

Marta Pequeña

Rio de Pescadores

Cofta Bara

Rio Escondido

Medanos della Magdalena.

Rio de las Palmas

Circulus

LA FLORIDA.
Auctore Hieron. Chiaues.

Cancri

Chaves, the Spanish royal cosmographer at the Casa de Contratación in Seville. The map is less detailed in its depiction of the interior American Indian settlements than the De Soto Map, and in fact, it denotes the American Indian communities quite differently. Thus, it is unlikely that the de Soto manuscript served as a reference for Chaves; rather, his map is based largely an account of de Soto's expedition given by Gonzalo de Oviedo. The Río del Espíritu Santo is shown entering the Gulf through *Mar Pequeña* and flowing down from sources arising in the east. It could be the case that the latter feature is a vague reflection of the Ohio River before its junction with the Mississippi.

La Florida is one of three maps printed on a single sheet in Ortelius's atlas, all by Spanish cartographers. It is remarkable that these maps appeared in such a widely distributed work, given that at the time Spain forbade the publication of maps. This is clearly evidence of Ortelius's wide range of contacts throughout Europe and his ability to obtain maps not available to others.

Title: *La Florida: Auctore Hieron, Chiaues, Cum Priuilegio*
Date Issued: 1584
Cartographer: Abraham Ortelius and Gerónimo de Chaves
Published: *Theatrum Orbis Terrarum. Additamentum III* (Antwerp, Netherlands)
Copperplate engraving, 6.1 x 8.9 inches
Newberry Library, VAULT oversize Ayer 135 .O7 1584

Jolliet and Marquette's Vision of the River

By the 1660s, French officials in Canada had begun to take note of a great river west and south of the Great Lakes. Canadian fur traders had been moving into this area in search of pelts (having overtaxed the beaver and other resources of the St. Lawrence River Valley, where they also faced competition from the Iroquois), and Jesuit missionaries soon followed. One of these missionaries was Father Claude-Jean Allouez, who in 1669 was engaged in evangelical labors along the Fox River in Wisconsin. From there he sent a dispatch to his superior stating that this "river leads by a six days' Voyage to the great River named Messi-Sipi." This letter, which was published in the *Jesuit Relations of 1669–70*, may have been the first mention in print of the Mississippi River by its present name.

Eager to seek out and exploit new economic resources, Canada's recently installed intendant, Jean Talon, sent Father Jacques Marquette and Louis Jolliet to explore the river and to determine where it led. Marquette had arrived in Canada in 1666, and Jolliet was a Canadian-born merchant and former Jesuit novice. For Father Marquette, the purpose of the expedition would be to "visit the nations who dwell along the Mississippi River" in hopes of furthering his missionary work. The French government, on the other hand, had more worldly ends in mind. There was some hope that the river would lead to the California Sea (and hence, serve as a passage to China); or, at the very least, that the river would lead to the riches found in the gold mines of New Mexico.

In May of 1673, the pair of explorers, along with five companions, set out in two canoes from the mission of Saint Ignace, which Marquette himself had founded, on the north shore of the Straits of Mackinac. They proceeded across the northern rim of Lake Michigan to the bottom of the protected Green Bay, and up the Fox River to a settlement of friendly Mascoutins and Miamis. From here they were guided to a portage over to the Wisconsin River, which would lead them directly to the Mississippi. They swiftly made their way downriver on the spring flood, mapping the mouths of the Missouri and Ohio rivers along the way. After reaching the mouth of the Arkansas River (at almost exactly thirty-four degrees north, and not far from where de Soto had died in 1542), they were advised by local American Indians that they were but five days from the sea (it was actually seven hundred miles), and that fierce armed warriors would be met along the way. The explorers surmised that these warriors might actually be Spanish soldiers, with whom France was currently at war; so, continuing on now carried the threat of capture by the Spanish. Marquette and Jolliet decided that they were satisfied with their great discovery—that the Mississippi flowed southward into the Gulf of Mexico, not eastward into the Atlantic near Virginia, nor westward into the California Sea—and resolved to make their return to Canada. On their return, they discovered a new route back to Lake Michigan along the Illinois and Des Plaines rivers, portaging to the Chicago River and the present-day site of Chicago. The following spring Jolliet returned to Montreal to report the expedition's findings to the new governor, Louis de Baude, comte de Frontenac. Unfortunately, his canoe overturned in the churning waters of the Sault Sainte Louis, and Jolliet lost all his records and maps; although he attempted to reconstruct this information from memory, much of it was lost.

The first map illustrated here summarizes Jolliet's recollection of the expedition's findings. Once thought to be one of Jolliet's original maps (closer inspection revealed that the handwriting and signature did not match), this map shows the Mississippi (named "Rivière de Baude," in honor of Frontenac) originating from three lakes well north of Lake Superior, curving slightly westward after its junction with the Arkansas, and emptying into the Gulf of Mexico (Le Sien de Mexique) in the northwestern third of the Gulf Coast. It also depicts two rivers entering the Mississippi from the west, and the cartouche contains a letter from Jolliet to Baude in which it is proposed that a river runs west from the Mississippi to the Mer Vermeille (Gulf of California). Jolliet locates iron ore deposits below a large river named "Ouabouskigou," a name that the French changed to Ouabache, and that the English then rendered Wabash. Here the term refers to the Ohio River, and not the modern Wabash.

Marquette also drew a map (1673–74) that shows the explorer's outbound and homeward routes, including the Mississippi as far south as the Arkansas River; it was the first map to depict Lake Winnebago, the Wisconsin and Illinois rivers, and the mouths of the Missouri and Ohio rivers. This map, along with Jolliet's map (next pages) would form the basis for an early model of the Mississippi River. This representation depicts the river running north and south and emptying into the Gulf of Mexico at approximately the same place as the old Río del Espíritu Santo and its bay; it details only the northern half of the river. The second map shown here, which was the first printed map to depict the Jolliet-Marquette discoveries, is an example of this type. Published in Melchisédech Thévenot's book, *Recueil de Voyages de Mr Thévenot*, Estienne Michallete's *Carte de la decouverte faite l'an 1665[sic; 1673] dans l'Amerique Septentrionale* was the first printed map of the Great River, and contains the first printed use of the names "Mitchisipi" and "Lake Michigan." (North is oriented to the right on this map.) As on Jolliet's manuscript map, the Mississippi curves slightly westward and there is no bay at the mouth of the river; however, the middle third of the river is shown to be much straighter than on the Jolliet map. There is a manuscript map in the Bibliothèque Nationale de France, that is almost identical to this printed map, and it may be the map from which the Michallete-Thévenot map is derived.

The almost straight-line depiction of the river on these maps is understandable if one keeps in mind that they were conceived by individuals working their way down the river from the Great Lakes. In this sense, they are akin to Native American cartographic traditions, which focus on itinerary and not on exact topography. Thus, one finds an emphasis on distinguishing landmarks, such river junctions and falls, as well as the relationship of these to Indian villages and easily discernable geographic features such as mineral deposits and lakes.

The next map is a variant of the Michallete-Thévenot map, and was published in Father Louis Hennepin's memoir of his 1680–81 travels. Father Hennepin was a Flemish recollect missionary who came to New France (Canada) in 1675. In 1678, he and René Robert Cavalier, sieur de La Salle, set out from Lake Ontario to prepare for a trip down the Mississippi River, which La Salle planned to make the backbone of a vast commercial empire. They traveled independently at first, and early in his journey Hennepin passed by Niagara Falls; he would become the first European to produce a written description of that awesome sight. In 1680, La Salle sent Hennepin and two other men on an expedition up the Mississippi: they were to explore as far as possible by canoe, making contact with Indians along the way, and to determine whether sailing vessels could be used for trade upriver. As Hennepin and his companions traveled northward, they were captured by a band of Dakota and not released until the following year. On an excursion with his captors, Hennepin observed an impressive falls in the river at the present-day site of Minneapolis; he named them the Falls of St. Anthony, after his patron saint St. Anthony of Padua.

Hennepin returned to France in 1681, and two years later published a book about his explorations entitled *Description de la Louisiane*. This book would become one of the most popular travelogues of North America published in the late seventeenth century, and it included the continental map shown here, *Carte de la Nouvelle France et de la Louisiane*

Title: *Nouvelle Decouverte de plusieurs Nations Dans la Nouvelle France En l'annee* 1673 *et* 1674
Date Issued: 1674
Cartographer: Louis Jolliet
Published: Manuscript
Pen and ink and watercolor, 26 x 33.9 inches
The John Carter Brown Library at Brown University, Cabinet B674 / 1 Ms

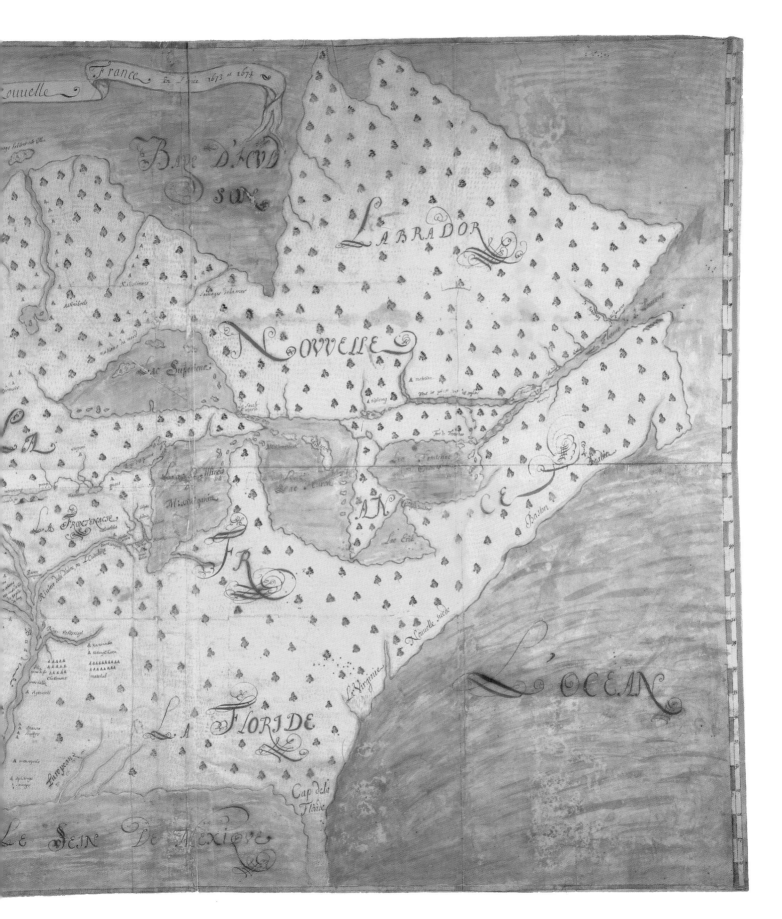

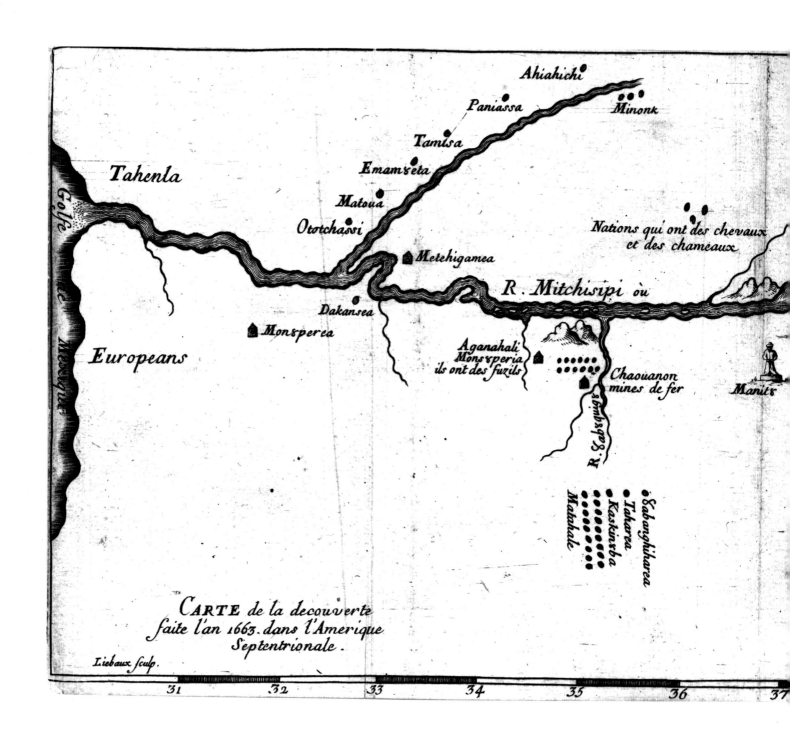

Tahenla

Golfe de Mexique

Europeans

Ahiahichi

Paniassa

Minonk

Tamisa

Emamseta

Matoua

Ototchassi

Nations qui ont des chevaux
et des chameaux

Metehigamea

R. Mitchisipi ou

Dakansea

Monsperea

Aganahali
Monsperia
ils ont des fuzils

Chaouanon
mines de fer

Manit's

R. Sasqbeg

Sabanghiharea
Tahasea
Kaskinsba
Matahali

CARTE de la decouverte
faite l'an 1663. dans l'Amerique
Septentrionale.

Liebaux sculp.

31   32   33   34   35   36   37

Title: *Carte de la decouverte faite l'an 1665 dans*
l'Amerique Septentrionale
Date Issued: 1681
Cartographer: Estienne Michallete
Published: *Recueil de Voyages de Mr. Thévenot* (Paris)
Copperplate engraving, 65 x 15.7 inches
Library and Archives of Canada, NMC-15380

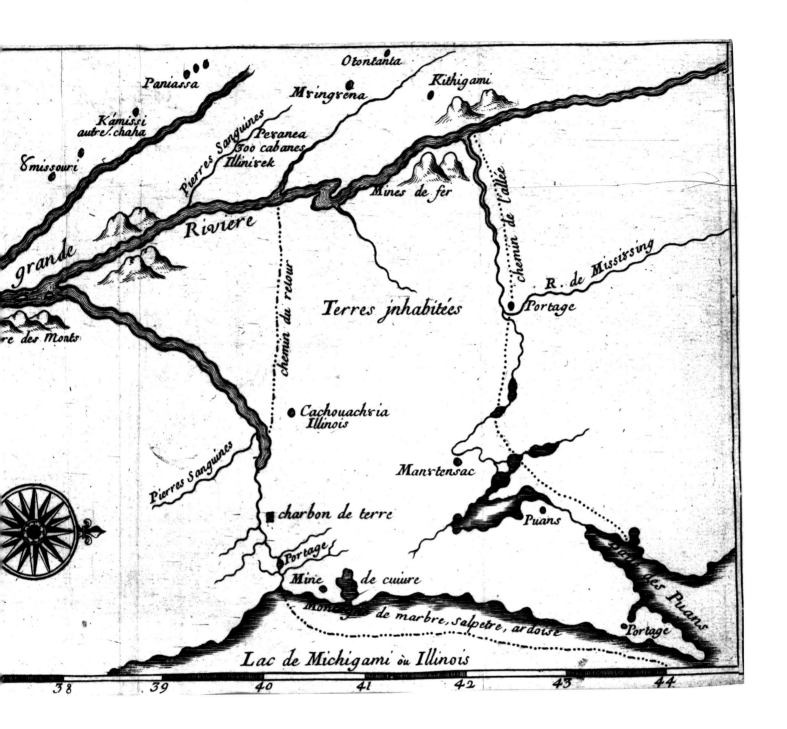

Otontanta

Paniassa

Mringrena

Kithigami

Kamissi
autre s. chaha

Pierres Sanguines

Pesanea
300 cabanes
Illinisek

8missouri

Mines de fer

Riviere

chemin de l'vallée

grande

R. de Misissing

re des Monts

Portage

Terres jnhabitées

chemin du retour

Cachouachria
Illinois

Manrtensac

Pierres Sanguines

charbon de terre

Puans

Portage

Mine de cuivre

Montagnes de marbre, salpetre, ardoise

Fleuve des Puans

Portage

Lac de Michigami ou Illinois

38   39   40   41   42   43   44

Nouvellement découverte. This map, which incorporates the northern part of the Michallete-Thévenot map, was the first printed map to use the name *"La Louisiane"* and to show the Falls of St. Anthony (Sault de St. Antoine de Padoü) and Lake Pepin (Lac de Pleurs, or Lake of Tears). The Mississippi (here called R. Colbert in honor of Jean-Baptiste Colbert, the French comptroller general of finances) is depicted as running due south as far as the Arkansas River (Mission des Recollets), and from there a dotted line extends the river in a slight southeasterly direction to a small sea along the coast. The map's impressive cartouche, which employs Christian and classical allegorical figures around the title, was engraved by Nicolas Guerard.

As the lower Mississippi was increasingly traveled by explorers more and more in touch with local Indians, the "fish-spine" representation of the river seen next began to appear. Such drawings are attributed to Henri de Tonti, another confederate of La Salle, who at the time of this map was the most experienced European Mississippi traveler. Similar drawings were made by those whom Tonti escorted down the river, including this one by Jacques Bureau. Again the emphasis is on the depiction of a route and not on exact topography. Thus, for example, the mouth of the Mississippi is schematized as straight against an east-west shore—a practice typical of Indian maps—

Title: *Carte de la Nouvelle France et de la Louisiane Nouvellement decouverte dediée Au Roy l'An 1685*
Date Issued: 1683
Cartographer: Louis Hennepin
Published: *Description de la Louisiane, Nouvellement Découvert au Sud Oüest de la Nouvelle France* (Paris)
Copperplate engraving, 11.6 x 18.9 inches
The Historic New Orleans Collection, Accession 73-988-L

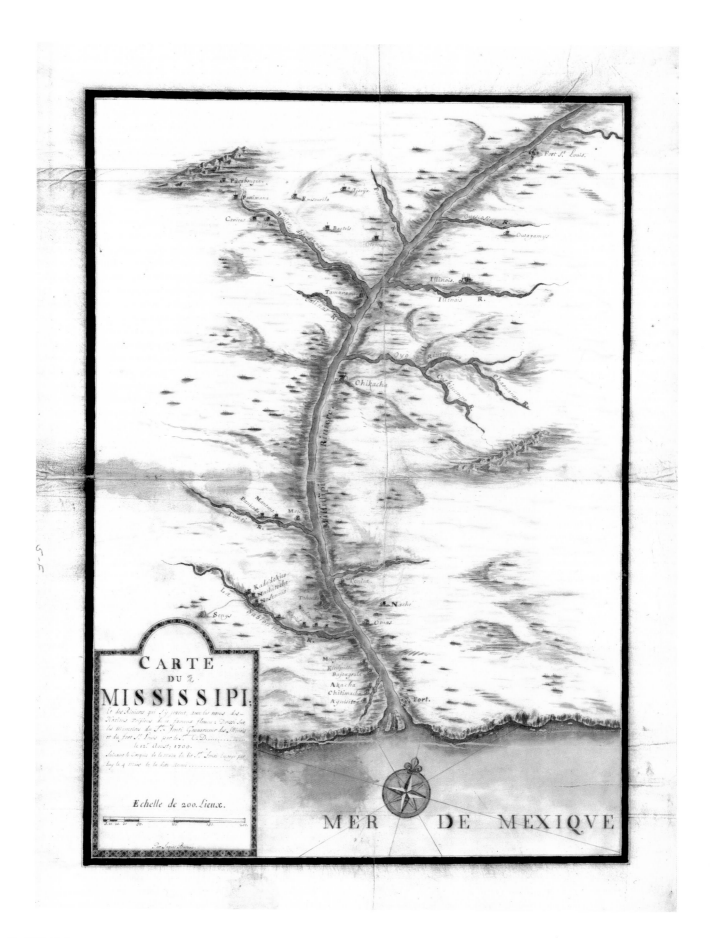

when Tonti knew from personal experience that river made a considerable bend at its mouth to the southeast.

A rather fanciful later example of an itinerary-type map is shown next. It depicts a large river, the "Rivière Longue" or "Rivière Morte" that flows into the Mississippi, and has a western extension that flows into a large salt lake; there is a large river just to the north and west of the salt lake, which, a note relays, the natives report flows to a western sea. Included on the map are illustrations of a two-hundred-person canoe, an eighty-pace house, and a medal, all used by the native people, called the "Taguglahur."

The discovery of the Rivière Longue (Long River) is credited to Louis-Armand de Lom d'Arce, Baron de Lahontan. Lahontan claimed to have come to Canada in 1683 at the age of seventeen as a marine lieutenant. He spent the next ten years in North America, during which he participated in an unsuccessful campaign against the Iroquois in 1684, served a stint as commandant at Fort Saint-Joseph in 1687, and explored territory along the Wisconsin and Mississippi rivers in 1688–89. During this last excursion, Lahontan reports that he ascended the Mississippi to a river flowing from the west that he came to call the Rivière Longue. His expedition traveled up this river for eight hundred miles, at which point, the story goes, Indians (the "Gnascsitares") told him that he was about 450 miles from a great salt lake that was near some high mountains. Moreover, Lahontan contends, these Indians had shown him a deerskin map that depicted a large river running to the western sea.

In 1703, Lahontan published an account of his journey on the Rivière Longue, along with his other travels throughout New France, in a book entitled *Nouveaux Voyages de Mr. le Baron de Lahontan dans l'Amérique septentrionale* (New Voyages to North America). At this time, travel narratives were the vogue in Europe, and interest in North America, which had been kindled by the *Jesuit Relations* and stoked by the accounts of Hennepin and Tonti, was greater than ever. Lahontan's book became immensely popular, and included a map of the Long River. The Rivière Longue, of course, was simply a product of Lahontan's fertile imagination. Although it served to arouse old hopes of finding a water route to the Pacific, even the most generous of interpretations does not allow one to identify it with any existing river. Nor can any of the aboriginal nations named along the river be identified. On the other hand, Lahontan's depiction of the Mississippi River Valley south to the area of modern St. Louis is fairly accurate.

Title: *Carte du Mississipi: et des Rivieres qui s'y jettent, avec les noms des Nations Voisines de ce Fameux Fleuve, dresse sur les memoires du Sr. Tonti, Gouverneur des Illinois et du fort St. Louis par le Sr. C. D. Le 12 Aoust, 1700, Suivant le croquis de la main du dit Sr. Tonti, envoye par luy le 4 Mars de la ditte anne?*
Date Issued: 1703
Cartographer: Jacques Bureau
Published: Manuscript
Watercolor and ink, 22.2 x 16.9 inches
American Geographical Society Library,
Scan map accession No. am005545

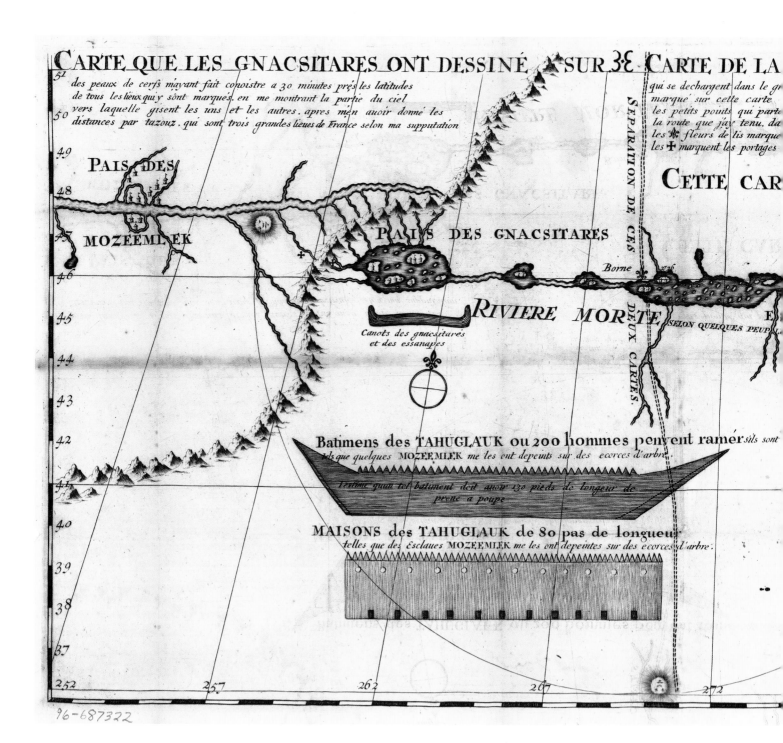

CARTE QUE LES GNACSITARES ONT DESSINÉ SUR 3E CARTE DE LA

des peaux de cerfs m'ayant fait conoistre a 30 minutes prés les latitudes
de tous les lieux qui y sont marqués, en me montrant la partie du ciel
vers laquelle gisent les uns et les autres, apres m'en avoir donné les
distances par tazouz, qui sont trois grandes lieües de France selon ma supputation

qui se dechargent dans le gr
marqué sur cette carte
les petits points qui parte
la route que j'ay tenu, da
les ✳ fleurs de lis marque
les ✝ marquent les portages

CETTE CAR

PAIS DES

MOZEEMLEK

PAIS DES GNACSITARES

Borne

RIVIERE MORTE

SELON QUELQUES PEUPL

Canots des gnacsitares
et des essanapes

Batimens des TAHUGLAUK ou 200 hommes peuvent ramér sils sont
tels que quelques MOZEEMLEK me les ont depeints sur des ecorces d'arbre

J'estime qu'un tel batiment doit avoir 130 pieds de longeur de
proüe a poupe

MAISONS des TAHUGLAUK de 80 pas de longueu
telles que des Esclaves MOZEEMLEK me les ont depeintes sur des ecorces d'arbre.

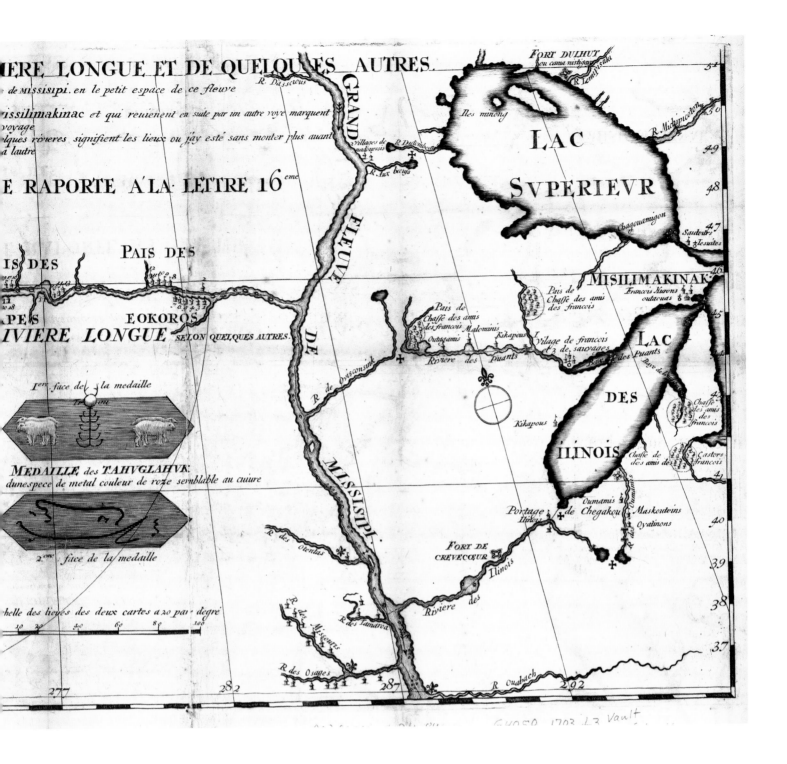

Title: *Carte Que les Gnacsitares Ont Dessiné Sur . . . [and] Carte de la Rivière Longue et de Quelques Autres,*
Qui Se Dechargent Dans le Grandfleuve de Missisipi

Date Issued: 1703

Cartographer: Louis Armand de Lom d'Arce, baron de Lahontan

Published: *Nouveaux voyages de M. le Baron Lahontan dans l'Amérique septentionale* (La Haye)

Two printed maps on one sheet, 11.8 x 26.8 inches

Library of Congress, Geography & Map Division, G4050 1703.L3 Vault

The Legacy of La Salle's Quest

René Robert Cavalier, sieur de La Salle, was a French explorer who came to Canada in 1667 to seek fortune and adventure. His brother Jean, a priest of St. Sulpice, had gone to New France the previous year. The Sulpicians—perhaps due to the influence of his brother—granted La Salle land near La Chine Rapids above Montreal, where he farmed, acquired a substantial interest in the fur trade, and sought to learn several American Indian languages. His Indian contacts told him stories of a great river system to the southwest, which La Salle thought was likely to flow into the Gulf of California, providing passage to China. Stirred by these reports, La Salle sold his holdings in 1669 and set out for the Great River. He claimed to have discovered the Ohio River, but abandoned his excursion short of the Mississippi, which would first be explored by the Jolliet-Marquette expedition in 1673.

By the time Jolliet returned to Montreal, La Salle had formed an alliance with the recently installed governor of New France, Louis de Baude, Comte de Frontenac. La Salle had found a kindred spirit in Frontenac, and the two planned to establish a vast political and commercial empire that would span the interior of North America. Backed by Governor Frontenac, La Salle began by building Fort Frontenac at present-day Kingston, Ontario, in July 1673, which was to serve as a base for controlling the fur trade in the Great Lakes area. He was installed there as seigneur in 1675 after a visit to the French court, and his dealings flourished despite opposition from Montreal merchants and Jesuit missionaries. In 1677, he again traveled to France, this time securing a five-year monopoly over the fur trade in the Illinois country (that is, the area south of the Great Lakes and west of Niagara Falls), as well as the right to explore the interior ("the western parts of New France") as far as Mexico.

La Salle returned to New France in 1678, accompanied by an Italian soldier of fortune, Henri de Tonti, who would become his most loyal friend and ally. Also accompanying him was Father Louis Hennepin, whom La Salle employed as a chaplain at Fort Frontenac. Convinced by now that the Mississippi emptied into the Gulf of Mexico (and not the Pacific Ocean), La Salle envisioned a fur-trading operation that included a chain of fortified trading posts across the Illinois country and down the Mississippi. He immediately set out to establish this enterprise. In 1679, he built the *Griffon*, the first commercial sailing vessel to ply the Great Lakes; he hoped to use the profits from carrying cargo as the means to help fund his empire. He sailed the *Griffon* from his shipyard above the Niagara River to Green Bay on Lake Michigan, and sent the ship back to Michillimakinac, filled with illegally acquired furs. La Salle then canoed down Lake Michigan to the mouth of the Miami River, where he built Fort St. Joseph. Pushing on, he built Fort Crevecœur on the Illinois River near present-day Peoria, where work was to commence on a second sailing ship.

La Salle's undertaking quickly faced financial ruin as the result of the wreck of the *Griffon*, the destruction and desertion of Fort Crevecœur, and the sinking of a supply ship coming from Montreal. Also, Father Hennepin, who had been sent down the Illinois River for the purpose of traveling up the Mississippi to the Wisconsin River and opening up trade along that route, had been captured by the Sioux and held captive for a year. Heavily in debt, La Salle was desperate to redeem his fortunes. He grittily determined to explore the Mississippi to its mouth, and in the spring of 1682, he and Tonti set out down the Great River. The adventurers reached the head of the river's bird's-foot delta, where on April 9, 1682, La Salle claimed the river and all the land that it drained for France. He called this territory "La Louisiane," or Louisiana, in honor of King Louis XIV. He named the river itself "Colbert" in honor of his patron at court, Jean-Baptiste Colbert, the French comptroller general of finances (whose help he would need for his next scheme). La Salle took a noon solar reading to estimate his latitude, which he incorrectly calculated as 28° 20' north, almost a full degree too far south.

His journey now fully documented, La Salle returned to the Illinois River where he built and wintered at Fort St. Louis on Starved Rock. While at the fort, La Salle received distressing news: Frontenac had been replaced as governor, and the new governor, Le Fevbre de la Barre, had seized all of La Salle's property and ordered him to surrender Fort St. Louis. La Salle refused, but his only recourse was a direct appeal to the king. He left immediately for France, where he arrived in late December 1683.

La Salle relayed his adventures to Louis XIV, telling the king of his desire to build a fortified settlement 180 miles from the mouth of the Great River he had descended; the fort would be used as a warehouse and exchange point for his trading operations. Perhaps on the advice of others at court, La Salle also mentioned that this colony could be used to assist the efforts of Diego de Peñalosa, the former governor of Mexico who had fled to Paris to avoid arrest by the Inquisition. Peñalosa had petitioned the crown for an outpost on the Texas coast at the mouth of the Río Bravo, from which he would raid nearby Mexican mines.

Cartographic evidence would be needed to sway the court, and La Salle worked with various geographers and cartographers to create a series of maps that attempted to reconcile his latitude for the mouth of the Mississippi with existing maps of the region. The result was a prototype on which the Mississippi below the Ohio swings far to the west in a great arc that is almost parallel to the Gulf Coast and then back to the southeast emerging on the Texas coast at twenty-eight degrees north (almost on the actual site of the Río Grande). This type of map was first drawn by Jean Baptiste-Louis Franquelin, a cartographer working in Canada.

Franquelin had first come to Canada in 1671 as a trader, but was subsequently recruited by Governor Frontenac to draw maps of New France, "since he was the only one in the colony equipped for this sort of work." In 1686, Franquelin was appointed by Louis XIV as Canada's first royal hydrographer, which meant that in addition to his regular cartographic duties, he was responsible for teaching navigation and hydrography to young river pilots and others seeking this information. Franquelin first drew a map based on La Salle's information in 1684; it has

Title: *Carte de l'Amerique Septrionale*
Date Issued: 1688
Cartographer: Jean Baptiste-Louis Franquelin
Published: Manuscript
Pen and ink and watercolor, 57.5 x 59.8 inches
Archives du Dépôt des Cartes et Plans de la Marine

been lost, and only a 1687 copy and a manuscript version from 1688 still exist. This last map is illustrated here: besides the misplaced Mississippi, note the small sea ("B. de Spiritus") on the coast—it is located where the Río del Espíritu Santo would typically be placed; note too the promontory south of the sea has begun to resemble the Mississippi Delta.

A second type of map derived from the La Salle expedition is shown next. It was drawn by Vincenzo Maria Coronelli, one of Italy's most celebrated cartographers. Coronelli drew, engraved, and printed over four hundred maps, and produced numerous globes as well. Among the latter was a magnificent pair of globes that he constructed for Louis XIV—one terrestrial, one celestial— each over 15 feet in diameter, drawn and painted by hand, and which could be entered by a special door. The present map is a gore from a 43.3-inch globe, one of the largest printed globes at that time (the gores were published in 1688). This gore depicts the central part of North America, and in particular, La Salle's trip down the

Mississippi. Unlike Franquelin, Coronelli did not abandon the southerly course of the Mississippi; he also maintains the slightly westward course of the river south of the Arkansas as shown on the Michallete-Thévenot map. In order to locate the river's mouth as dictated by La Salle, Coronelli displaces the Mississippi well to the west; as a result, the Wisconsin and Illinois rivers are shown as far longer than they actually are. On the other hand, the elongated S-curve of the river's southwestward and then southeastward course is not distorted as on Franquelin's map. Coronelli also represents the lower river with a fork (La Fourche) at its mouth, perhaps a representation of Bayou Lafourche. A vestigial Bahia del Espíritu Santo and Small Sea remain on the north Gulf Coast, although no rivers are seen flowing into it—despite the name "Río del Espíritu Santo" next to the Small Sea.

In April 1684, La Salle received the royal support he sought: not only was his Canadian property restored, the crown would underwrite an expedition to the Mississippi through the Gulf of Mexico, where he was to establish a colony "a secure distance" from the river. France and Spain were at war at the time, and this colony was to serve as a base for striking Mexico, harassing Spanish shipping, and obstructing English expansion; it would also serve as a warm water port for La Salle's Mississippi Valley fur trade. La Salle's royal backing included four ships, one hundred soldiers, and various supplies and privileges for his colony.

After an aborted initial departure, La Salle's fleet set sail on August 1, 1684. The voyage was beset by numerous misfortunes, including the desertion of some of La Salle's men in Antilles; these men would be captured by the Spanish, to whom they divulged La Salle's plans to place a colony on the "Micipipi." After landing on the Gulf Coast in late December, La Salle reckoned that he was too far north, and set a course to the west and then to the south. He landed his colonists at Matagorda Bay on the Texas coast on February 20, 1685, believing he was not far from the Mississippi.

There, La Salle built a small outpost, christened Fort St. Louis, which survived for almost four years before it succumbed to an Indian raid. By this time, La Salle was dead. He had explored westward from Fort St. Louis, reaching the Rio Grande and ascending it as far as the site of present-day Langtry. At last resigned to the fact that he had landed west of the Mississippi, he made two easterly marches hoping to find the Great River. He was murdered by one of his companions on the second expedition, near the Trinity River in Texas. Seven members of the group endured, continuing to the

Title: [Half-globe gore of mid–North America]
Date Issued: 1688
Cartographer: Vincenzo Maria Coronelli
Published: *Libro dei Globi* (Venice, Italy)
Copperplate engraving, 2.8 x 1.6 inches
Newberry Library, VAULT oversize Ayer 135 C8 1696 v. 1, no. 199

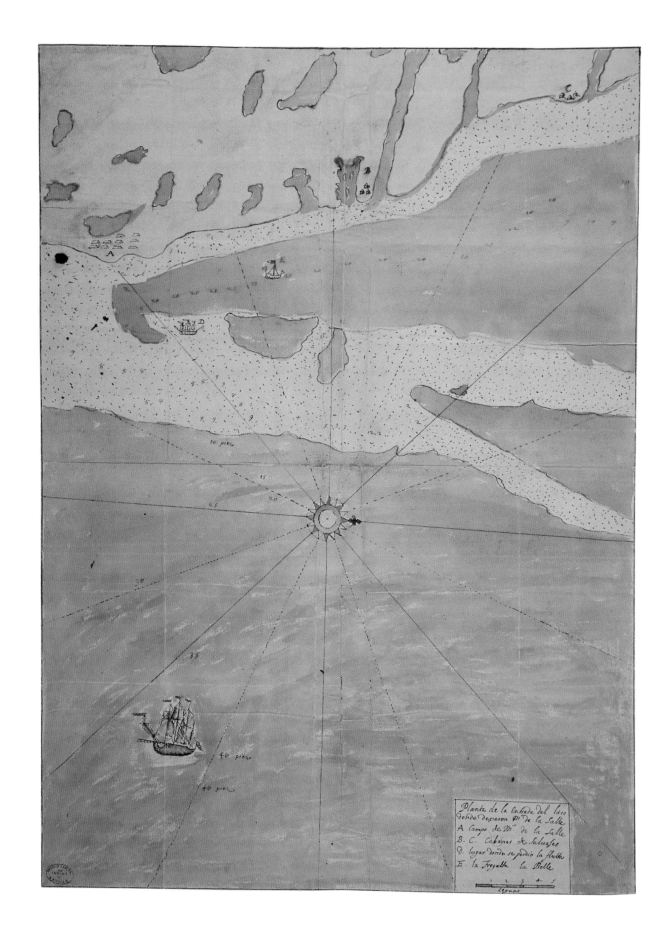

Arkansas River, where they came across members of a party Tonti had left when he came down the river in 1686, expecting to find La Salle working his way upriver. Five of La Salle's men—including his brother Jean, Father Anastase Douay, and Henri Joutel, each of whom would later write of the expedition—made their way back to Canada, and eventually France.

How is it that La Salle missed the Mississippi, landing in Texas instead? Although historians have long debated the reasons for La Salle's misplaced landing, the maps illustrated here indicate that La Salle landed precisely where he thought the Mississippi should be. He knew that Spanish charts placed the Río del Espíritu Santo much further east. Given, however, the (erroneous) latitude he had recorded at the river's mouth, La Salle concluded that the Mississippi was not the same river as Alonso Álvarez de Pineda's Río del Espíritu Santo or Hernando de Soto's "Great River." Indeed, he equated the Mississippi with the Río Escondido, a river that first appeared on maps in the mid-sixteenth century as entering the Gulf at its western end with a latitude that corresponded with the one La Salle had taken at the mouth of the Mississippi: "If all the maps are not worthless," he concluded, "the mouth of the River Colbert is near Mexico . . . this Escondido assuredly is the Mississippi."

Although La Salle's grand venture ended in failure, his explorations had a profound effect on Mississippi River cartography. He was the first to show that the Mississippi entered the Gulf of Mexico (as Marquette and Jolliet had earlier surmised). And his "intrusion" into the Gulf set off a renewal in Spanish exploration of the region as they set out to find his colony. As we shall see, these efforts produced the first new mapping of the Gulf Coast, on which the Mississippi delta appears in the right shape and in the appropriate place.

Spanish efforts to locate La Salle's settlement were successful, as shown on the last map illustrated here. This map shows Matagorda Bay, Texas, indicating water depths, shoals, and land areas. The letter "A" indicates the remains of La Salle's camp, while the letter "E" identifies the wreck of the *Belle*, La Salle's ship, which was excavated in the 1990s by marine archeologists.

Title: *Planta de la Entrada del laco Donde Dexaron Mr. de las Salle [Bahia del Espritu Santo]*
Date Issued: 1687
Cartographer: Pedro Ronquillo
Published: Manuscript
Pen and ink and watercolor, 15.4 x 21.7 inches
Archivo General de Indias, México, 616

CHAPTER 2

COLONIZING THE GREAT RIVER'S VALLEY

The Colony of Louisiana

In 1682, René Robert Cavalier, sieur de La Salle, claimed all the land drained by the Mississippi River for the French crown; he christened this territory "La Louisiane" in honor of Louis XIV. La Salle envisioned a grand fur-trading enterprise that included fortified trading posts strung across the Mississippi River and Great Lakes, but tragically failed in his venture. Throughout the 1690s, various parties in France and Canada—including La Salle's brother (the Abbé Jean Cavalier), the Jesuits, and La Salle's lieutenant (Henri Tonti)—all proposed reviving his dream. Such an undertaking would require royal support, however, and that would not be forthcoming—for France was at war.

In 1697, France formally ended its nine-year imperial war with the British and their allies (known in North America as King William's War) by signing the Treaty of Ryswick. This pact recognized France's right to possess the Mississippi Valley, but thus far neither the crown nor private interests had asserted France's claim to the region. Moreover, the British had been making incursions into the area as early as 1690. Indeed, in 1698 Dr. Daniel Coxe, a London merchant, formed the Anglo-Dutch Carolana Company, a joint-stock company with the expressed purpose of founding a colony at the mouth of the Mississippi. It was primarily as a response to the English threat that France established the colony of Louisiana.

In 1698, Louis Phélypeaux, Comte de Pontchartrain, the minister of the marine, ordered Pierre Le Moyne, sieur d'Iberville, to find "the mouth [of the Mississippi] … select a good site which can be defended with few men, and … block entry to the river by other nations." A native of Montreal, Iberville had earned this command on account of his aristocratic background and his reputation as a soldier fighting the British in Canada. After chancing upon the Mississippi's bird's-foot delta in March 1699, Iberville and his brother, Jean Baptiste Le Moyne, sieur de Bienville, explored the lower river in search of proof that this was indeed the river that La Salle had claimed for France. Confirmation came in the form of a letter written by La Salle's lieutenant; Tonti had left the letter with a group of American Indians in 1686 when he had come in search of La Salle's settlement. Iberville also located various Indian villages during his expedition, and gleaned information about the tributaries and overflow outlets of the Mississippi within the area of modern Louisiana. Iberville was unable, however, to find a suitable site for a fort along the river. Accordingly, he returned to the coast, and after locating a channel of sufficient depth to accommodate seagoing ships, ordered the construction of a fort on the eastern side of Biloxi Bay in April 1699. This temporary fort was christened "Fort Maurepas" (now modern-day Ocean Springs, Mississippi) and was strategically situated between the Mississippi and a Spanish base at Pensacola, Florida. Iberville then sailed for France in May 1699, leaving behind a garrison of eighty-one men, including his brother Bienville.

Bienville, who was second in command at the fort, would come across an English corvette ascending the Mississippi later that year. While exploring the lower river with five men in two canoes, Bienville met Captain William Bond, who was leading an expedition sponsored by Dr. Coxe's Carolana Company. Bienville ordered Bond out of the French king's river, bluffing him with a threat to call for support. Two decades later in a report to the crown, Bienville would recall that he "obliged them [the English] to abandon their enterprise." The location of this encounter—just south of the eventual site of New Orleans—would henceforth be known as "English Turn."

Iberville returned to Biloxi in January 1700, and upon learning of his brother's encounter with Bond, ordered the construction of Fort de Mississipi, also known as Fort de La Boulaye, near the mouth of the Mississippi. He also sought out contact with several Indian tribes of the region, seeking to secure their allegiance in a common front against British ambitions in the Mississippi basin. Returning once again to France, Iberville lobbied for a strong commitment to the fledgling colony. The crown authorized a third expedition for the purpose of founding a naval base at Mobile, and approved Iberville's strategy to forge economic and strategic alliances with the native population. Iberville returned to Louisiana in December 1701 and undertook construction of a modest installation on the west bank of the Mobile River near present day Mobile, Alabama, which he would call "Fort Saint-Louis." He confirmed his brother as commandant, and with the assistance of Henri Tonti, began to implement his Indian program. After a four-month sojourn in Louisiana, Iberville sailed for France, never to return to the colony he had founded.

The first map shown here was drawn by Nicolas de Fer in 1701: it depicts the Louisiana colony in its infancy, and highlights the voyages of La Salle and Iberville. The legend gives a brief history of La Salle's expedition, while the cartouche dramatizes the explorer's tragic fate at the hands of his own men. (The title incorrectly cites the year of La Salle's 1682 "discovery" of the Mississippi.) La Salle's ill-fated colony at Matagorda Bay is marked, as is the route that the Spanish explorer and governor of Mexico, Alsonso de León, took to find the ruins of this settlement. Although the lower Mississippi and its tributaries are not well defined, this map clearly illustrates Iberville's route along the modern Bayou Manchac and the Amire River to lakes Maurepas and Pontchartrain. Using information provided by Iberville, this map also locates Indian villages, as well as Fort Maurepas and Fort de Mississipi. De Fer distorts the Mississippi Sound and Lake Pontchartrain on this map, perhaps as a means to provide details. On the other hand, the relationship between the Mississippi, Lake Pontchartrain, and the Gulf of Mexico is better realized than on earlier maps. This map was clearly meant to secure France's claim to the Mississippi basin by documenting its effective occupation by the French; in addition, it

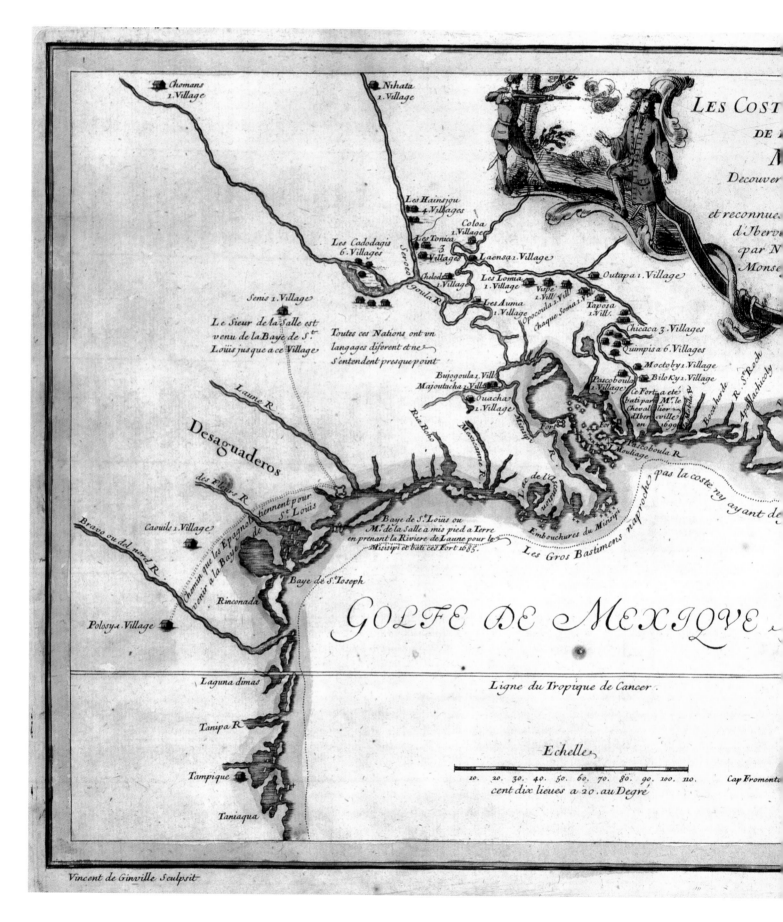

Chomans 1. Village

Nihata 1. Village

Les Hainsiou 4. Villages

Coloa 1. Village

Les Cadodagis 6. Villages

Les Tonica 3. Villages

Laensa 1. Village

Chelod 1. Village

Les Lomia 1. Village

Outapa 1. Village

Senis 1. Village

Vispe 1. Vill. 1. Vill.

Le Sieur de la Salle est venu de la Baye de St. Louïs jusque a ce Village

Les Auma 1. Village

Opocoula 1. Village

Chaque Soma 1. Village

Taposa 1. Vill.

Toutes ces Nations ont un langages diferent et ne s'entendent presque point

Chicaca 3. Villages

Quimpis a 6. Villages

Moctoby 1. Village

Bujogoula 1. Vill.

Biloxy 1. Village

R. St. Roch

Majoutacha 1. Village

Pascoboula 1. Village

Ouacha 1. Village

Ce Fort a eté bati par Mr. le Chevallier d'Iberville en 1699.

Laune R.

R. a Boho

Desaguaderos

Mexicaine R.

Fort

Pascoboula R. Mouliage

des Fleurs R.

tiennent pour St. Louïs

Bravo ou del nord R.

Caouils 1. Village

Chemin que les Epagnols de la Baye de venir a la Baye

Baye de St. Louïs ou Mr. de la Salle a mis pied a Terre en prenant la Riviere de Laune pour le Misisipi et bâti ce Fort 1685.

Lac de l'Ascension

naproche pas la coste ny ayant de

Embouchures du Misisipi

Les Gros Bastimens

Polosy 1. Village

Rinconada

Baye de St. Ioseph

GOLFE DE MEXIQVE

Laguna dimas

Ligne du Tropique de Cancer.

Tanipa R.

Echelle

Tampique

10. 20. 30. 40. 50. 60. 70. 80. 90. 100. 110.

Cap Fromento

cent dix lieues a 20. au Degré

Taniaqua

Title: *Les Costes aux Environs de la Rivière de Misisipi, Decouvertes par Mr. de la Salle en 1683 et reconnues par Mr. le Chevallier d'Iberville en 1698 et 1699*

Date Issued: 1701

Cartographer: Nicolas de Fer

Published: *L'Atlas Curieux ou le Monde représenté dabs des Cartes Générales et Particulieres du Ciel et de la Terre divisé tant en ses Quarte Principales Parties que par États et Provinces et orné par des Plans et Descriptions des Villes Capitables et principales et des plus superbes Edifices qui les Embelissent . . .* (Paris)

Copperplate engraving, 11 x 15.3 inches

The Historic Collection of New Orleans, Accession 1976.147

records the French understanding of the Gulf Coast and its ethnogeography as reported by Iberville.

The second map here may have in part been based on Captain Bond's 1699 exploration of the area. It was the prototype for a series of English maps that portray the Mississippi as forked before it reaches its delta; this fork creates an island west of the main channel. Maps of this mold usually have an additional fork in the western channel, which creates a smaller island on the Gulf Coast. There is an inset map of the delta on this chart, making it clear that the river fork is not just another version of the delta. The position of this fork might lead one to believe that it is a reflection of another river, probably the Atchafalaya. Or, it may be a misplaced fusion of Bayou Lafourche and some coastal rivers that appear on earlier maps of the area. The Mississippi Sound and its islands are more correctly represented on this map than on the de Fer map, and this map contains the Bayou Manchac-Amire River-lakes Maurepas-Pontchartrain overflow. Note the attempt to substantiate a British claim to the area by the printing of "Part of Carolina" across the Gulf Coast.

Title: A Chart of the Bay of Mexico
Date Issued: 1702
Cartographers: Richard Mount and Thomas Page
Published: Separately (London)
Copperplate engraving, 18.5 x 22.8 inches
The Historic Collection of New Orleans, Accession 1991.127

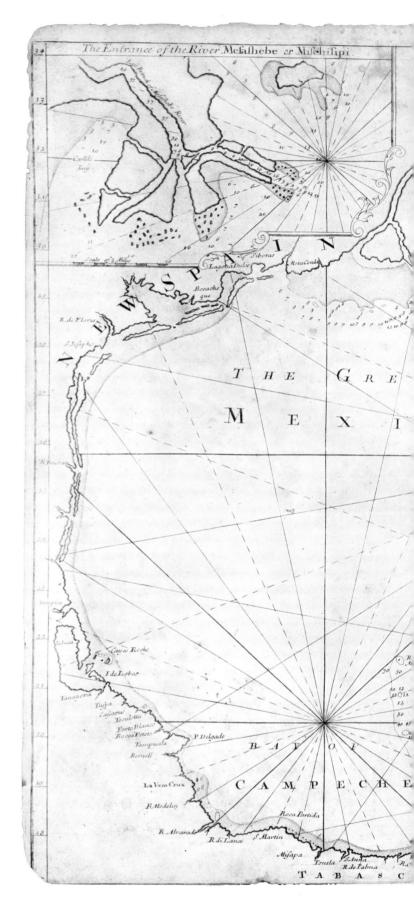

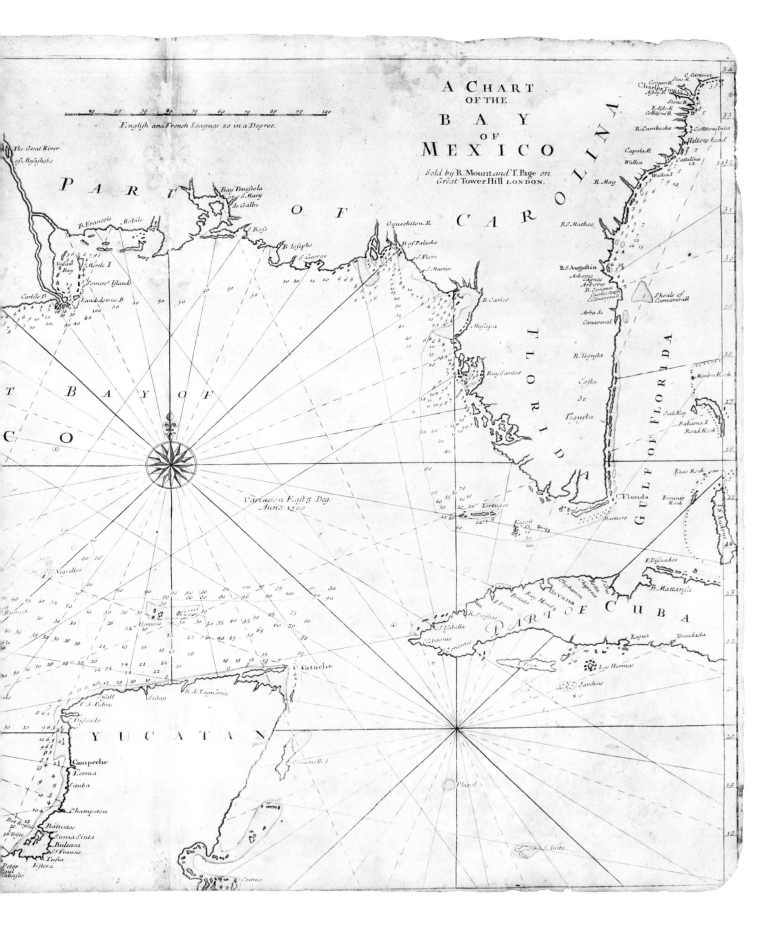

A CHART
OF THE
BAY
OF
MEXICO

Sold by R. Mount and T. Page on
Great Tower Hill LONDON.

English and French Leagues 20 in a Degree.

PART OF CAROLINA

FLORIDA

GULF OF FLORIDA

BAY OF MEXICO

PART OF CUBA

YUCATAN

Variation East 5 Deg.
Anno 1700

The Great River of Misasebe

Bay Tenescola or S.t Mary de Galbe

B. Francois   Mobile

S.t Rose

B. Iosepho

S.t George

Nadau Bay

Merile I.

Somers Island

Carlile B.

Landsdowne B.

Neavilles

Moranes

Campeche
Lerma
Situba

Champeton

Batustos
Zuma S.ta
Buleasa
S.t Francis
Tusta
Estera
Peter
Balasco

Port Royall
Trifte

C. Catoche

R. de Laguaime

T.all
V. de Pedro
Disseado

Seian

Cozumeli I.

Placel

Oquechiton R.
B.t of Palache
S.t Pierre
S.t Martin

B. Carlos

Musapa

Bay Santos

Costa de Tegusta

R. Tegusta

Tortugas
R. tos.t
Martiere

C. Florida

B.S. Augustin
Arbores cagnas
Arbores
B. Coriente
Carlos Caslt
C. Canaveral

Arba de Canaveral

Shoals of Canaverall

R.S. Matheo

R. May

Cooper R.
Ashly R.
Charles Town

E. Islo R.
Colliton R.

B. Camboche

Capola R.
Wallea

Seco   C. Carteret

Stone R.

Colliton Inlet

Heltons head

Cattalina
Wallea I.

Nimbre Rock

Isle Key
Bahama I.
Road Rock

Isaac Rock

Bimini Rock

S. Andros

Havana
Bay Hendy
Boratto
Chabarin
Chagoria

E. Disseados

B. Mattansa

S.t Isabella
R. Picefroy
Chabani
C. Corientes

C. Pina

Los Hermos

Jardins

Jagua   Trinidada

S. Anito

Cosmos

The Business of Colonizing

Louisiana struggled to survive in its infancy and the French crown—its treasury depleted by war and Louis XIV's lavish expenses—was in no position to nurture the fledgling colony. So, after thirteen unprofitable years, Louis XIV, the Sun King, and his advisors came up with a plan to support the development of the Mississippi colony without royal expense—it would place Louisiana in private hands. On September 14, 1712, financier and nobleman Antoine Crozat was awarded a royal charter that gave him a trading monopoly in the colony for fifteen years. Crozat, reportedly one of the wealthiest men in Europe, sent Antoine de Lamothe Cadillac to oversee the colony. Cadillac, who was also an investor in Crozat's venture, was to locate the reported silver and gold mines in Louisiana, establish tobacco plantations, and develop commerce with the Spaniards. He arrived in Mobile in May 1713 and proved himself to be completely inadequate to the task. After five years Crozat conceded that his venture into colonizing was a failure; in August 1717 he successfully petitioned the king for a release from his charter, and Louisiana was once again a ward of the bankrupt crown.

John Law, a Scottish financier, immediately seized the opportunity to take over the colony. Law had made his reputation in Paris the previous year by founding a private bank authorized to issue paper currency, and was an acquaintance of the young King Louis XV's regent, Philippe d'Orléans. Law approached the regent with the offer to again privatize Louisiana, and within a month was granted a twenty-five-year proprietorship with a commercial monopoly over the colony.

Law exaggerated the wealth of Louisiana to promote investment in his company (he had, for example, gold ingots "from the mines of Louisiana" displayed in Paris shop windows). Maps were also used as propaganda, including the singular example by Guillaume de L'Isle shown here. Although designed chiefly for commercial reasons, this map is a landmark in Mississippi Valley cartography. Based on twenty years of research, it was widely copied and was the chief source for all maps of the Mississippi for at least fifty years. De L'Isle credits several sources for his map, including François Le Maire, a missionary based at Mobile who drew reasonably accurate maps, as well as Louis Antoine Juchereau de Saint Denis (who, acting on Cadillac's behalf, undertook an expedition to the Rio Grande seeking out trade with neighboring Spanish settlements and established Natchitoches in 1714). Many of the details on this map can also be traced to American Indian informants, who briefed explorers such as La Salle on the location of rivers, names and features of villages, and other critical data. Reissued as late as 1783, this was the first large-scale map to accurately depict the lower river and Gulf region, the first printed map to mention Texas (Mission de los Teijas), and the first modern map to trace the expedition of de

Soto–Moscoto. It also highlights the more recent expeditions of La Salle (1687), Alsonso de León (1689), Henri Tonti (1702), Louis de Saint Denis (1713 and 1716), and Jean-Baptiste Le Moyne de Bienville. This map clearly had a political aim, as it shows a very broad Louisiana, extending from a tributary of the Rio Grande to the Appalachians; and it lays claim to Carolina—a pronouncement that would raise the ire of British colonial officials.

Unlike Crozat, Law thought that the profitability of Louisiana hinged on its large-scale settlement—for it would take considerable numbers to defend the territory and to exploit the region's natural resources. Accordingly, his company encouraged immigration to Louisiana, and agreed to send both settlers and slaves to the colony. Voluntary French settlers were rare, however, and for a while French authorities sent indentured servants and inmates of Parisian prisons to the colony. Law's company agents also convinced residents of impoverished German principalities to immigrate to Louisiana. Once they had arrived in Louisiana, colonists found that Law's company had invested very little to help them establish themselves in their new homeland. The second image shown here depicts the colonial headquarters of Law's company at New Biloxi, a rather crude depot located across the bay from Fort Maurepas or "Old Biloxi." Colonists would be landed at Ship Island in the bay and then brought to New Biloxi before being transported to various inland concessions.

After a period of excessive speculation, Law's company suffered a spectacular collapse in 1720, and scores of investors faced financial ruin. The episode became known as the "Mississippi Bubble," and John Law became a reviled figure throughout Europe. In 1734 the German publisher Matthäus Seutter published his splendidly engraved map of Louisiana, which is modeled after an earlier promotional map for Law's company by Nicolas de Fer. As seen here, Seutter's map is known for the satirical illustration of Law's investment scheme in its title-piece. We see a female personification of the Mississippi River—precariously perched upon a bubble—pouring jewels and riches from her shell. A banner waves immediately above her and reads "boldness brings fortune." Further above her is a winged personification of Fame, who holds a trumpet with a banner that announces, "God is second." Cherubs above the cartouche, along with a female figure whose banner reads "What is hope?" are issuing stock for the company; another group of cherubs is blowing bubbles in the foreground surrounded by piles of worthless stock, while others work cutting up the valueless stock certificates. In the background, two investors—speculators who have taken their profit—are shown sneaking away, leaving other desperate investors to fling themselves out of a small tree. In the foreground we see other disconsolate investors, including one who tries to impale himself on his sword. Above them is a cherub who upends an empty money bag.

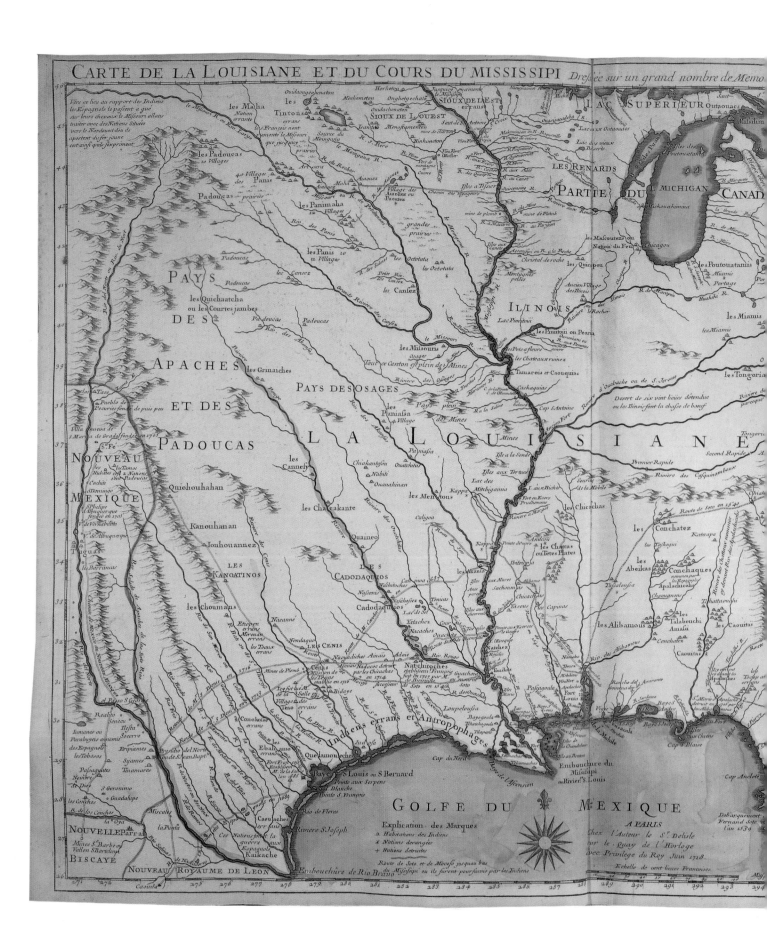

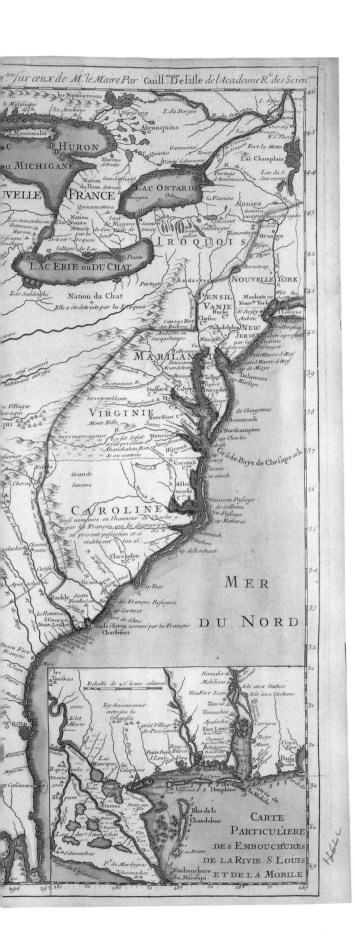

Title: *Carte de la Louisiane et du Cours de Mississipi Dressée sur un grand nombre de Memoires entrau.^{tres} sur ceux de Mr. le Maire...*
Date Issued: 1718
Cartographer: Guillaume de L'Isle
Published: Separately (Paris)
Copperplate engraving, 21.3 x 28.7 inches
Collection of Cohen & Taliaferro, LLC.

NEXT PAGES
Title: *Veuë du camp de la concession de Monseigneur Law, au Nouveaux Biloxy, coste de la Louisianne*
Date Issued: 1720
Cartographer: Jean-Baptiste Michel Le Bouteux
Published: Manuscript
Pen-and-ink drawing, 19.3 x 39 inches
Newberry Library, Artifacts cage oversize Ayer MS map 30 sheet 77

A. Magazin de 80. pieds de long sur 25. pds. de large
B. Tente de Monsieur Alias Estinatien directeur general
C. Tente de Mr. le Veni second directeur
D. Tente du Sr. Le Bouteux sous directeur
E. Tente du Sr. Navarre Chirurgien Major
F. Tente de Mr. le Saint Aumonier
G. Maison du R. P. Maximin aumonier
H. Tente du Sr. Libre Inspecteur du tabac
I. La grande rue formée par les baraques des ouvriers aux extremites et au milieu delaquelle sont les tentes des off. conducteurs et sous off.
L. Corps de la Caserne des hors. liden. de Gorde.
M. Corps de Garde.
N. Tentes servant d'Aviso
O. Maison du Boucher chargé du
P. Forges, l'armurier, et le Coutelier
Q. le four
R. Baraque de l'apoticaire et des g.
S. hopital

VEUË
DU CAMP
DE
LA CONCESSION
DE
MONSEIGNEUR
LAW.
AU NOUVEAU
BILOXY, COSTE
DE LA
LOUISIANNE

Title : *Accurata delineatio celeberrimæ Regionis Ludovicianæ vel Gallice Louisiane ol. Cauadæ et Floridæ adpellatione in Septemtrionali America . . .*

Date Issued: 1730

Cartographer: Matthäus Seutter

Published: *Atlas Novus* (Augsburg, Germany)

Copperplate engraving, 20.2 x 23 inches

University of Western Ontario, Serge A. Sauer Map Library

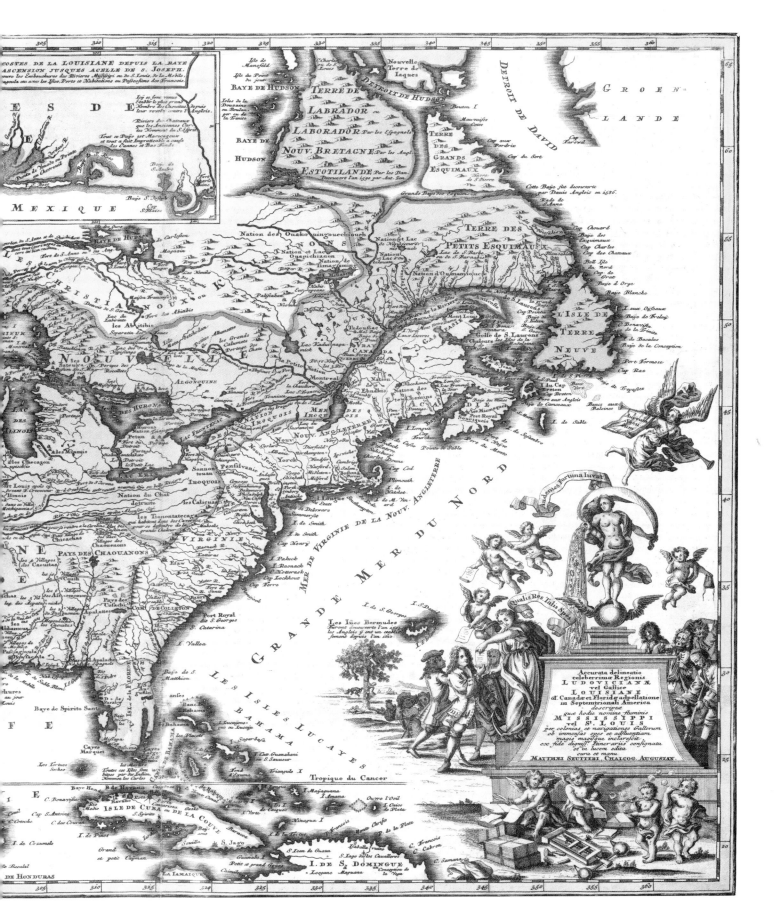

COSTES DE LA LOUISIANE DEPUIS LA BAYE
ASCENSION JUSQUES ACELLE DE S. JOSEPH.

MEXIQUE

Baye S. Joseph
Cap. S. Blaise

DETROIT DE DAVID

GROEN-
LANDE

BAYE DE HUDSON

TERRE DE
LABRADOR ou
LABORADOR Par les Espagnols
Nouv. Bretagne Par les Angl.
Estotilande Par les Dan.

BAYE DE
HUDSON

TERRE
DES
GRANDS
ESQUIMAUX

Cap du Sort

TERRE DES
PETITS ESQUIMAUX

L'ISLE DE
TERRE
NEUVE

Nation des Ouako uingouechiouch

HURONS

NOUVELLE

DES HURONS

ALGONQUINE

VRAIE
CANADA

Golfe de S. Laurens

CHRISTIANOUX ou KILISTINONS

FRANCE

MER DES
IROQUOIS

NOUV. ANGLETERRE

IROQUOIS

VIRGINIE

PAYS DES CHAOUANONS

MER DE VIRGINIE DE LA NOUV. ANGLETERRE

GRANDE MER DU NORD

Les Isles Bermudes

Audentes fortuna Iuvat

ISLE DE LA FLORIDE

Baye de Spirito Santo

LES ISLES LUCAYES

BAHAMA

Qualis Res Talis Spei

Tropique du Cancer

ISLE DE CUBA
DE LA COUVE

LA IAMAIQUE

I. DE St. DOMINGUE

DE HONDURAS

Accurata delineatio
celeberrimæ Regionis
LUDOVICIANÆ
vel Gallice
LOUISIANE
à Canada et Florida appellatione
in Septentrionali America
descriptæ
quæ hodie nomine fluminis
MISSISSIPPI
vel St. LOUIS
per colonias et navigationes Gallorum
ob immensas opes et adfluentiam
magis magisque inclarescit.
eoc fide dignissis Itinerariis consignata
et in lucem edita
cura et manu
MATTHEI SEUTTERI, CHALCOG. AUGUSTÆ.

Colonial Settlement along the Mississippi

The first communities along the Mississippi River were not military outposts or colonial settlements, but evangelical missions. In 1699 the Seminary of Foreign Missions in Quebec sent three missionaries to found Cahokia, the first permanent European settlement on the Mississippi. Named after a tribe of Illinois Indians, Cahokia was located on the east side of the river south of present-day St. Louis, and would become a center of French influence in the upper Mississippi Valley. In 1703 Kaskaskia was founded as a Jesuit mission about fifty miles south of Cahokia, on the west bank of the Kaskaskia River, just east of the Mississippi. This site allowed boats to escape the turbulence of the Mississippi and dock on the bank of a much calmer river. Also named after an Illinois Indian tribe, Kaskaskia would develop as an important French trading post and a farming community. It would later serve as the capital of the Illinois Territory (1809–18) and briefly as the state capital of Illinois (1818–20).

The first map shown here was drawn in 1769 by Thomas Hutchins, who would become geographer to the United States, and is derived from a French manuscript now preserved in Paris. It situates a string of colonial settlements that grew up between Cahokia and Kaskaskia along the eastern bank of the Mississippi. These villages were located in the fertile bottom-land below the river bluffs (indicated by the hachures) that is part of what is now known as the American Bottoms, a sixty-mile-long strip of floodplain that became the breadbasket of Louisiana. From the north is Cahokia, then "St. Phillips" (Saint-Philippe, 1721), and what Hutchins calls "Fort Charters," the French Fort de Chartres (1720). Further south is Prairie du Rocher (1719), and finally the village of Kaskaskia. On the west side of the river is St. Genevieve (c. 1750) and St. Louis (1764) at the top of the map.

In 1716, Jean Baptiste Le Moyne, sieur de Bienville, ordered the construction of Fort Rosalie at the site of present-day Natchez, Mississippi. The fort was named after the wife of the Comte de Pontchartrain, the minister of the marine, and served as the primary French stronghold and trading post among the Natchez Indians. Although little more than a small, crudely palisaded fort, a large French settlement soon developed around its perimeter. This settlement grew to more than one thousand farmers growing tobacco, wheat, and other crops in the rich land that surrounded the fort. On November 29, 1729, the Natchez—angered by the French commandant's plan to relocate the tribe's Great Village in order to establish a plantation there—massacred most of the area's white population.

A small sketch by Dumont de Montigny depicts the area just before this event. Fort Rosalie is shown at the center of the map, situated on a bluff above the Mississippi River ("Fleuve St. Louis"). On the hillsides surrounding the fort are the various farms, which Dumont indicates had considerable cultivated areas around them. Also shown is a "village sauvage," most likely the site of the Great Village that precipitated the massacre (now preserved as a mound site in Natchez). Note that this village had a circular palisade at its center, in contrast to the square palisade generally employed by Europeans. It is also clear that the isolated farms around the fort were particularly vulnerable to attacks like the one of 1729.

New Orleans was founded in 1718 by Bienville on behalf of John Law and the Company of the West. It was named in honor of the regent, Philippe d'Orléans, who had awarded Law and his company the commercial monopoly over the colony of Louisiana. Bienville picked a deep water site about fifty miles up the main branch of the river that guarded the natural portage between the Mississippi River and Bayou St. John, leading to Lake Pontchartrain. From this upriver site, the settlement would thus only serve as a Gulf port, but could also be used to efficiently monitor river traffic and guard against foreign intrusion. New Orleans became the capital of Louisiana in 1722, one year after French engineer Adrien de Pauger had laid out a permanent street plan. As seen on the beautiful, albeit somewhat fanciful, manuscript here, Pauger used a rectangular and uniform grid street system and the town had a narrow retaining wall along the riverfront and a public square (Place d'Armes), which opened onto the river. Signed by Thierry, a king's engineer, this plan is dated 1755 and portrays many of the city's existing major landmarks. It shows more buildings and gardens than existed at the time, depicting the city as built to its edges. This idealized vision was undoubtedly meant to encourage settlers to come to New Orleans.

In 1720, large numbers of German families began to arrive in Louisiana. These families had suffered horribly during the Thirty Years War and subsequent French Occupation, and were persuaded by Law's Company of the West that great riches awaited them in the new colony. When they arrived, they found otherwise: they were given small plots of land and a few primitive tools, and found mostly hardship instead of their promised wealth. Many of these pioneers settled upriver from New Orleans along a section of the river that came to be called the "Cote des Allemands" (German Coast), roughly in the area of what is now known as St. John the Baptist Parish. This region is depicted on the next two maps illustrated here. The first is a remarkable anonymous manuscript that records land ownership along the river in the area surrounding New Orleans circa 1723, and even marks the buildings within each landholding. Note the characteristic French "long-lots" along the river — long, narrow land concessions that allowed each landowner access to the waterway. Shown in the lower left is the "Habitations des Allemands" in its first decade of settlement. François Saucier's beautiful 1749 map of the region around Lakes Pontchartrain and Maurepas shows the German Coast as a well-established settlement and the American Indian "village sauvage" of the Colapissas. Saucier demarcates the fresh water and brackish water swamps along the southern shore of Lake Pontchartrain and also shows roads, cultivated land, fortifications, and the grid plan for New Orleans.

The next two maps depict early French settlement along the lower Mississippi and Gulf Coast. The first is a bird's-eye view of the Louisiana coast drawn by François Chereau that includes waterways, islands, settlements, forts, and Indian villages, all numbered and keyed to an index below the image. There are obvious inaccuracies in the map—New Orleans, for example, is on the wrong side of Lake Pontchartrain and is too close to the Gulf of Mexico. Nevertheless, it is a beautiful illustration, rich in detail, and clearly designed for a European market hungry for information about the French colony. The second map is a classic in the annals of Louisiana cartography: drawn by D'Anville in 1732, it accurately renders the lower Mississippi, the Arkansas, the Red, the Osage, and the lower Missouri rivers and is one of the earliest detailed portrayals of French settlement in the Gulf Coast area. The inset on the right side of the map features the Mississippi basin up to a point north of its confluence with the Missouri River.

In 1762 the governor of Louisiana granted New Orleans resident Gilbert Maxent a fur-trading monopoly with the Indian tribes living on the Missouri River and the western bank of the Mississippi. Maxent entered into a partnership with Pierre Laclede, who agreed to build and manage a trading post near the tribes. In August 1763, Laclede and his thirteen-year-old stepson Auguste Chouteau led an expedition to the confluence of the Missouri and Mississippi rivers, where they determined that the land was too low and swampy to build an outpost. They retraced their route eighteen miles back down the Mississippi until they spied a break in the sandstone bluffs that lined the west side of the river. It was there—on top of a gently sloping plateau that gave easy access to the river—that they would build the trading post that became the capital of the Illinois country.

In February 1764 Chouteau led a party of thirty men back to the site, laid out the town, and began its construction. It was named St. Louis in honor of Louis IX, the patron saint of the current French monarch, Louis XV. As seen in the plan of the city here, Chouteau's layout employed a uniform grid pattern similar to that of other French colonial cities of the day, especially New Orleans. This diagram also includes fortifications that were proposed for St. Louis by General Georges Henri Victor Collot, a daring French spy who had visited the area in 1796. Two forts, which were never built, are shown in insets; the city's plan includes existing fortifications, a creek with bridges, the Grand Etang (pond), the public square, and a Catholic church. St. Louis was in Spanish possession at the time, and Collot was convinced that a fortified St. Louis would be the key to the control of the region between the Alleghenies and the Rocky Mountains.

Collot explored the entire Mississippi-Ohio region in 1796 and wrote about his travels in *Voyage dans L'Amérique Septentrionale*. Printed in 1804, its publication was delayed by the author's death until 1826. Collot had hoped that by undertaking and

Title: A Plan of the Several Villages in the Illinois Country
Date Issued: 1778
Cartographer: Thomas Hutchins
Published: *A Topographical Description of Virginia, Pennsylvania, Maryland, and North Carolina, Comprehending the Rivers Ohio, Kenhawa, Sioto, Cherokee, Wabash, Illinois, Mississippi, etcetera* (London)
Uncolored printed map, 7.5 x 5.1 inches
David Rumsey Collection, Image No. 5045002

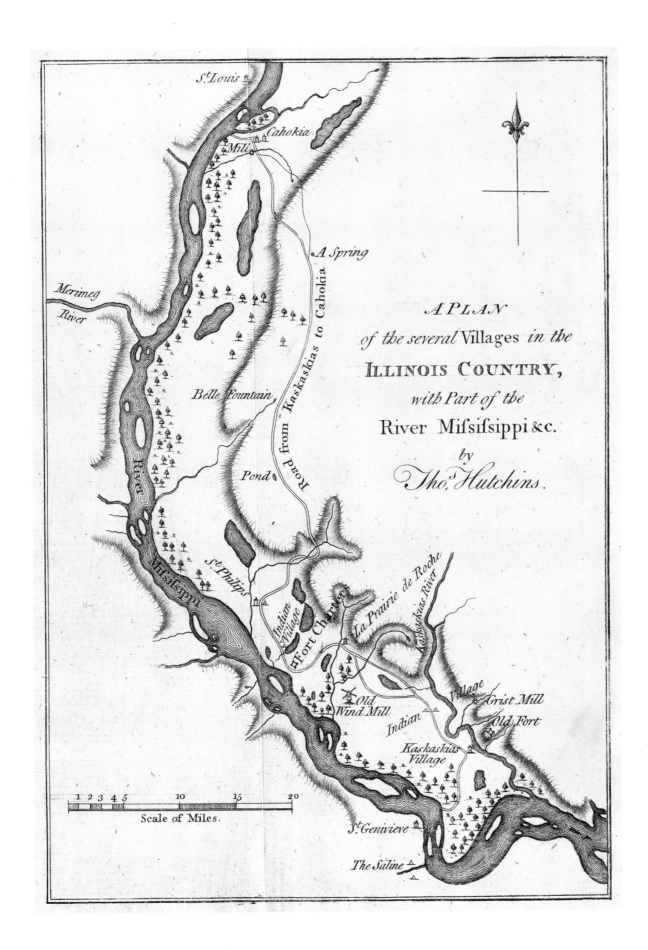

St. Louis

Cahokia

Mill

Merimeg River

A Spring

Road from Kaskaskias to Cahokia

Belle Fountain

Pond

River

Mississippi

St. Philips

Indian Village

Fort Charters

La Prairie de Roche

Kaskaskias River

Old Wind Mill

Indian

Village

Grist Mill

Old Fort

Kaskaskias Village

St. Genivieve

The Saline

A PLAN
of the several Villages in the
ILLINOIS COUNTRY,
with Part of the
River Mississippi &c.
by
Thos. Hutchins.

1 2 3 4 5   10   15   20
Scale of Miles.

59

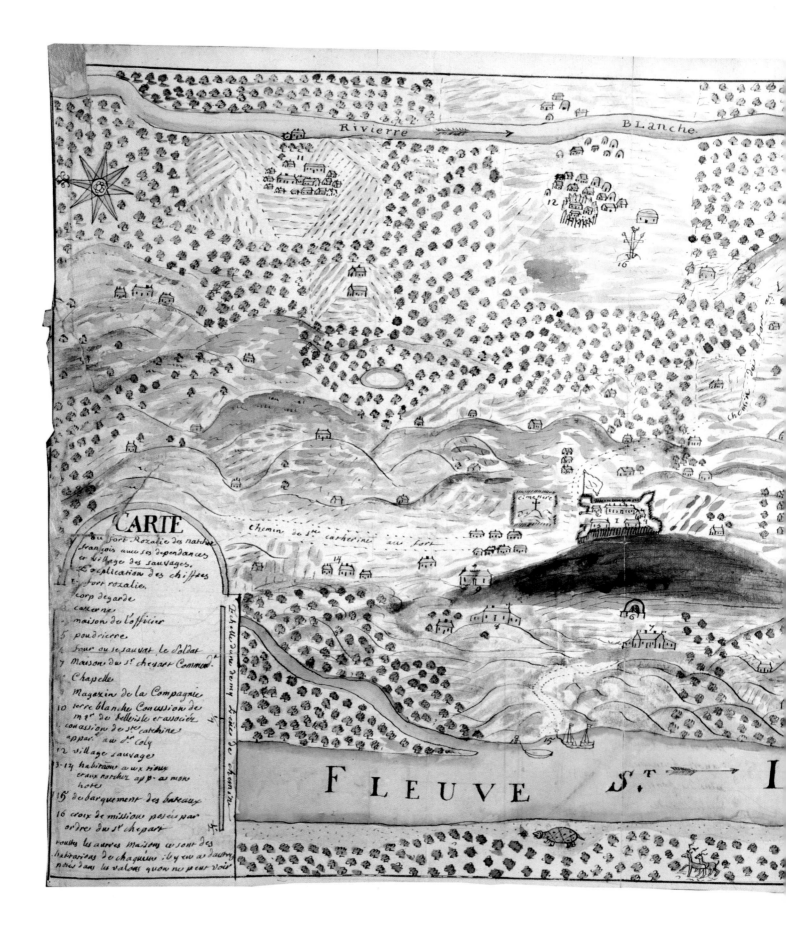

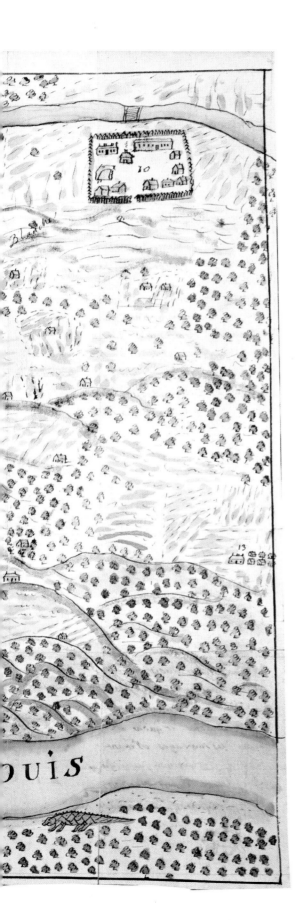

Title: *Carte du Fort Rozalie des Natches François avec ses Dependances et Village des Sauvages*
Date Issued: 1747
Cartographer: Jean François Benjamin Dumont de Montigny
Published: Manuscript
Pen and ink and watercolor, 13.2 x 17.5 inches
Newberry Library, VAULT oversize Ayer MS 257 map 9

NEXT PAGES
Title: *Plan de la Ville la Nouvelle Orleans Capitale de la Province de la Loûisiane*
Date Issued: 1755
Cartographer: Sieur Thierry
Published: Manuscript
Pen and ink and watercolor, 16.1 x 28 inches
The Historic New Orleans Collection, Accession 1939.8

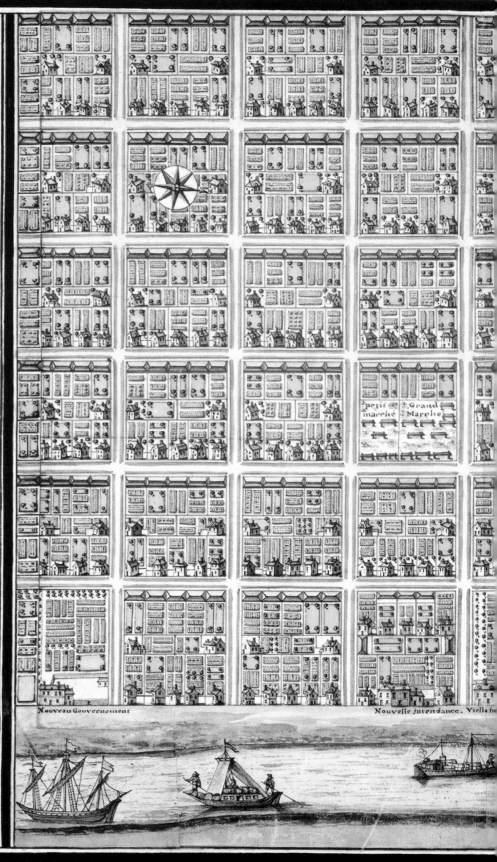

PLAN DE LA VILLE LA NOUVELLE ORLEANS CAPITALE DE LA PROVINCE DE LA LOÜISIANE

fut decouverte en 1680. par M.^r cavalier de rouen et par le pere hennepin Recolle a yant remonte le fleuve S. laurent au travers de tous les lac qu'il traver sé jla riviere en pays Riviere des jli nois juquau fleuve miſſiſipi jl ny a vait que quel qu petit fort, C'eſt en l'an 1720. que M.^r le duc D'orleans Re' gent y fit rant porter vne colonie fit Bâtire vne ville dit la nouvelle Orleans du Régne de fa Maj.^{te} louis ^{XV.} Cette ville a 600.T. de long et 335.T. de large les principales maifons font Bâ ties de Brique et couvertes de tuille, les autres maifons font Bâties de bois cou vertes de même Cette province eſt tre's fertille

TABLE

les jeſuittes

A. les Capucin B. la prifon C. le Corps de Garde D. maifon du procureure General E. les cazernes F. pavillion des officies G. les arfenaux H. les magazin du Roy I. maifon du Garde magazin K. maifon du doien des Confeillers L. maifon du major M. maifon de l'aide major N. mai fon de Broſſe un de plus Riche O. jar din des plantes du Roy P. vielle mai fon des Religieufe Q. hopital R. nouvel le maifon des Religieufe S. maifon des penfionnaires T. ancien Gouverne ment

Echelle de 100. Toifes

Deſſiné mis au net par leſieur Thierry Geographe Ancien deſſinateur du Bu reau des fortifications es Bâtiment du Roy 1755.

Nouveau Gouvernement

petit Marché   Grand Marché

Nouvelle Intendance. Vielle

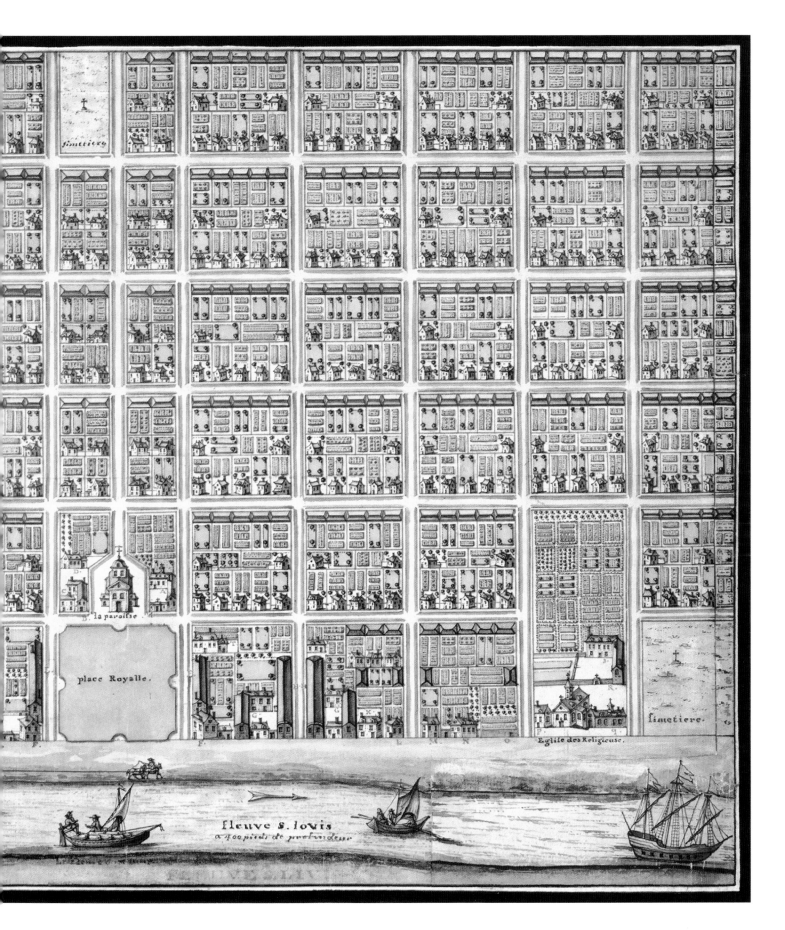

fimetiere.

la paroisse.

place Royalle.

Eglife des Religieuse.

fimetiere.

fleuve s. louis
a 400 pieds de profondeur

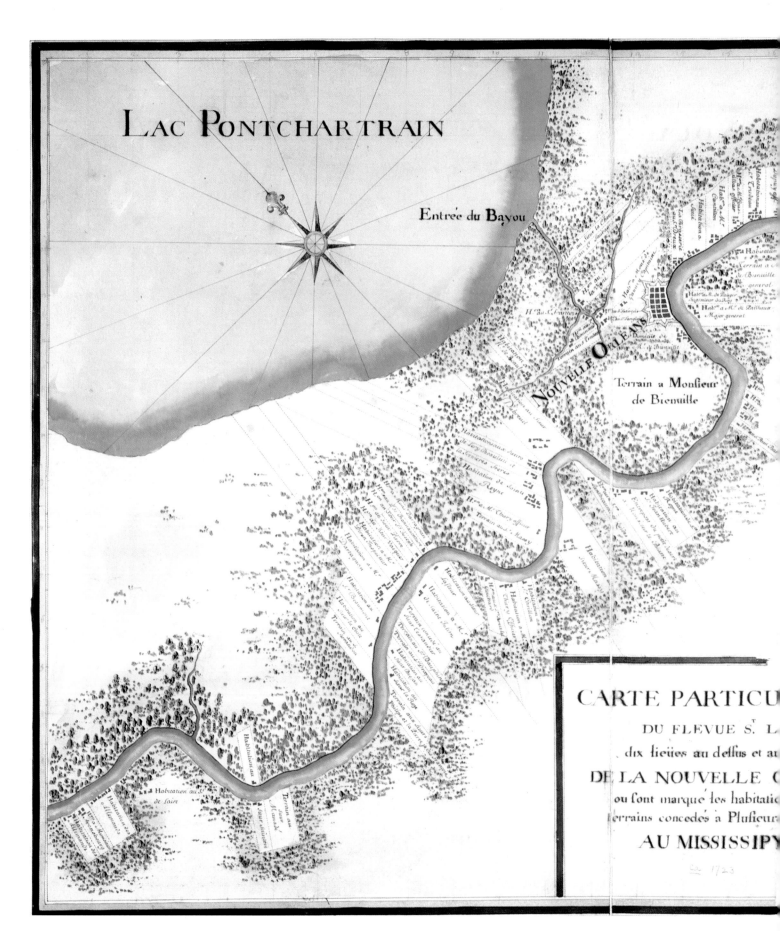

LAC PONTCHARTRAIN

Entrée du Bayou

NOUVELLE ORLEANS

Terrain a Monfieur
de Bienuille

CARTE PARTICU

DU FLEVUE St L

dix lieües au deſſus et au

DE LA NOUVELLE C

ou ſont marqué les habitatio

terrains concedés a Pluſieur

AU MISSISSIPY

1723

publishing this study, he could entice his government into considering the repossession of its former territory. Of course, by the time of its release, France had already sold this land to the United States in the Louisiana Purchase.

Collot's narrative is accompanied by thirty-six maps, plans, and views, and which together contain a wealth of information regarding the topography, fortifications, settlements, and other resources of the Mississippi River Valley. The map shown here is a manuscript map that Collot drew in 1796, and which was later duplicated for the book. It shows the course of the Mississippi from St. Louis to its mouth, including any development he observed along the riverbanks of this route. There are seven inset plans of fortifications and their surrounding settlements along the river: St. Louis des Illinois 1796, Plan du Cap Girardo 1796, Plan du Fort de la Nlle. Madrid, Plan du Fort des Ecores à Margot, Plan du Nogales, Plan du Baton Rouge, and Fort des Natchez.

Title: *Carte Particuliere du Fleuve St. Louis dix Lieües au Dessus de la Nouvelle Orleans: Ou sont Marqué les Habitations et les Terrains Concedés à Plusiers Particuliers au Mississipy*
Date Issued: 1723
Cartographer: Anonymous
Published: Manuscript
Pen and ink and watercolor, 19.3 x 26.8 inches
Newberry Library, Ayer MS Map 30 sheet 80

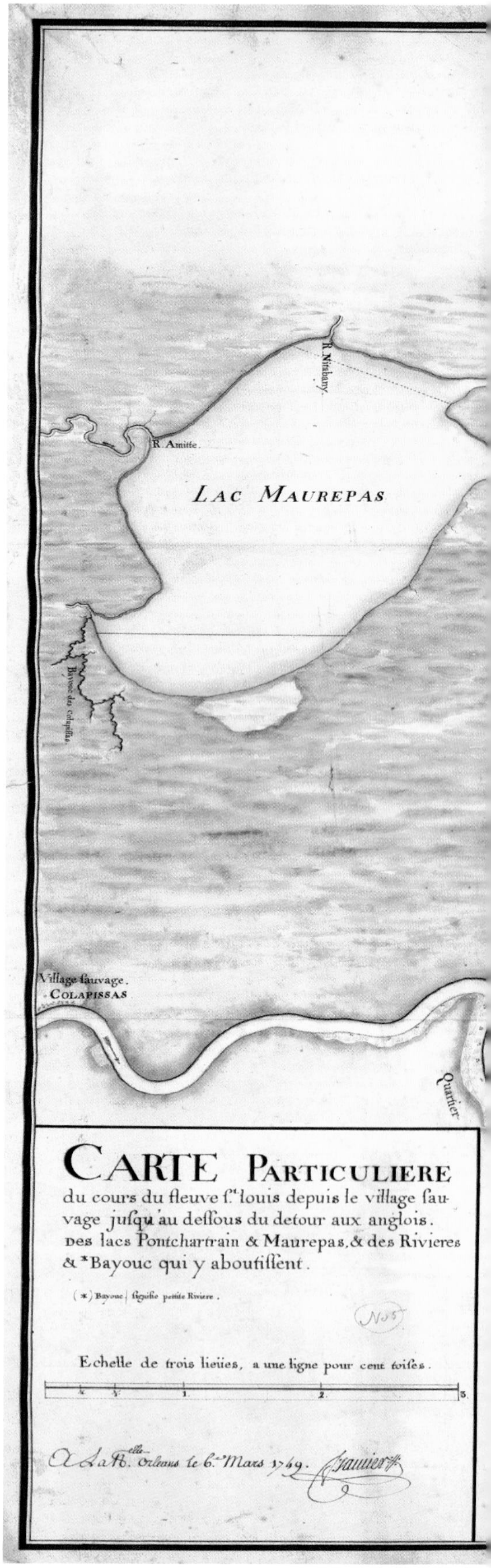

CARTE PARTICULIERE du cours du fleuve f.ᵗ louis depuis le village fau-vage jufqu'au deffous du detour aux anglois. des lacs Pontchartrain & Maurepas, & des Rivieres & *Bayouc qui y aboutiffent.

(*) Bayouc / fignifie petite Riviere .

Echelle de trois lieües, a une ligne pour cent toifes .

A la f̃.ᵉˡˡᵉ Orleans le 6.ᵉ Mars 1749.

Title: *Carte Particuliere du Cours Dufleuve St. Louis depuis le Village Sauvage jusqu'au Dessous du Detour aux Angloix, des lacs Pontchartrain & Maurepas & des Rivières & Bayouc quiy aboutissent*

Date Issued: 1749

Cartographer: François Saucier

Published: Manuscript

Pen and ink and watercolor, 13.8 x 18.5 inches

Library of Congress, Geography & Map Division, G4042.M5 1749 .S3 Vault

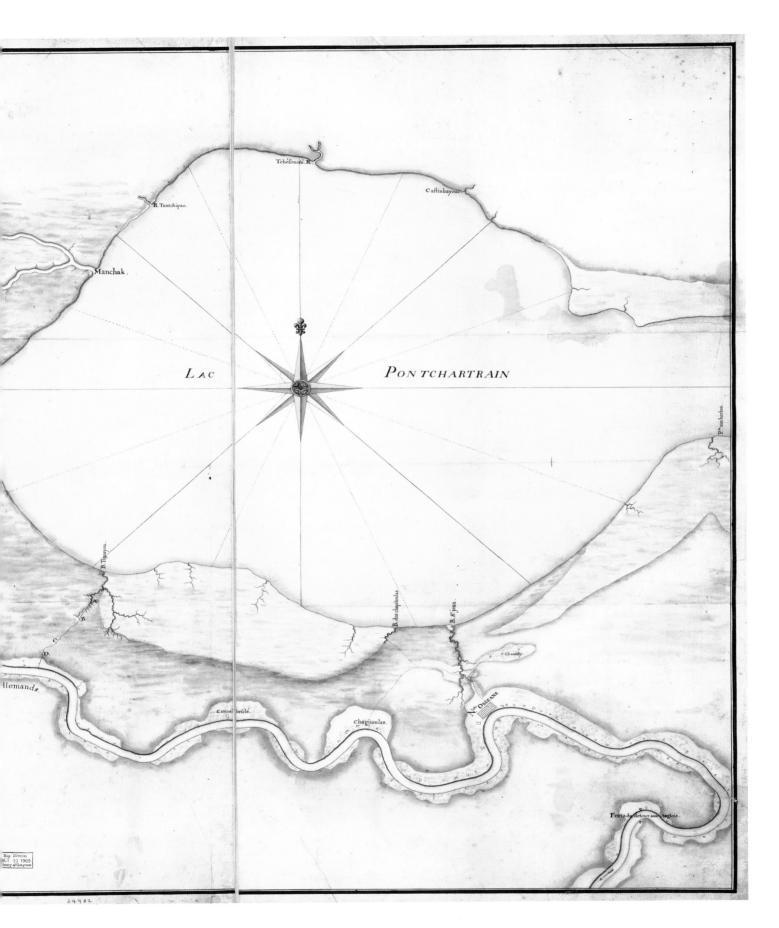

LAC *Tchefoncte R.*

Caftinbayoue.

R. Tantchipao.

Manchak.

PON TCHARTRAIN

Pte unchartes.

B. Tiguayou.

B. des chapitoulas.

B. St. Jean.

St. Chantily.

Hemands.

C.
D.
B.

Canne brule.

Chapitoulas.

N.lle ORLEANS

Forts du detour aux Anglois.

67

Missisipi fl.

GOLFE DE

a Paris chez Chereau le jeune

1. Embouchure du Missisipi   5. Nouveau Fort Louis
2. la Nouvele Orleans   6. Vieux Fort Louis
3. Lac de Pontchartrain   7. Isle Dauphine
4. Lac de Maurepas   8. Isle de la Chandeleur

LE MISSISIPI
ou la Louisiane
Dans l'Amerique
Septentrionale

9. Pe...
10. M...
11. Ge...
12. Ba...

13. Charle Fort
14. Riviere du St Esprit
15. Vilages des Indiens
16. Debarquement des Fran=
:cois.

...cola
...le Riviere
...nador Riviere
...c Ste Rose

Title: *Le Missisipi ou la Louisiane dans l'Amerique Septentrionale*
Date Issued: c. 1720
Cartographer: François Chereau
Published: Nicolas Bonnart (Paris)
Colored printed map, 7.9 x 12.2 inches
The Historic New Orleans Collection, Accession 1959.210

NEXT PAGES

top left:
Title: *Carte de la Louisiane*
Date Issued: 1732
Cartographer: Jean Baptiste Bourguignon D'Anville
Published: [*General Atlas*] (Paris)
Printed map, 22.4 x 40.6 inches
David Rumsey Collection, Image No. 2603037

top right:
Title: *Plan de la Ville de Illinois sur le Mississipi:*
Avec les Differents Projets de la Fortifier
Date Issued: 1764
Cartographer: George de Bois St. Lys
Published: Manuscript
Pen and ink and watercolor, 12.2 x 16.5 inches
Missouri Historical Society Library, Map St. Louis 1796 No. 3

bottom:
Title: *Carte Particuliere du Cours du Mississippi depuis le*
Missouri et le Pays des Illinois jusqu'a l'Embourche de ce Fleuve
Date Issued: 1826
Cartographer: Georges Henri Victor Collot
Published: *Voyage dans L'Amérique Septentrionale* (Paris)
Colored manuscript map, 35.4 x 126 inches
Service Historique de la Marine à Vincennes, Recueil 66, No. 7

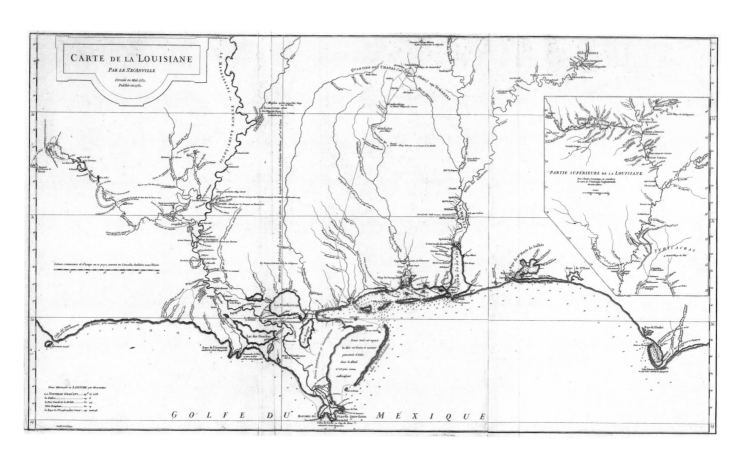

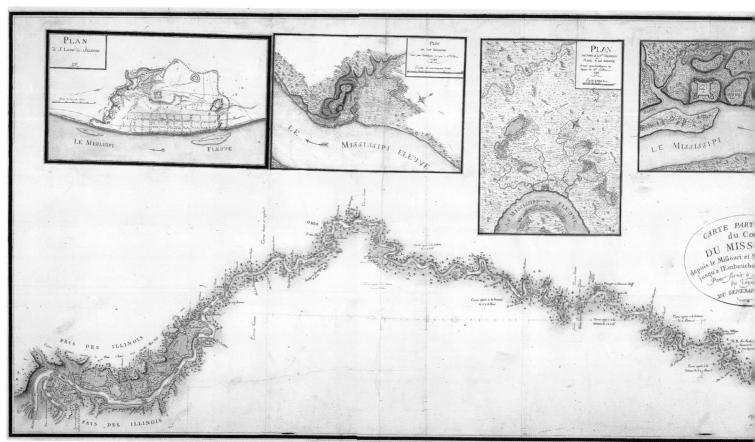

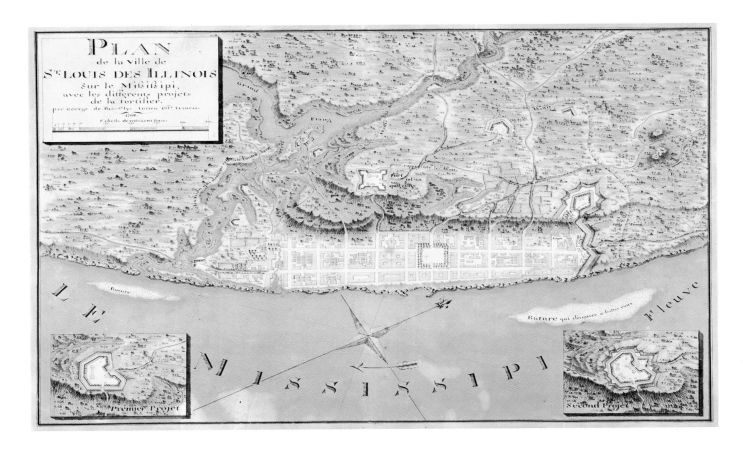

PLAN
de la Ville de
St LOUIS DES ILLINOIS
sur le Missisipi,
avec les differents projets
de la fortifier.
par George de Bois St Ly. Ancien Off. François
1796.
Echelle de troi cent toises

Premier Projet

Second Projet

LE MISSISSIPI Fleuve

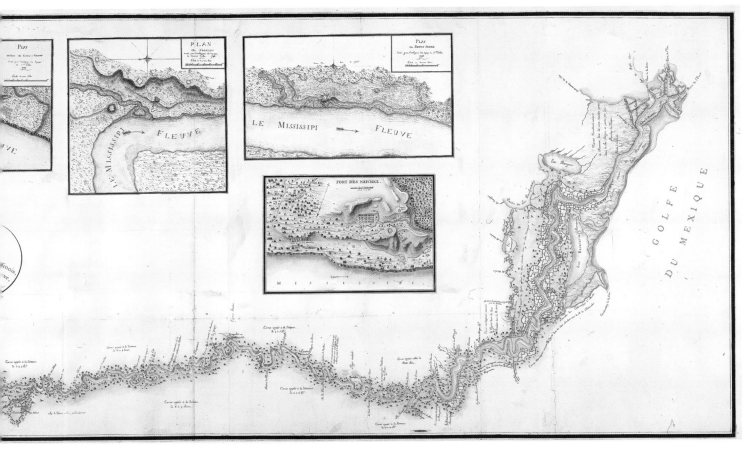

PLAN

PLAN
de Natchez

PLAS
de Baton Rouge

LE MISSISSIPI FLEUVE

LE MISSISSIPI FLEUVE

FORT DES NATCHEZ

MISSISSIPI

GOLFE DU MEXIQUE

British Designs on the Mississippi Valley

The colony of Louisiana had been organized primarily as a means to prevent British intrusion into lands that the French deemed their legitimate possessions. The British, on the other hand, disputed the extent of France's claims. French colonial authorities claimed sovereignty over a vast area comprising about one-third of the North American continent, roughly including Canada, the Great Lakes region, the Ohio Valley, and all lands west of the Appalachian Mountains to the Mississippi River as far south as the Gulf of Mexico. The British claims were asserted through the various colonies, but amounted to an area no less extensive: Virginia and Pennsylvania both claimed rights to the Ohio Valley; Massachusetts (which included present-day Maine) claimed lands that extended beyond the border with Canada; and Carolina claimed both Spanish Florida and French Louisiana.

Colonial officials appealed to evidence of all sorts—official correspondence, royal proclamations, memoranda, plans, and so forth—to defend their territorial claims. Maps in particular were used to summarize and defend these claims, and the result was an eighteenth-century "map war" between France and England. This conflict stimulated the production of a series of maps that culminated in what has become known in the annals of American cartography as "the year of the great maps." More than that, however, this cartographic skirmish helped to solidify the irreconcilability of the French and British positions and would thus help push them onto a path of a more deliberate confrontation.

As seen earlier, the first shot in this campaign was De L'Isle's 1718 map, *Carte de la Louisiane*, which was intended to circumscribe and minimize Britain's territorial claims; in particular, De L'Isle characterized "Caroline" as discovered, named, settled, and possessed by France. The English rejoinder to the "impertinent" map of De L'Isle is shown here. Published by Herman Moll in 1720, it shows the border lines as specified by De L'Isle in blue and notes that this amounts to a claim on land that had already been claimed and settled by the English. In fact, Moll suggests, the real British border of Carolina (shown in yellow) is westward into a region along the Mississippi River—land that was also claimed by France. Moll depicts Spanish claims in red.

There is a sense in which De L'Isle wins this round—by the terrestrial accuracy of his map. Moll notes De L'Isle as a source for his map, and closely follows De L'Isle's depiction of Texas and the lower Mississippi. Moreover, Moll's inset, "A Map of ye Mouth of Mississippi," is identical to an inset on De L'Isle's map. De L'Isle was the first cartographer to place "Texas" on a map, and Moll does likewise: "Mission de los Teyas Sett. In 1716." Moll would seem to gain an edge because his synthesis of a number of contemporary sources gives him greater accuracy in other regions represented on these maps. He makes a glaring mistake, however—one that De L'Isle had earlier set right. Moll depicts Lahontan's fictitious Rivière Longue (the "Morte or Longo") flowing eastward from "La Hontan's Limit" across the northern plains to the Mississippi. Although De L'Isle had depicted the Rivière Longue on earlier maps, by 1718 he had corrected the error.

Nicolas Bellin softened French claims with his 1732 edition of *Carte de la Louisiane et des Pays Voisins*, according to which the English colonies (which now include Carolina) are closely contained east of the Appalachian Mountains. In 1733, Henry Popple published his massive *A Map of the British Empire in America*, which limits the French territories to a narrow strip along the Mississippi River from the Gulf of Mexico to the fork of the Ohio River, the coastal areas of Louisiana, the north bank of the St. Lawrence River between Lake Ontario and the Emboucheure — St. John's Island, the Cape Breton Islands, and Anticoste Island. The series of volleys in this battle culminated in 1755 with the production of a number of maps that are considered among the most important in American cartography. The British maps that year were uncompromising. Thomas Bowen, on his 1755 *Map of the British and French Settlements in North America . . . ,* notes that "the bounds of Virginia and New England by Charters, May 28, 1609 and Nov. 3, 1620," extend "from the Atlantic Ocean to the South Sea." A map published in London that year by "a Society of Anti-Gallicans" was entitled "A new and accurate map of the English empire in North America: Representing their rightful claim as confirm'd by charters, and the formal surrender of their Indian friends; likewise the encroachments of the French, with the several forts they have unjustly erected therein." Produced by William Herbert and Robert Sayer, the boundaries of Georgia, North and South Carolina, and Virginia range westward on this map beyond the Mississippi.

The greatest of the maps in the year of great maps was John Mitchell's *A Map of the British and French Dominions in North America*. Shown here, it has been described as the most important map in North American history, and is the only map known to have been drawn by Dr. John Mitchell. Born in Virginia and educated in Edinburgh, Mitchell was an early American renaissance man: he practiced medicine in Virginia, where he also conducted botanical research. Edmund Berkeley notes in his biography of Mitchell that he "was for a time perhaps the ablest scientific investigator in North America," and that Mitchell "has a place in the early history of American botany, zoology, physiology, medicine, cartography, climatology, and agriculture, to say nothing of politics."

After falling ill, Mitchell quit Virginia and sailed to London in May 1746 to regain his health. At the time, the only large-scale map of North America produced in Britain was Popple's, a map which also had been made to draw attention to the French threat to British claims and to promote British settlement in the colonies. Mitchell was dissatisfied with this map, however, for it made geographic omissions and errors, and it did not — in Mitchell's judgment — adequately depict the French threat to Britain's domain, which now included numerous forts along the Mississippi and its tributaries that, in effect, encircled the British colonies. Accordingly, Mitchell set out to make his own map.

Determined to make the most comprehensive and up-to-date map of North America possible, Mitchell spent the next five years gathering data for his chart. He referred to contemporary maps of every North American province (maps that were supplied by the provincial governors) and gained access to the manuscript maps and geographic records in the archives of the London Board of Trade and Plantations. Much of this material had been

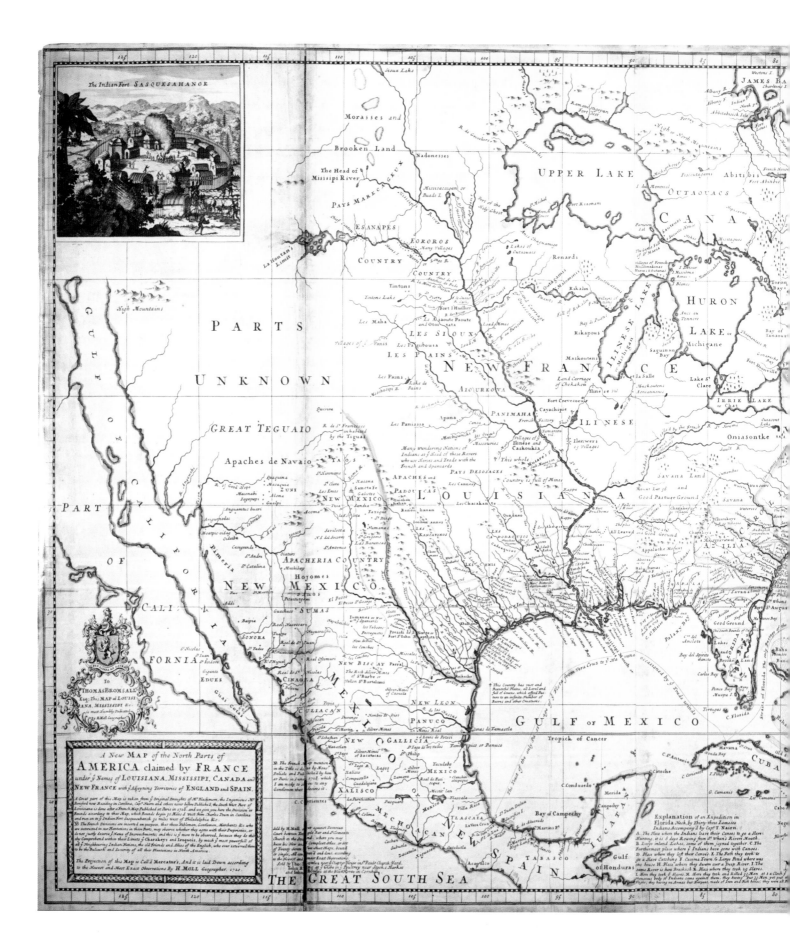

Title: A new map of ye north parts of America, claimed by France under ye names of Louisiana, Mississipi, Canada & New France, with the adjoyning territories of England & Spain
Date Issued: 1720
Cartographer: Herman Moll
Published: Separately (London)
Copperplate engraving, 24 x 39.8 inches
Newberry Library, VAULT drawer Graff 2855

gathered using the most sophisticated methods of the time: latitudinal determinations were made by the quadrant, which had been independently invented in 1731 by John Hadley and Thomas Godfrey, and longitudinal reckonings were made using the chronometer devised by John Harrison in 1735. The result was a map so accurate that it has been appealed to in the resolution of eighteenth-, nineteenth-, and even twentieth-century border disputes. Some of these cases include the Webster-Ashburton Treaty of 1842, the Quebec boundary definition of 1871, the Canada-Labrador boundary case of 1926, the Wisconsin-Michigan boundary case of 1926, and the Delaware-New Jersey dispute of 1932.

Mitchell's map was used by British and American negotiators at the Treaty of Paris of 1783, which ended the American Revolution and established the independence of the American colonies. The "treaty map" contains extensive notes, and shows topographical features, principal roads, the location of Indian villages, and dates of various settlements. In copious notes, Mitchell defends British territorial claims, remarking, for example, that by their charters Virginia and New England stretch "from Sea to Sea"; the coloring on the copy of the map shown here depicts the western borders of Virginia, the Carolinas, and Georgia as extending well beyond the Mississippi, presumably to the Pacific Ocean.

Title: A map of the British and French dominions in North America, with the roads, distances, limits, and extent of the settlements, humbly inscribed to the Right Honourable the Earl of Halifax, and the other Right Honourable the Lords Commissioners for Trade & Plantations
Date Issued: 1755
Cartographer: John Mitchell
Published: Separately (London)
Copperplate engraving, 53.5 x 76.8 inches
Library of Congress, Geography & Map Division,
G3300 1755 .M51 Vault

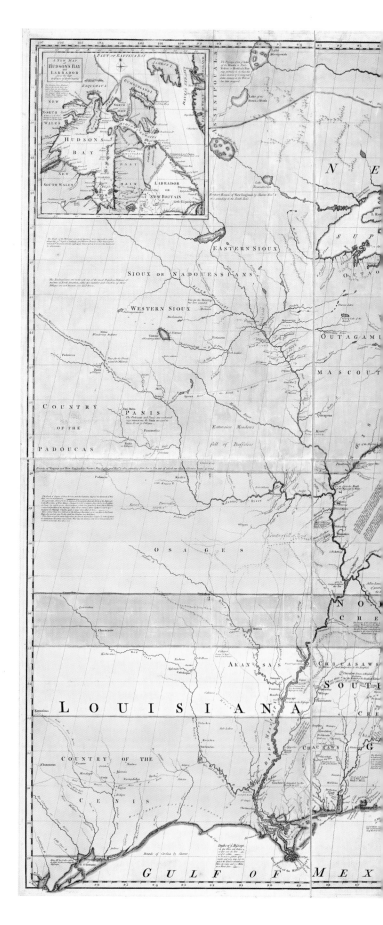

A MAP of the
British and French Dominions in
North America
WITH THE
Roads, Distances, Limits, and Extent of the
SETTLEMENTS,
Humbly Inscribed to the Right Honourable
The Earl of Halifax
And the other Right Honourable
The Lords Commissioners for Trade & Plantations,
By their Lordships
Most Obliged
and very humble Servant
Jn. Mitchell

Spanish Louisiana

The French and Indian War, known in Europe as the Seven Years War, in which Great Britain and France fought over their international empires, concluded in 1763. The British were the undisputed victors, and by the Treaty of Paris gained title to Canada. Spain, which had joined France late in the conflict, ceded Florida to Britain but in return received most of Louisiana (now the western half of the Mississippi River basin) and the Isle of Nouvelle Orleans (New Orleans and its environs).

The Spanish were at first reluctant to take on the colony, but in the end, Louisiana was deemed more valuable than Florida. In particular, Spain saw Louisiana as an important buffer between the British colonies and the vast wealth of New Spain. On the other hand, Louisiana had been a disastrous drain on France's finances, and so the French deemed possession of its Caribbean sugar islands as more valuable than that of a colony that had never made a profit.

Cartographers worked feverishly to portray the new political landscape on the North American continent, and a flurry of maps ensued. An early attempt to depict the situation was done by the colorist of the first map shown here. This attractive map was drawn by Nicolas Bellin in 1763, and focuses on the center of the continent ranging west to the Rio Grande ("R du Nord ou Rio Bravo") and east to the Atlantic. As shown here, the Mississippi River serves as the line of demarcation between Spanish and British possessions: the lands west of the Mississippi that were now Spanish territory are colored yellow; the British territory east of the river is highlighted in red. Of course, this mistakenly represents the Isle of Orleans, which is east of the river, as a British possession.

The Spanish understood that the best way to prevent British control of Louisiana was to occupy and settle the colony. Accordingly, they granted land to loyal Catholics of any nationality: French, German, and Irish Catholic settlers all came to make their claims; even Anglo-Americans were allowed to immigrate—provided they converted to Catholicism. The settlement at New Madrid in Missouri along the Mississippi River was a direct result of this program. Although the citizens of New Madrid were not Spaniards, they could be expected to detest the British and deter any of their designs west of the Mississippi, especially on the fur trade along the Missouri River.

The Spanish also encouraged the emigration of French Catholic Acadians from present-day Nova Scotia and its environs to Louisiana. During their 1754–63 conquest of Canada, the British ruthlessly expelled nearly ten thousand Acadians, many of whom eventually did migrate to Louisiana, some settling in what became known as the "Acadian Coast" of the Mississippi River (along the banks of the river in what are now the parishes of Ascension and St. James). These immigrants flourished in their new home, interacting and intermarrying with their American, Spanish, Indian, and African neighbors, and soon spread up and down the river.

In 1778, the Spanish settled seven hundred Canary Islanders, known as Isleños, in Louisiana. Africans made up the largest group of immigrants to Spanish Louisiana, albeit forced, and by the end of Spain's nearly forty-year reign in Louisiana, slaves made up about 55 percent of the population. A census taken in 1799 showed that the liberal Spanish immigration policy had its desired effect: the population of Louisiana had increased to fifty thousand, an increase of about 500 percent since 1763.

Spanish authorities during this period prohibited the circulation of maps as a matter of national security, and so printed Spanish maps of Louisiana are rare. The Spanish did strive to scientifically study the geography of their new colony, and the manuscript map (shown on the following pages) pays careful attention to major waterways and to the location of American Indian nations. Drawn around the time of the Treaty of Paris negotiations, it depicts the British colonies of Virginia and Carolina as extending west to the Mississippi; what would become the Spanish province of "Luisiana" lies west of the river.

This map was clearly meant to emphasize the natural advantage the Mississippi afforded the Spanish for the defense of their western lands, and over the years Spain adopted various means to safeguard the river: a series of small posts was established along the river south of its confluence with the Ohio, including Nogales (1790, present-day Vicksburg) and a fort on Chickasaw Bluffs above the river (1795, now modern-day Memphis); a fleet of Spanish gunboats patrolled the river in an attempt to regulate commercial and military traffic. Taking advantage of the American Revolution, the Spanish declared war on Britain in 1779 and were able to gain complete control of the lower Mississippi and Gulf Coast through a series of military victories.

The Treaty of Paris of 1783 ended the American Revolution, and by this accord Great Britain granted the United States full use of the Mississippi River "from its source to the ocean." That same year the British returned East and West Florida to Spain, but their pact with the Spanish contained no guarantee of river access to the Americans. Moreover, the Spanish crown was rightfully concerned about the westward movement of the American population into the fertile territory bordering Spanish Louisiana. In particular, the Spanish feared that land acquisition along the Mississippi would stimulate unlawful traffic in its colonial borderlands and encourage incursion into New Spain. It therefore refused to recognize the British treaty provisions and closed the river to non-Spanish vessels in July 1784.

In 1784 American foreign minister John Jay negotiated a surrender of America's rights to the Mississippi for twenty-five years in exchange for commercial privileges in Spanish markets favorable to the New England fishing industry. This plan predictably raised very strong objections in the trans-Appalachian settlements, especially in Kentucky. On the other hand, as far as some conservative New Englanders were concerned, if closing the Mississippi to American navigation would provide a boon to the Atlantic states, then so be it. Threats of secession ensued on both sides, including a group of New Englanders that were so alarmed by westward expansion that they adopted Montesquieu's dictum that a republic could survive only if it occupied a small territory. James Madison had a vision of a different kind of republic—a pluralistic one—and argued that

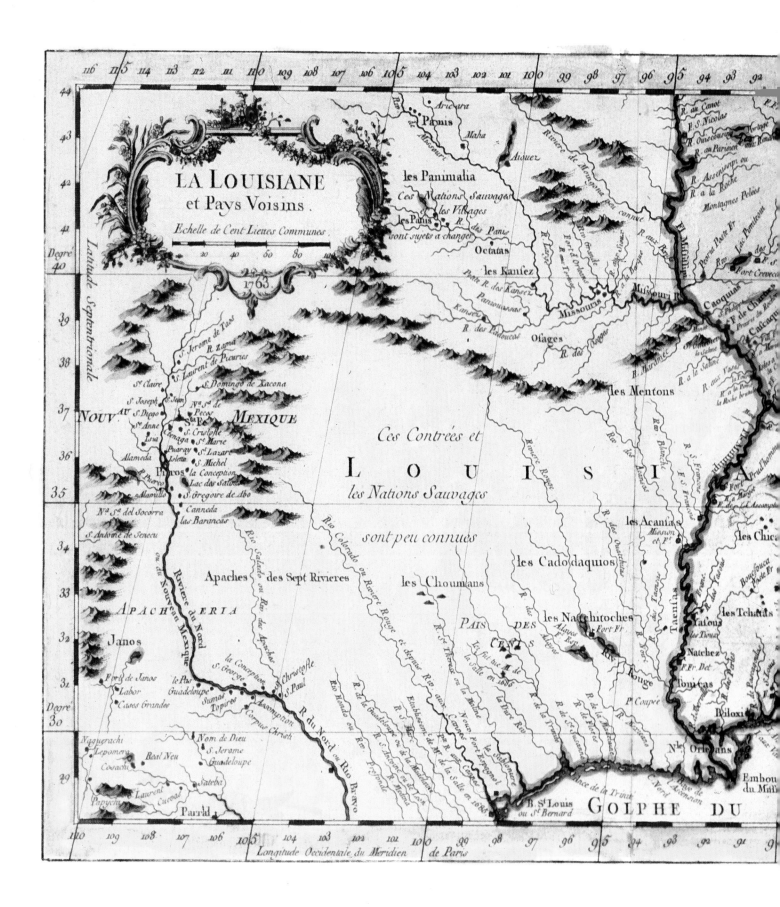

a large, extended, heterogeneous country could support republican values better than a small country dominated by special interests. Madison won the day, as he mustered forces in Congress to defeat the treaty's ratification. Thus it was that the Mississippi River came to play a central role in the determination of a young nation's image of itself and its power.

The issue of river navigation would remain unresolved for eleven years until President Washington—unnerved by the specter of disorder in Kentucky—sent Thomas Pinckney as his envoy extraordinary to the Court of Spain. The Spanish had just suffered military defeats at the hands of the French, and were in a mood to compromise. Furthermore, Spain had been unable to stem the advance of American settlers and frontiersmen into its Louisiana and Florida borderlands, and was ready to concede that its colonial authority had been seriously undermined. Pinckney skillfully concluded the Treaty of San Lorenzo in 1795—commonly referred to as Pinckney's Treaty—which defined Spanish and American boundaries, granted navigation rights on the Mississippi River, and allowed for American docking privileges in New Orleans. By 1802, New Orleans had been transformed into one of the busiest ports in North America.

Title: *La Louisiane et Pays Voisins*
Date Issued: 1763
Cartographer: Jacques Nicolas Bellin
Published: Separately (Paris)
Copperplate engraving, 13.4 x 19.3 inches
The Historic New Orleans Collection, Accession 1975.35

Title: [*Mapa realizado hacia 1760, contemporáneo del Tratado de Paris, en el que figura La Luisiana, a la izquierda del Mississipi, con la Ciudad de Nueva Orleans*]

Date Issued: c. 1760

Cartographer: Anonymous

Published: Manuscript

Pen and ink and watercolor, 6.7 x 9 inches

Archivo Histórico Nacional, Sección Estatdo,
Maps y Planos, No. 16

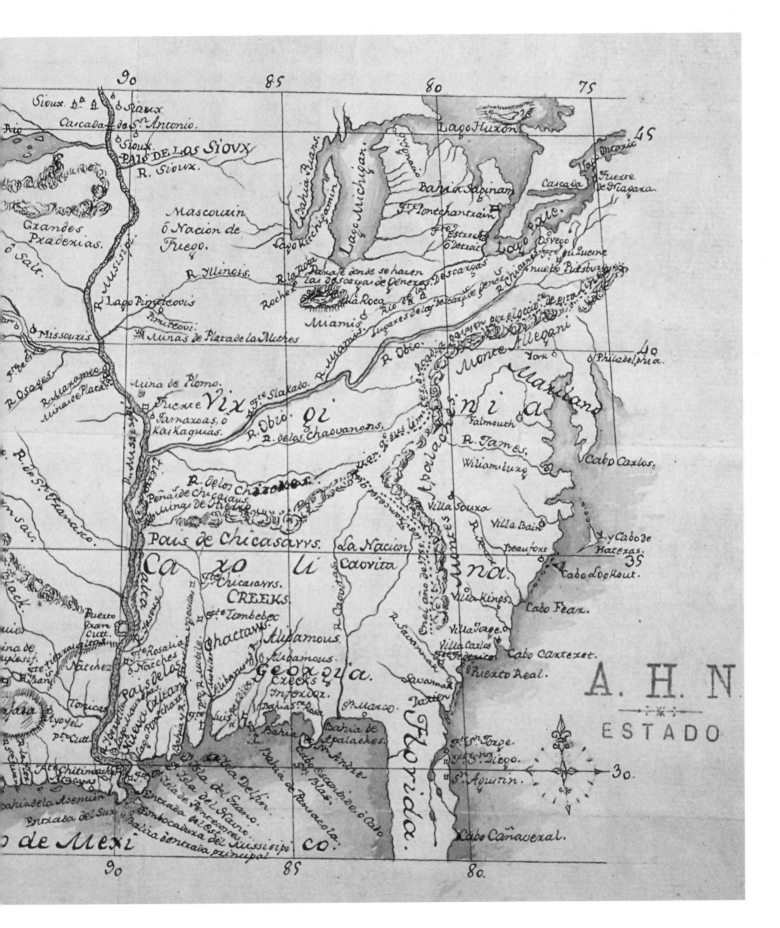

British Maps of the Mississippi

The Treaty of Paris of 1763 had established the Mississippi River as the boundary separating the British and the Spanish empires in North America. The Spanish viewed the river as a natural as much as a symbolic boundary; in particular, the Mississippi would serve as a barrier to British encroachment on Spanish territory to the west. Great Britain, on the other hand, intended to use the river as a means to exploit the Mississippi Valley fur trade. This plan faced a large obstacle, however, for although the British had gained the right to navigate the river, its major port, New Orleans, was under Spanish control.

The first step in the British commercial scheme was to occupy and garrison several locations on the east bank of the river in the Illinois country. A military detachment was dispatched from Mobile to the Illinois country early in 1764; they ascended the Mississippi to a point near the mouth of the Red River, where an attack by Tunica Indians forced them to abandon their mission. A few months later, Lieutenant Phillip Pittman, disguised as a Frenchman, set out upriver with a band of Creole traders. Fearing detection, he returned to Mobile before reaching the Illinois country. Failing in their southern approaches, the British worked their way down the Ohio River and took possession of Fort Chartres in October 1765.

That same year the Thirty-Fourth Regiment of Foot spent five months working its way up the Mississippi under the command of Major Robert Farmer. Pittman served as an engineer on the expedition, which surveyed the Mississippi Valley and charted the river's course from Fort de la Balise, built by the French on the east pass of the river's mouth in 1734, to Fort Chartres in the Illinois country. Pittman published an account of this excursion in 1770 as *The Present State of the European Settlements on the Mississippi*. He notes that the report "was originally wrote at the request and for the perusal only, of the secretary of state for the colonies"; it was the first book in English to describe the French towns from New Orleans to St. Louis and is notable for Pittman's sympathetic description of the situation of the native peoples, who in his words, were "oppressed" by the French. Included with the publication were a three-sheet map of the Mississippi River from Fort Balize to Fort Chartres, a draft of the Iberville River, and plans of Mobile, New Orleans, Fort Rosalie, and Kaskaskia.

Shown here is a single-sheet map of the Mississippi drawn by another member of the Thirty-Fourth Regiment, Lieutenant John Ross. It was first published in 1772, and is based upon the surveys made by the 1765 expedition and on earlier plans by the French cartographer Jean Baptiste Bourguignon d'Anville. This large-scale map was reissued in 1775 in Thomas Jefferys's *The American Atlas*, which at the time was the major cartographic reference for America. The map itself is amazing in its detail as it depicts the course of the river and its tributaries from just below St. Louis to its mouth; included is information on settlements, abandoned French forts,

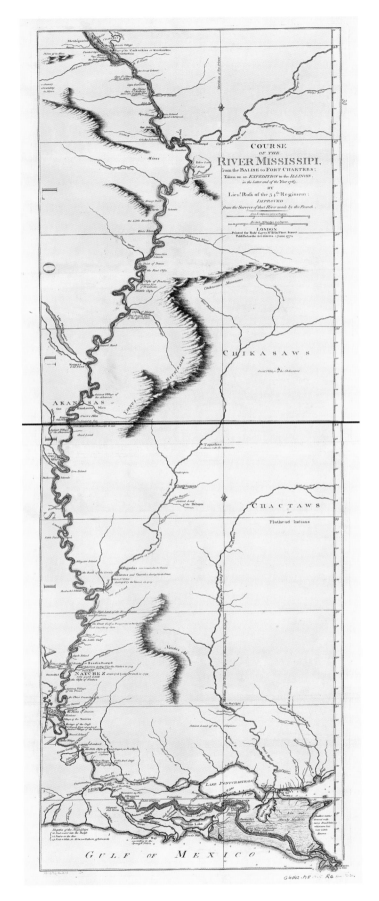

ancient American Indian sites, portages, quarries, mines, and other natural resources the expedition encountered along the way.

The next map is a British manuscript map that depicts the province of West Florida and the Spanish-held Isle of Orleans. Probably drawn shortly after the signing of the Treaty of Paris, it illustrates the Mississippi River from its mouth to the Ohio River, various interior streams, the area's coastline, as well as European and American Indian settlements. It contains an inaccurately sketched line marking the province's eastern boundary with the note: "This line being proposed to be the eastern boundary of the New Collony is supposed to run parrallel to the R. Mississipi and to continue in this direction 'till it strikes on the R. Ohio." Another note discusses the depth of the water along a route from the Mississippi to the Gulf of Mexico via the Iberville River (Bayou Manchac), Amite River, and lakes Maurepas and Pontchartrain. The note relates that there is not a sufficient water supply to permit year-round traffic on the Iberville, but adds that "it is immagin'd that by a trifling expense the waters of the Mississipi might be turned thro' that channell and thereby render the navigation good at all seasons in the year."

Title: Course of the River Mississipi, from the Balise to Fort Chartres: Taken on an Expedition to the Illinois, in the latter end of the year 1765, Improved from the Surveys of that River made by the French
Date Issued: 1772
Cartographer: Lieut. John Ross
Published: Separately (London)
Copperplate engraving, 44.5 x 13.8 inches
Library of Congress, Geography & Map Division,
G4042.M5 1765 .R6 Vault Oversize: Am. 5-30

What this proposes is the creation of a water bypass of the lower Mississippi River above New Orleans, a route that would circumvent the Spanish restrictions on British trade in Louisiana. The British immediately began to develop plans for the bypass, which, as shown on the next map, included the establishment of a settlement at the junction of the Mississippi and Iberville rivers. This location is clearly delineated on the map, and an inset depicts the harbor of the proposed settlement. Published by *Gentlemen's Magazine* in 1772, the map is from a larger, more detailed manuscript created by Elias Dumford, who served as surveyor-general of British West Florida at Pensacola.

Their lands in the Mississippi Valley never produced the commercial benefits the British envisioned. Although they did manage to garrison several positions on the east bank of the river, they would never gain control of the river, nor were they permitted an *entrepôt* at New Orleans. Furthermore, the British plans for a New Orleans bypass, which included enlarging and settling the Iberville River, never came to fruition. Great Britain would hold the eastern part of Louisiana ceded by France in 1763 for twenty years, until it too was driven out of the territory by its rebellious colonies.

Title: A Plan of West Florida, the Isle of Orleans, and Some Part of the Spanish Dominions to the Westward of the Mississippi
Date Issued: *c.* 1763
Cartographer: Anonymous
Published: Manuscript
Pen and ink and watercolor, 57.5 x 20 inches
Library of Congress, Geography & Map Division,
G3980 1763 .P5 Vault

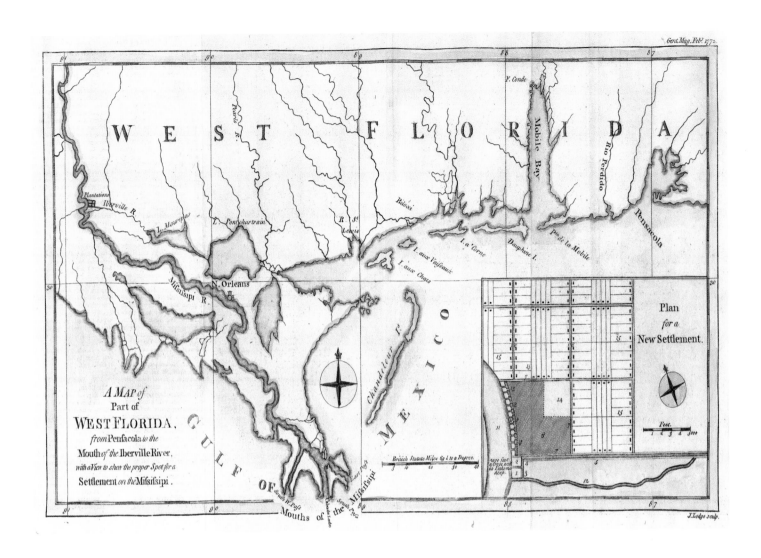

Title: A Map of Part of West Florida from Pensacola to the Mouth of the Iberville River with a View to show the proper Spot for a Settlement on the Mississippi

Date Issued: 1772

Cartographer: Elias Dumford

Published: *Gentlemen's Magazine* (London)

Printed map, 8.3 x 15.7 inches

Author's Collection

The End of the Colonial Era

By the end of the eighteenth century, Spain was a weak imperial power that was in no way capable of defending its North American possessions. In part to avoid the ignoble conquest of this territory by British or American forces, King Carlos IV agreed to retrocede Louisiana back to France, along with the Floridas, which Spain had claimed since 1492. This transfer of authority was a cause of great concern for the United States, for in its westward expansion, navigation of the Mississippi River and access to the Port of New Orleans had become critical to American commerce. Indeed, the very existence of new settlers in the valleys of the Cumberland, Tennessee, and Ohio rivers depended on their right to use the Mississippi River freely and to make transshipment of their exports at New Orleans. The situation reached a crisis point in October 1802 when the Spanish crown signed a decree transferring the territory to France; the Spanish agent in New Orleans, acting on orders from the Spanish court, revoked the right of deposit, or temporary storage, of American goods at New Orleans for transshipment.

President Thomas Jefferson and Secretary of State James Madison worked to resolve the issue through diplomatic channels, but rebellious factions in the West began to call for war and—along with the opposition Federalist Party—advocated secession by the western territories in order to seize control of the lower Mississippi and New Orleans. Tensions mounted, and the president reacted to the urgency of the situation. In January 1803, he sent James Monroe to Paris as a minister extraordinary; Monroe was to join Robert Livingston, the United States minister to France, in negotiations to obtain land east of the Mississippi from the French. Monroe carried a letter of instructions composed by Madison, and approved by Jefferson, that allocated up to ten million dollars for the purchase of New Orleans and all or part of the Floridas. Failing that, Monroe was to endeavor to purchase only New Orleans, or, at the very least, to secure American access to the Mississippi and its southernmost port.

In the meantime, Napoleon Bonaparte's plan to reestablish the French empire in America faced troubles of its own. The French army had failed to quell a rebellion in its sugar-rich colony of Saint Domingue (present-day Haiti) and a renewed war with Great Britain loomed on the horizon. France's minister of finance, François de Barbé-Marbois, who had repeatedly questioned Louisiana's worth, advised Napoleon that the value of Louisiana would be greatly diminished without Saint Domingue; moreover, he notified the ruler that France's financial stringencies ruled out any defense of the Mississippi Valley, which would undoubtedly be invaded by the British from Canada in the event of war. Napoleon, despite his assurances to Spain that he would not cede the territory to a third party, agreed with Barbé-Marbois that best way to cut their losses was to offer all of Louisiana to the United States.

Monroe arrived in Paris the day after Napoleon's foreign minister, Charles Maurice de Talleyrand, informed Livingston that France was willing to sell all of Louisiana. Although the American ministers had neither instructions nor the authority to make such a purchase, the negotiations that followed moved swiftly to a conclusion. On April 30, 1803, they reached an agreement to purchase the Louisiana territory, including New Orleans, for fifteen million dollars. Precisely what the United States had purchased was unclear: the wording of the treaty was vague, it did not give assurances that West Florida was part of the agreement, nor did it clearly describe the boundaries of Louisiana.

Of course, the boundaries of Louisiana had never been delineated on the previous treaties that transferred the colony's ownership between France and Spain, and indeed, most of the territory to be exchanged had not yet been surveyed or mapped in any detail. All that the negotiators in Paris knew was that the region historically had been bordered on the south by the Gulf of Mexico and on the east by the Mississippi River between its mouth and its uncertain headwaters. If they had consulted the most accurate and comprehensive map of the continent available to them, it would probably have been Aaron Arrowsmith's 1802 *Map Exhibiting All the New Discoveries in the Interior Parts of North America.*

This map (shown on the following pages) leaves much of the trans-Mississippi west to the imagination, although it does depict a "Stoney Mountain" range approximately where the Rockies are located. The Missouri River is given a course from the Rocky Mountains to St. Louis, and its headwaters are sketched in some detail. This depiction, which was derived from Peter Fidler's drawing of a map made by the Blackfoot Indian Ac Ko Mo Ki, shows a number of small streams that join into two branches of the Missouri that flow almost due east. The southern branch of the Missouri appears to be the main branch of the river and connects to the Knife River; the northern branch is a reasonable representation of the actual course of the Missouri.

The map also includes a caption near the southern sources of the Missouri that states "Hereabout the Mountains divide into several low Ridges"; near this note, the headwaters of the Rio Grande and Colorado also appear. The Great Lake River is shown on the western slopes of the mountain range and is connected to the Columbia River with a dotted line. Another note claims that via this route one can descend to the sea in eight days. Putting this all together, the implication could be drawn that by traversing the southern branches of the Missouri system, one might discover a core drainage system of "several low ridges" that contained not only the headwaters of the Missouri, Colorado, and Rio Grande, but also the southern branches of the Great River of the West or Columbia. This, of course, would be the long-sought Northwest Passage to the Pacific Ocean.

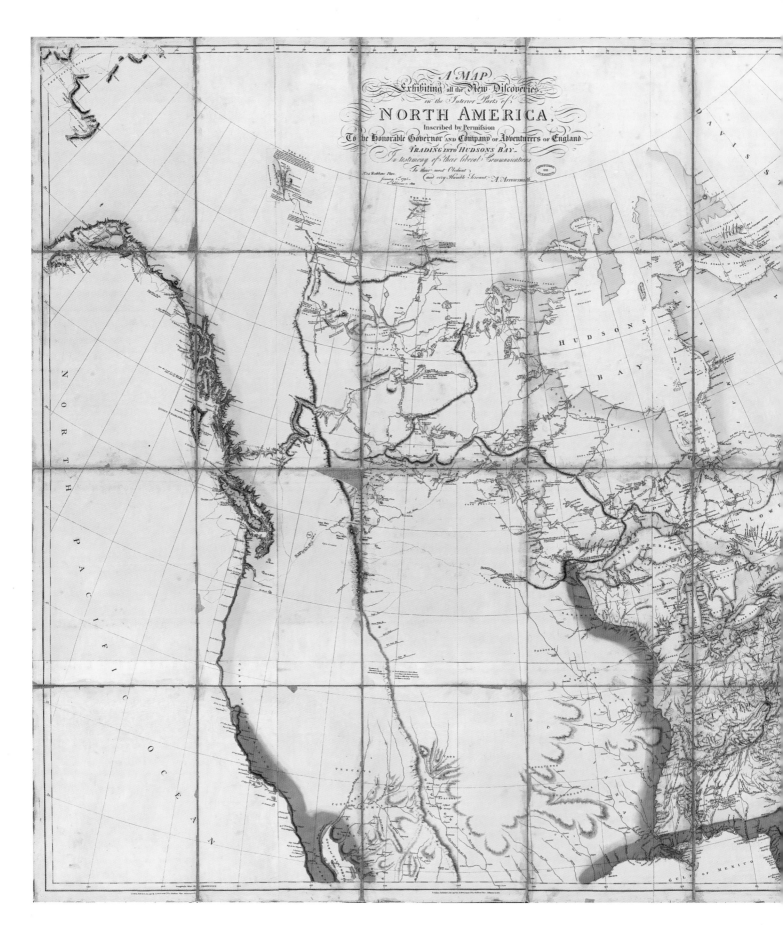

Title: Map exhibiting all the New Discoveries in the Interior Parts of North America: Inscribed by permission to the Honorable Governor and Company of Adventurers of England trading into Hudsons Bay in testimony of their Liberal Communications

Date Issued: 1802

Cartographer: Aaron Arrowsmith

Published: Separately (London)

Copperplate engraving, 49.2 x 57.5 inches

Library of Congress, Geography & Map Division, G3300 1802 A7 Vault Casetop

CHAPTER 3

MAPPING THE LOWER RIVER AND ITS DELTA

Correcting La Salle's Mistake

René Robert Cavalier, sieur de La Salle, descended the Mississippi to its mouth in 1682, where, it appears, he miscalculated the location of the Great River's mouth — a mistake that would have a profound effect on French maps of North America for the next two decades. La Salle communicated his findings to a young mapmaker in Canada, Jean Baptiste-Louis Franquelin, who promptly began producing a series of maps that illustrated La Salle's geographic notions (see Chapter 1). In drawing his maps, Franquelin used a model of the Gulf Coast that was then popular in France, as exemplified on the maps of Nicolas Sanson and Alexis-Hubert Jaillot. This coastline had first been drawn in 1631 by the Dutch cartographer Hessel Gerritz, and it subsequently appeared on Dutch maps created by Willem J. Blaeu, Jan Jansson, and Nicolass Visscher. What Franquelin simply did was locate the mouth of the Mississippi as dictated by La Salle on the Gerritz coastline.

Franquelin's maps showed the river's mouth far to the west on the Texas coast, almost on the actual site of the mouth of the Rio Grande. This setting proved to be very favorable to La Salle's appeal for royal assistance to establish a colony near the river's mouth. For as depicted on these maps, the Mississippi emptied into the Gulf not far from the mines of New Spain, a

resource coveted by the French crown. In 1684 La Salle led an expedition, sponsored by Louis XIV, back to the mouth of the Mississippi. He failed to locate the river, and landed at present-day Matagorda Bay on the Texas coast. In 1865 the Spanish learned of La Salle's landing and set out immediately to find his colony, which they considered an encroachment on their sovereign territory.

The Spanish search for La Salle's colony had two fronts. The first was led by Alsonso de León, governor of Coahuila, Mexico, who set out on a series of land expeditions that culminated in April 1689 with the discovery of the remains of La Salle's ill-fated settlement. León later ransomed a number of Frenchmen captured by local Indians, including two brothers, Jean Baptiste and Pierre Talon, whose accounts enabled the Spanish to piece together an account of what had happened to La Salle's colony. The second front was by sea, in the form of several naval expeditions of the Spanish Windward Fleet piloted by Juan Enríquez Barroto. The first sailed west from Apalachee early in 1686 to the Northeast Pass of the Mississippi, which Enríquez Barroto described as a "Palisaded River" because of the logs, mud clumps, and small mud islands he found there. A second voyage left Veracruz at the end of the same year and sailed into Matagorda Bay where wreckage from La Salle's fleet was discovered. From there, the expedition worked its way north and east along the Gulf Coast, which Enríquez Barroto, aided by other pilots, carefully observed and recorded. After working their way to the mouth of Mississippi and on to Mobile Bay, the voyageurs returned to Veracruz in July 1687.

Enríquez Barroto constructed a map based on the data gathered on these voyages, which has since been lost. Most of the information on the map was preserved, however, on a manuscript drawn in 1696 by another pilot of the Windward Fleet, Juan Bisente. This map locates the Mississippi's delta in the middle of the Gulf Coast, and correctly depicts the lower river as having a southeastward-trending course. Bisente and his map were captured by the French in a sea battle off the island of Santo Domingo in January 1697; also captured were the Talon brothers, who were repatriated to French service.

This double triumph—the capture of Bisente and his map and the return of the Talon brothers—enabled the French to correct La Salle's mistaken geography, and by 1701 the information on Bisente's map had been largely incorporated into maps of Louisiana drawn by Nicolas de Fer and by Guillaume De L'Isle. (De Fer's printed and hand-colored 1701 map is shown in Chapter 2; De L'Isle drew various manuscript maps around the same time.) Both mapmakers used Bisente's toponyms and relied on his chart for essential elements of their maps, including the location of the Mississippi's delta. In addition, both supplemented their depictions with information supplied by Iberville's initial exploration of the Gulf Coast and the lower river.

By 1703 De L'Isle had reworked his manuscript maps into the great map seen here. Based on the Enríquez Barroto–Bisente map, information received from Iberville's further explorations, and perhaps on material from the voyage of Captain Bond, it is the first printed map to show the actual course of the Mississippi from below the Red River to the Gulf of Mexico. It accurately depicts details concerning the Great River and its tributaries and distributaries, including the "Fork"—that is, Bayou Lafourche. The Mississippi Sound, Mobile and Pensacola bays, and other coastal features are also correctly presented. The map does not fare as well in depicting interior features—the Chattahoochee River, for example, is shown rising in a lake. Nonetheless, this map was a remarkable cartographic achievement that would influence later representations of the Mississippi Valley; its success also guaranteed that the work of Enríquez Barroto and Bisente would survive, albeit in French guise. The second edition of the map is seen here, which De L'Isle published himself from the address, Quai de Horloge.

Title: *Carte du Mexique et de la Floride des Terres Angloises et des Isles Antilles du Course et des Environs de la Riviere Mississipi*

Date Issued: 1708

Cartographer: Guillaume De L'Isle

Published: [*Atlas de Geographie*] (Paris)

Cooperplate engraving, 18.9 x 25.6 inches

David Rumsey Collection, Image No. 4764099

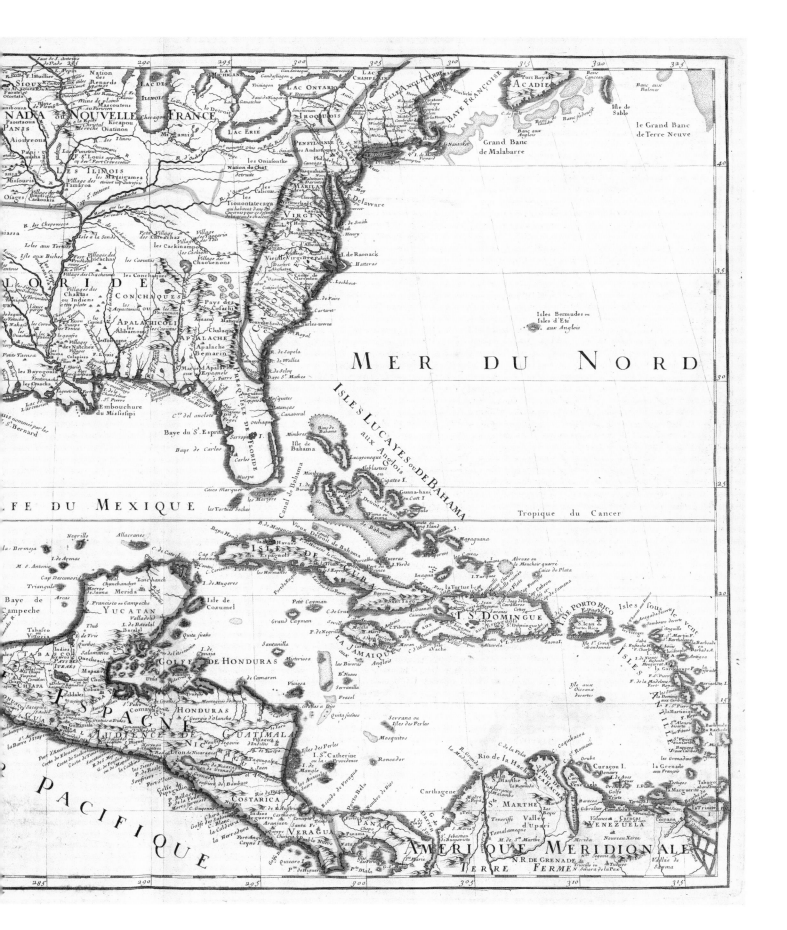

The Soupart Map of 1716

The first map illustrated here filled a large void in the cartography of the Gulf Coast region. Little is known about its creator, not even his given name, although the best guess is that Soupart was a pilot on the French brigantine *Dauphine*. His map covers the coastline from Tampa Bay to Calcasieu Lake, contains twenty-six place names, and illustrates the heartland of the young Louisiana colony—the area from Pensacola to the Mississippi River Delta—in far greater detail than any other earlier representation. Mobile Bay is particularly detailed, indicating that Soupart had surveyed its environs thoroughly. There are three legends that extend from the mouth of Mobile Bay into the Gulf: they provide information about Dauphine Island, passages to the bay, and the destruction of Fort Ste. Marie des Apalaches by the Alibamoux Indians in 1705. Also shown are the islands, navigable channels, inlets, and rivers between Mobile Bay and Lake Pontchartrain, providing naval intelligence for what would become a major route to New Orleans. Note also the various kinks and convolutions in the course of the lower Mississippi, a feature also found on other maps of the Louisiana colony, especially those that focused on the coastline. The map's edges are charred, possibly from the August 1719 fire that destroyed the *Dauphine* in Pensacola Bay.

Soupart's map was largely incorporated into maps published by de L'Isle and de Fer in 1718. In fact, both of these maps contain an inset map of the Gulf Coast that is for the most part a copy of Soupart's depiction of this region. De L'Isle's *Carte de la Louisiane* (as seen in Chapter 2) gives the Mississippi—both on the general map and on the inset map—a straighter course than does Soupart; also shown is a cluster of lakes below the Mississippi, a feature not shown on Soupart's map. This latter feature can be found on a map drawn by the French draftsman Sieur Vermale in 1717, which in turn is a copy of a (now lost) general map of Louisiana drawn by a missionary in the colony, François le Maire. Le Maire was interested in Louisiana geography, could draw reasonably accurate maps, and had access to the French court; and he would prove to be an important resource as de L'Isle and other mapmakers worked to render more realistic depictions of the French colony. Indeed, de L'Isle relied heavily on the memoirs and manuscript maps of Father le Maire in the production of his 1718 map.

The most literal expression of Soupart's survey can be found on de Fer's four-sheet 1718 map, *Le Cours du Missisipi, ou de St. Louis*. Shown here are the two western sheets (the left side) of this map. The lower-left sheet is derived from a 1701 de L'Isle manuscript map entitled *Cartes des environs du Missisipi*; de L'Isle never published this map, but de Fer started issuing a version of it in 1715 under the title *La Rivière de Missisipi, et ses*

Environs. He added a few embellishments and released it again in 1718 as *Partie Meridionale de la Rivière de Missisipi et ses Environs*. This last map forms the lower sheet seen here, its title either trimmed off or concealed when the sheets were pasted together. The upper sheet is an inset of the Gulf that was de Fer's version of Soupart's map. Note that de Fer utilizes Soupart's twisting course of the Mississippi, but also added the cluster of lakes first found on Vermale's map.

De Fer's four-sheet map enjoyed a wide circulation, thanks to its publication in volume six of Abraham Châtelain's 1719 *Atlas Historique*. Entitled *Carte de la Nouvelle France*, this reduced, one-sheet version of the original was widely copied by later mapmakers, despite the fact that the general map contained information about Texas that had been greatly improved by de L'Isle's 1718 map. Moreover, these same mapmakers seem unconcerned that the Soupart inset was more current and even contradicted the main map itself. De L'Isle's map was also widely copied by other cartographers, ranging from Herman Moll to Johan Baptiste Homann. Some of these copies included the inset of the Gulf Coast, but all exploited the Soupart information contained on de L'Isle's general map of Louisiana. It was thus through the maps of Guillaume de L'Isle and Nicolas de Fer that Soupart's survey would remain the basic model of the Gulf Coast until the middle of the eighteenth century.

NOUVEAU LA · L · O · V

MEXIQUE S · I · A

S · E

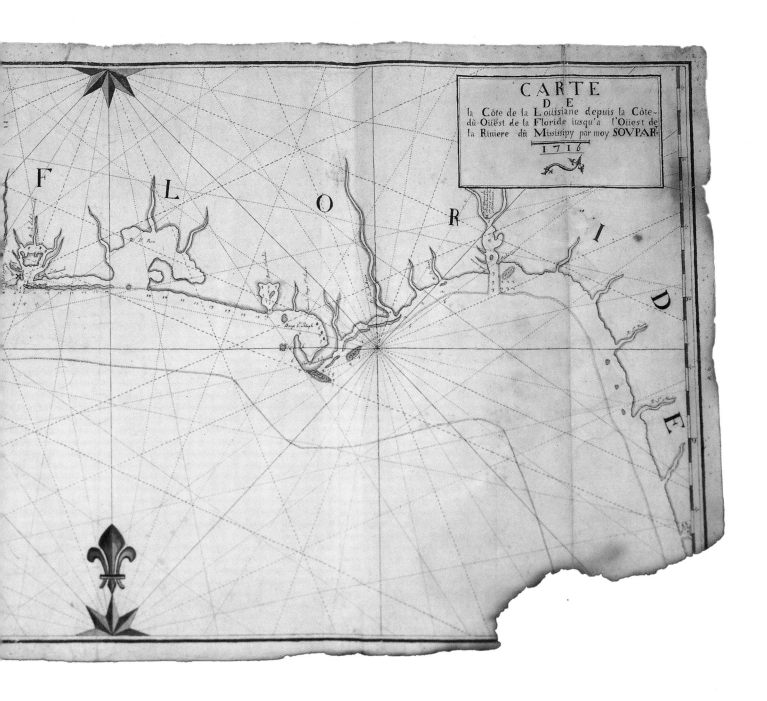

Title: *Carte de la Côte de la Loüisiane depuis la Côte du Qüest de la Floride jusqu'a l'Ouest de la Rivière du Mississipy par moy Soupart*

Date Issued: 1716

Cartographer: Soupart

Published: Manuscript

Pen and ink, 16.7 x 44.3 inches

Arthur Holzheimer Collection

The Isle of Orleans

French cartographers often referred to New Orleans and its environs as the "Isle of Orleans," and this manuscript map depicts the Mississippi River Delta as worthy of this name—that is, as a conglomeration of islands separated by waterways. The map covers a portion of the Gulf Coast from the Atchafalaya River, Louisiana, to St. Joseph Bay, Florida, and includes the coastline, coastal features, extensive soundings, interior streams, and European and American Indian settlements. The soundings and depiction of interior waterways make it clear that this was a navigational chart of an important shipping corridor; indeed this shipping lane was frequently mapped in the latter half of the eighteenth century. Lafargue pays special attention to a passage from the Mississippi River to the Gulf of Mexico via Bayou Manchac and lakes Maurepas and Pontchartrain, a route also carefully studied by the British.

Title: *Le Cours du Missisipi, ou de St. Louis, Fameuse Riviére de l'Amerique Septentrionale aux environs de laquelle se trouve le pais appelle Louisiane*
Date Issued: 1718
Cartographer: Nicolas de Fer
Published: Separately (Paris)
Copperplate engraving, 37 x 24 inches
Newberry Library, 4042.M5 1718 .F3

NEXT PAGES
Title: *Carte de la Coste de la Province de la Louisiane et des Bouches du Micissipy ou Fleuve St. Louis*
Date Issued: 1768
Cartographer: Jean Lafargue
Published: Manuscript
Pen and ink and watercolor, 18.5 x 37.8 inches
Library of Congress, Geography & Map Division,
G4012.C6 1768 .L3 Vault

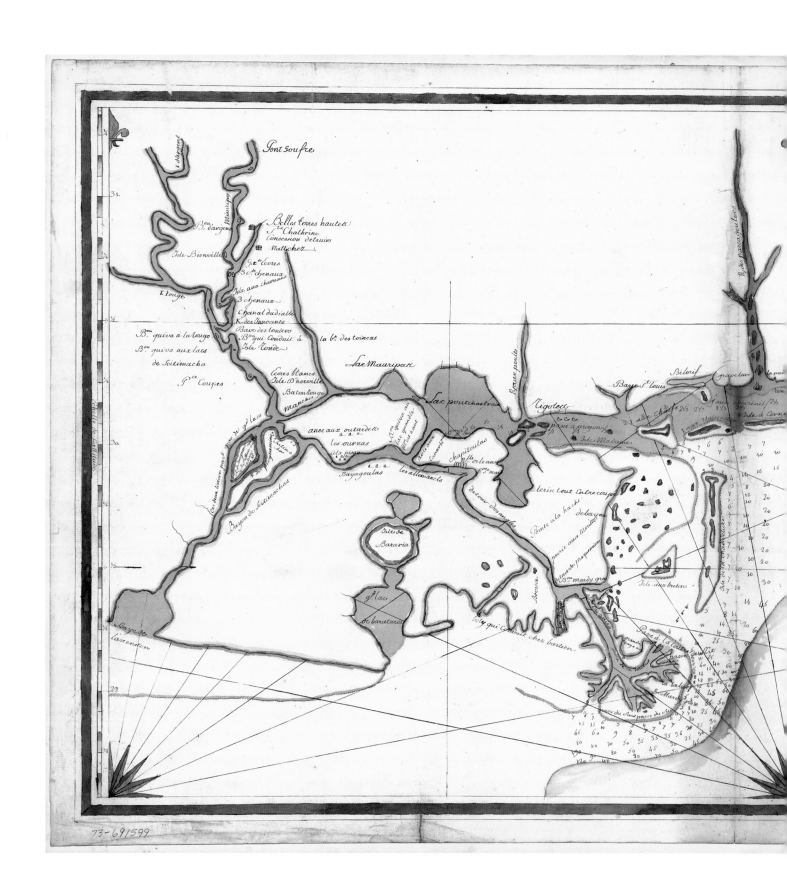

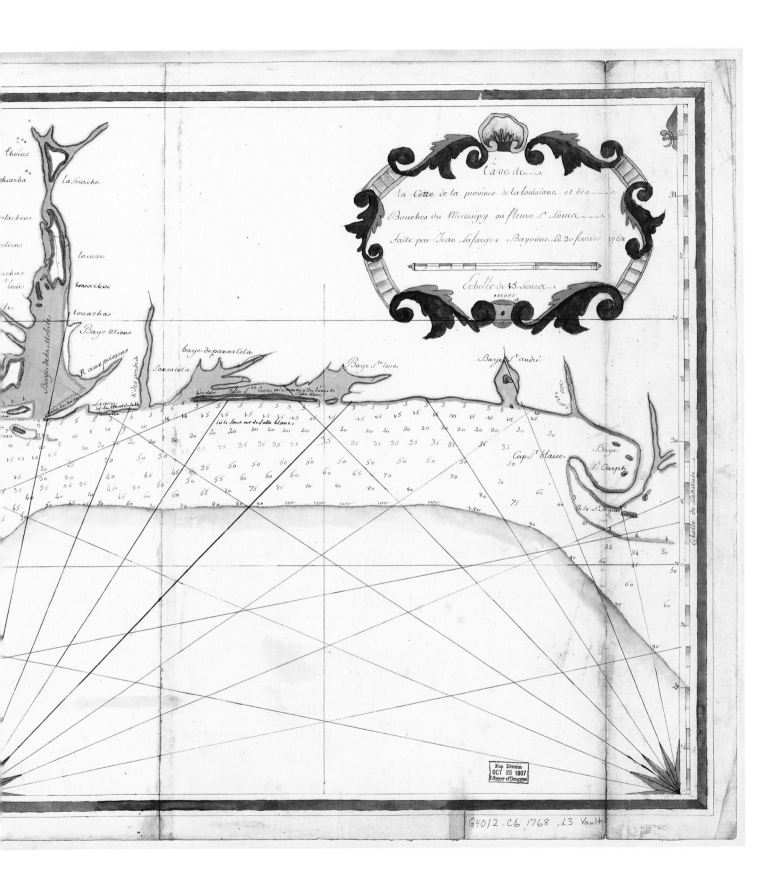

A Chart from the Atlantic Neptune

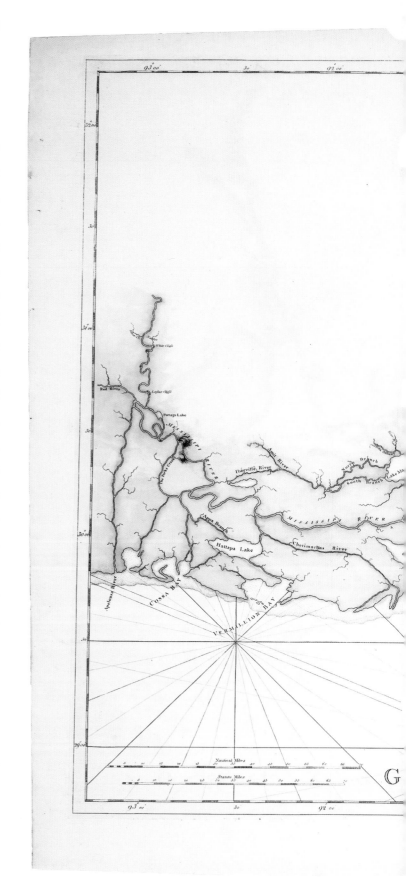

his map is from a magnificent four-volume atlas of sea charts and views of the eastern and southern coasts of North America published during the American Revolutionary War. The *Atlantic Neptune* was produced by Joseph Frederick Wallet Des Barres and is considered a landmark in American cartography: it represents the first systematic survey of the Atlantic coast of North America, and spans from the St. Lawrence River and Nova Scotia to Florida, the Caribbean, and the Gulf of Mexico. The charts in the *Atlantic Neptune* are highly detailed and artistic, contain both hydrographical and topographical information, and were based on surveys of such accuracy that they were in use as the standard charts of the East Coast for over fifty years. The atlas also contains charts that record various episodes during the American Revolutionary War, such as the events leading to the surrender of Charleston, South Carolina. Thus, the *Atlantic Neptune* is a unique document of the moment the American colonies broke away from Britain. This chart of the Gulf Coast focuses on the lower Mississippi and Mobile rivers.

Title: [Chart of the Gulf Coast from Pensacola to the Apelousa River, including the Mobile and lower Mississippi rivers]
Date Issued: 1779
Cartographer: Joseph Frederick Wallet Des Barres
Published: *Atlantic Neptune* (London)
Copperplate engraving, 29.1 x 20.5 inches
National Maritime Museum, K0877

CHAPTER 4

THE SEARCH FOR THE GREAT RIVER'S SOURCE

In January 1803 President Thomas Jefferson secretly sought to send an expedition up the Missouri River, which coursed through lands that at the time were claimed by France. The purpose of this mission would be to locate the Northwest Passage (the hypothetical northwestern water route to the Pacific Ocean), as well as to set up an American fur-trading enterprise in alliance with northern Indian tribes. The Louisiana Purchase would change the significance of this mission, for the Lewis and Clark Expedition would now explore and report on the western reaches of the United States.

While Lewis and Clark were at the headwaters of the Missouri far to the west, General James Wilkinson, governor of the newly designated Upper Louisiana Territory, took it upon himself to send an expedition to locate the source of the Mississippi. The area had been explored in 1798 by the intrepid British-Canadian geographer David Thompson, who deemed Turtle Lake to be the source of the Mississippi (and is so marked on Thompson's monumental 1814 *Map of the North-West Territory of the Province of Canada from Actual Survey during the years 1792–1812*).

In the summer of 1805 Wilkinson ordered Lieutenant Zebulon Pike to lead a reconnaissance to locate the source of the Mississippi River, collect geographic information about the region of its headwaters, negotiate peace treaties with local Indian tribes, and assert the legal claim of the United States to the area. Pike had little training to conduct such an expedition and only a limited idea of what he was to accomplish. Nevertheless, he and twenty soldiers set out from St. Louis and ascended the Mississippi to a point near Little Falls in Minnesota, where they made a winter camp on the west side of the river. From there, Pike and a small contingent of his party headed overland by sled to present-day Leech Lake, which he mistakenly identified as the "main" source of the Mississippi (he also identified Red Cedar Lake as the river's "upper source.") After negotiating with the Dakota for the purchase of 155,000 acres of land at the junction of the Mississippi and Minnesota rivers (the future site of Fort Snelling), Pike made his way back to St. Louis, where he arrived at the end of April 1806.

Using Pike's field notes and sketch maps. Wilkinson's cartographer Antoine Nau compiled an oversized four-sheet manuscript map of the upper Mississippi River, which, as seen here, was reduced and redrawn by Nicholas King. The map is generally limited to the area along Pike's route up the Mississippi, although the Des Moines River and its tributaries are also depicted (as based on information Pike obtained from traders). Four trading posts built by the Mackinac Fur Trading Company are shown along the river, confirmation of British influence among the Fox and Sauk Indians in the region. Pike's winter stockade is located, as well as the land grant Pike obtained from the Dakota. This map was largely incorporated by William Clark into his 1814 milestone work, *A Map of Lewis and Clark's Track Across the Western Portion of North America, from the Mississippi to the Pacific Ocean* (see Chapter 5).

A succession of explorers would soon follow Pike's lead, all seeking the "true source" of the Mississippi River. In 1820 Governor Lewis Cass of the Michigan Territory led an expedition that ventured into the headwater's region as far as Red Cedar Lake, which his party rechristened "Cass Lake"; there they learned from local Indians that the origin of the Mississippi lay about fifty miles to the "west-northwest" (it is actually to the southwest). Cass decided not to press on, however, as the depth of the waterway was too low to proceed by canoe. The Italian explorer Giacomo Costantino Beltrami was next to search for the Great River's source. In 1823 Beltrami joined the expedition of Major Stephen H. Long, who was surveying the region of the Red

River Valley. Animosities soon developed between Beltrami and Long, and Beltrami left the group to set out on a personal quest to find the source of the Mississippi. He traced the Great River back to a lake that he named Julia, after his deceased friend Countess Giulia Spada de Medici (this lake had been surveyed by Thompson twenty-five years earlier). Beltrami, who believed that Lake Julia was the source not only of the Mississippi, but the Red River as well, wrote an account of his Minnesota explorations in 1824, which was published in New Orleans as *La Découverte des Sources du Mississippi et de la Rivière Sanglante*. In 1828, an expanded English translation of this narrative was printed in London, which included a folding map that detailed his view of the geography of the headwaters of the Mississippi. On this chart he makes note of "Doe lake, W. source of the Mississippi"; his guide had advised him of the existence of this lake, which at time was known by its French name, Lac la Biche.

Another excursion to the northern woods of Minnesota was organized by Henry Schoolcraft in 1832. Schoolcraft had been to the area once before, when he served as the mineralogist for General Cass's 1820 reconnaissance of the area; he was currently working as the Office of Indian Affairs agent to the

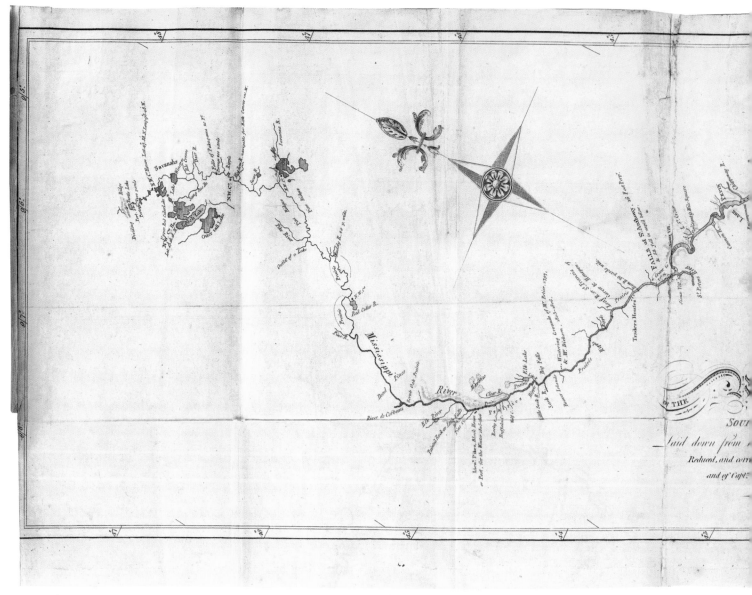

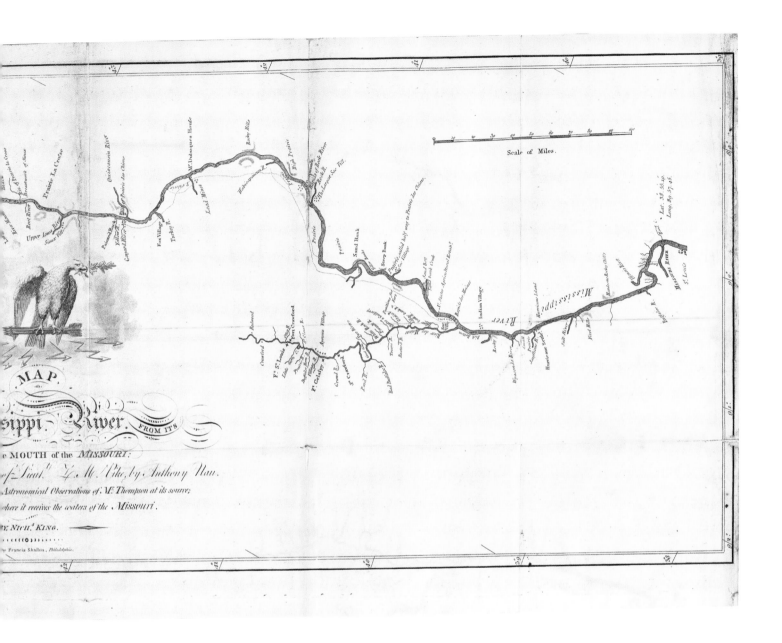

Title: Map of the Mississippi River from its Source to the Mouth of the Missouri, laid down from the notes of Lieut. Z. M. Pike by Anthony Nau, reduced and corrected by the Astronomical Observations of Mr. Thompson at its source, and of Captn. M. Lewis, where it receives the waters of the Missouri

Date Issued: 1810

Cartographer: Nicholas King

Published: *An Account of Expeditions to the Sources of the Mississippi, and Through the Western Parts of Louisiana, to the Sources of the Arkansaw, Kans, La Platte, and Pierre Jaun, Rivers: During the Years 1805, 1806, and 1807, and a Tour through the Interior Parts of New Spain, when conducted through these Provinces, by order of the Captain-General, in the year 1807*, by Z. M. Pike, illustrated by Maps and Charts (Philadelphia)

Copperplate engraving, 8.7 x 5.5 inches

David Rumsey Collection

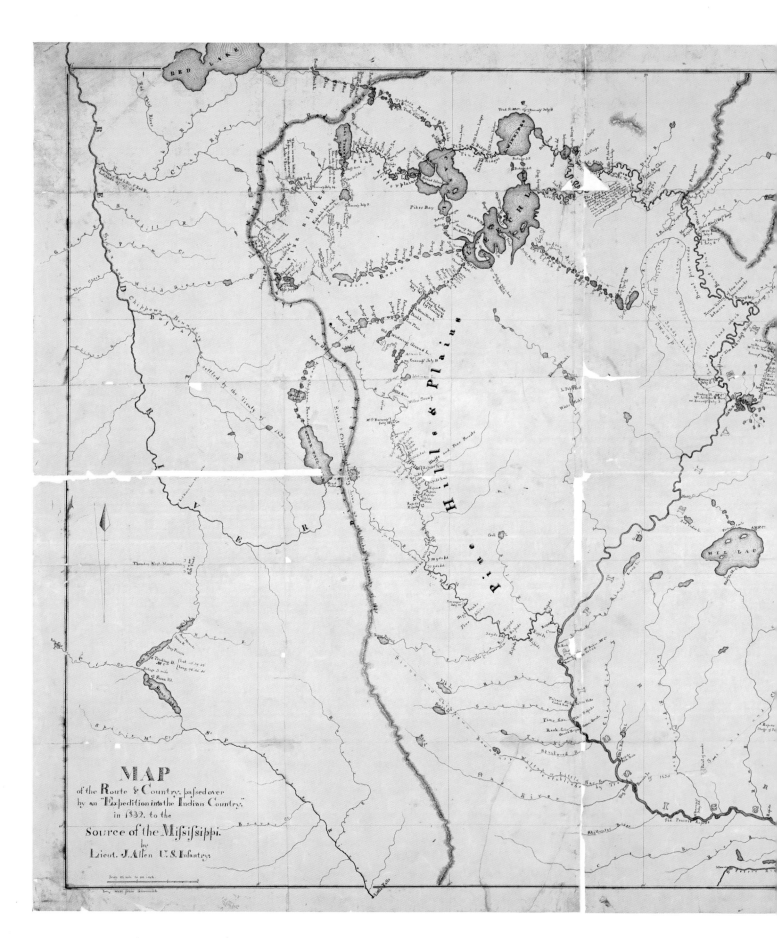

MAP
of the Route & Country, passed over
by an "Expedition into the Indian Country,"
in 1832, to the
Source of the Mississippi.
by
Lieut. J. Allen U.S. Infantry.

Title: Map of the Route & Country, passed over by an "Expedition into the Indian Country," in 1832, to the Source of the Mississippi

Date Issued: 1832

Cartographer: Lt. James Allen

Published: Manuscript

Pen and ink, 29.9 x 37.4 inches

National Archives, RG 77, CWMF, Misc. 13

northern tribes. In his presentation to Cass, who was now secretary of war under President Andrew Jackson, Schoolcraft stated that the primary purpose of this expedition would be to seek an end to the recurring Ojibwa-Dakota skirmishes that were threatening the new settlements in the northwest, and to conduct an investigation into the influence of British traders on these conflicts. Before the expedition would get underway, Schoolcraft's mission would be expanded to include a thorough study of the area's fur trade and the vaccination of the local Indians against smallpox. There was also another object Schoolcraft had in mind: after receiving his orders, he told Cass that if he did "not see the 'veritable source' of the Mississippi this time, it will not be from a want of effort."

When Schoolcraft initially approached Cass with his plans, he asked that an officer from the Corps of Engineers accompany him to map the route of the expedition. Cass agreed, but due to the high demand for the skills of the Corps officers, was unable to supply one in time for Schoolcraft's trip; instead, Cass sent Lieutenant James Allen, an infantry officer detailed to topographical duty. Allen was to map the expedition's route, report on the country's geology, and record observations of the wildlife they encountered along the way. Following the route of the Cass excursion twelve years earlier, Schoolcraft and his party made their way to the shores of Cass Lake; from there they were guided by the Ojibwa chief Ozawindib to Lac la Biche, which they were assured was the true source of the Father of Waters. Schoolcraft renamed it Lake Itasca, a word he coined from the Latin *veritas caput* ("true head"). The expedition was covered widely

by the American media and Schoolcraft followed up with his own account of the discovery, published in 1834 as *Narrative of an Expedition Through the Upper Mississippi River to Itasca Lake*.

Based on compass bearings, Allen's manuscript map of the expedition (shown on previous pages) delineates the area west of Lake Superior to the Red River and north of Fort Snelling. Numerous American Indian villages are located, as are the Dakota (Sioux) and Ojibwa (Chippewa) boundary lines as established by the 1825 Treaty of Prairie du Chien. Towns, place names, and six "Trading Houses" of the A. F. Co. (the American Fur Company) are shown. The river systems are located and a few topographic details are pointed out, including a chain of hills that is meant to depict the dividing line between the watersheds of the Mississippi and Red rivers. Many canoe routes and portages are indicated. The "Source of the Mississippi" is located by latitude and longitude, but curiously it is not yet named.

The next map depicted is the sole cartographic effort of the French mathematician and astronomer, Joseph Nicollet. Nicollet had immigrated to the United States shortly after suffering financial ruin in the 1830 collapse of the French stock market. He had previously distinguished himself on the basis of his mathematical and astronomical studies, and while still in his thirties was decorated with the medal of the Legion of Honor. Obliged to make a new beginning, Nicollet's intention was to make a "scientific tour" of his adopted homeland "with the view of contributing to the progressive increase of knowledge in the physical geography of North America."

He began in 1832 by independently working his way through the South and the lower valley of the Mississippi, reaching St. Louis in 1835. With the help and encouragement of Ferdinand Hassler, the head of the United States Coast Survey, Nicollet proceeded north to explore the Great River's upper basin. Working with a telescope, chronometer, and barometer, he spent the years 1836 and 1837 recording the first accurate longitudes, latitudes, and altitudes of many landmarks in this region. He corrected, for example, Pike's location of the embouchement of the Crow Wing River, which according to Nicollet had created a "great disorder in the geography of this region." He also took great interest in the language and culture of the American Indians he met, and believed that the Ojibwa language, which belongs to the Algonquin linguistic group, was geographically "richer than ours."

Nicollet spent the winter of 1837–38 at Fort Snelling, where he drew the first of the manuscript maps that became the foundation for the 1843 map shown here. On the basis of the work exhibited by this manuscript, Nicollet was selected to lead the first expedition of the newly formed Corps of Topological Engineers to complete a scientific mapping of the upper Mississippi watershed; that is, "to make a complete examination of between the Mississippi and Missouri rivers, as far north as the British line, and to embody the whole of his labors in a map and general report for public use." With John C. Frémont serving as his chief assistant, and armed with the latest scientific instruments available, Nicollet traveled in 1838 westward from Fort Snelling to the Pipestone Quarry, through the Coteau des Prairies of present-day southwestern

Minnesota and eastern South Dakota, and back down the Minnesota River to the fort. The following year he headed an expedition up the Missouri River to Fort Pierre (South Dakota) and overland across the James and Sheyenne rivers northward to Devils Lake in what is now North Dakota.

Nicollet moved to Washington, D.C. in 1840 to compile his *Report intended to Illustrate a Map of the Hydrographical Basin of the Upper Mississippi River* and to draft its accompanying map. The map would be based on ninety thousand longitude and latitude readings, on altitudes measured with barometers, and on the accumulation of a wealth of other geographical data that filled sixty-seven manuscript map sheets. In 1841, the U.S. Senate authorized the printing of a large-scale version of his map, which after a year's delay, was published in 1842. The delay was due to a disagreement between Nicollet and the chief of the Topographical Bureau, Colonel John James Abert. Nicollet insisted on including all of the region's topographical features on the map, whereas Abert thought this to be an unneeded complication. Abert prevailed, and the first printed six-sheet version of Nicollet's map did not include the hachuring denoting barometrically determined land heights.

As seen here, a second version that is truer to Nicollet's intent was published shortly after his death in 1843; it uses a smaller scale and restores much of the hachuring, although as Nicollet had complained, this version is too small to show much of this detail. A little more than a decade after Nicollet's death, Lieutenant Gouverneur K. Warren of the U.S. Army Corps of Topographical Engineers acclaimed the Frenchman's map as "one of the

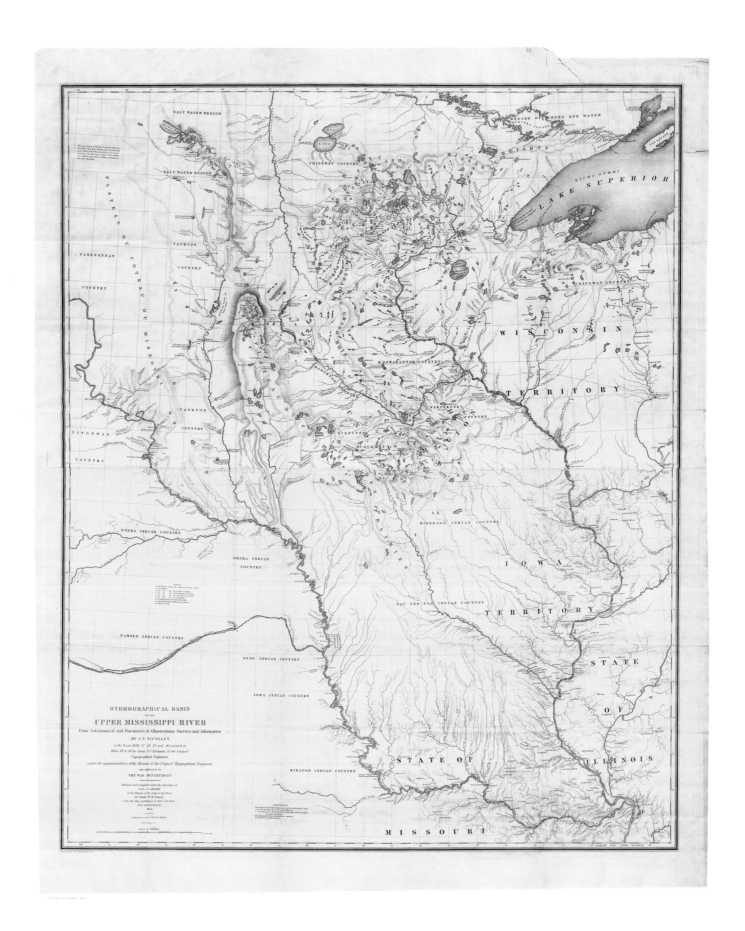

greatest contributions ever made to American geography." Nicollet had fulfilled his desire to expand the geographic knowledge of North America, and the accuracy of his map was such that it remained the standard for Midwest maps until the era of modern mapping.

In his survey of Lake Itasca, Nicollet carefully identified five streams that fed the lake. The largest of these tributaries, now known as Nicollet Creek, flows into the western arm of Lake Itasca from the southwest. After tracing this waterway back to a spring, he cited the geographical maxim "that the sources of a river are those which are most distant from the mouth," and recorded that this was "truly the infant Mississippi; all others below, its feeders and tributaries." In making these remarks, Nicollet did not consider himself to be overturning Schoolcraft's findings; rather, he was simply completing the work entailed by his predecessor's discovery.

In spite of Nicollet's conclusions, there remained those who still sought the "true source" of the Mississippi. Thus, for example, Julius Chambers visited Lake Itasca in 1872, convinced that all other explorers had stopped short of the Mississippi's source. He followed another creek from the west arm of Lake Itasca to Elk Lake, which he dubbed "Dolly Yarden" (after his canoe) and pronounced that this lake was "the source" of the Mississippi. In 1881, Captain Willard Glazier likewise proclaimed Elk Lake to be the source of the Mississippi, which with self-aggrandizing flair he renamed Lake Glazier. Whereas Chambers' declaration had been largely ignored, Glazier's received serious attention, for several reasons. For one, he was already a popular figure who had written several books on the history of the Civil War. This, in turn, made it easy for him to promote his claim for fame, which he did in earnest. In 1884 his biography, entitled *Sword and Pen*, was published. It included an account of his canoe trip from Leech Lake to Itasca Lake and Elk Lake, and thence down the Mississippi, and contained a map of the sources of the river. His 1887 publication, *Down the River*, retold the story and included a redrawn map with several new place names. *Mississippi Headwaters*, released in 1893, was the narrative of Glazier's 1891 expedition to the area; this second journey was

Title: Hydrological Basin of the Upper Mississippi River from Astronomical and Barometrical Observations Surveys and Information

Date Issued: 1843

Cartographer: Joseph N. Nicollet and William H. Emory

Published: *Report intended to Illustrate a Map of the Hydrographical Basin of the Upper Mississippi River*, by I. N. Nicollet (Washington, D.C.)

Copperplate engraving, 36.2 x 30.7 inches

David Rumsey Collection, Image No. 2488001

intended to reinforce his naming of Lake Glazier as the source of the Mississippi.

It would not be long before Glazier's campaign was discredited. As early as December 1886, an article in *Science* magazine supported the earlier findings of Nicollet. It was then noticed that the account of Glazier's expedition contained many passages lifted directly from Schoolcraft's earlier works; moreover, his map of the Mississippi headwaters clearly exaggerated the geography of the area in his favor, showing, for example, Lake Glazier in faulty proportion to Lake Itasca (whereby the former incorrectly appears to be almost as large as the latter). In 1887 the Minnesota Historical Society took up the fight and sought not only to repudiate Glazier's claim, but to rebuff his renaming of Elk Lake. Two years later, this organization commissioned yet another survey of the region, to be led by Jacob V. Brower. The purpose of this survey would be to determine "what is the true and actual source of the Mississippi river."

The conclusion of Brower's survey was that the true source of the Mississippi was neither Elk Lake (as proclaimed by Glazier) nor Lake Itasca (as Schoolcraft thought), nor even Nicollet Creek (Nicollet's "cradled Hercules"); rather, the source of the Great River lies in what is called the "Greater Ultimate Reservoir"—a marshy area of springs and lakes that receives its water supply from aerial precipitation. The results of Brower's last hydrographic survey are depicted on the map shown here. Note the many lakes that lie within the Ultimate Greater Reservoir, including the Hernando de Soto, Allen, Picard, Mikenna, Little Elk, Triplets, Whipple, Morrison, and Floating Moss; various streams can be seen to advance from them. The Mississippi is depicted "in an unbroken channel" as flowing from Nicollet's middle lake via Nicollet's Creek into Lake Itasca. The Minnesota Historical Society successfully lobbied to have the headwaters region depicted on this map preserved as Itasca State Park, and Brower served as its first commissioner.

Title: Detailed Hydrographic Chart of the Ultimate Source of the Mississippi River
Date Issued: 1891
Cartographer: Jacob V. Brower
Published: Separately (St. Paul, Minnesota)
Lithograph, 24.8 x 16.9 inches
Minnesota Historical Society, G 4142.I88 1891.B77 4F

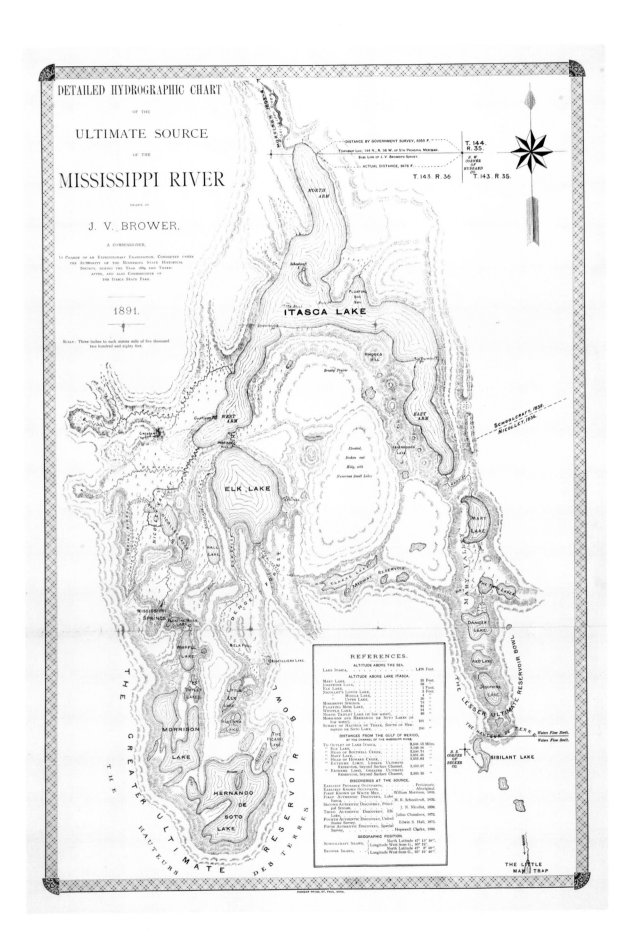

DETAILED HYDROGRAPHIC CHART

OF THE

ULTIMATE SOURCE

OF THE

MISSISSIPPI RIVER

DRAWN BY

J. V. BROWER,

A COMMISSIONER,

In Charge of an Expeditionary Examination, Conducted under the Authority of the Minnesota State Historical Society, during the Year 1889 and Thereafter, and also Commissioner of the Itasca State Park.

1891.

Scale: Three inches to each statute mile of five thousand two hundred and eighty feet.

DISTANCE BY GOVERNMENT SURVEY, 8350 F.
Township Line, 144 N., R. 36 W., of 5th Principal Meridian.
Base Line of J. V. Brower's Survey.
ACTUAL DISTANCE, 8476 F.

T. 144. R. 35.
N. W. CORNER OF HUBBARD CO.
T. 143. R. 36 | T. 143. R. 35.

NORTH ARM

Schoolcraft I.

FLOATING BOG BAY

ITASCA LAKE

RHODES HILL

WEST ARM

EAST ARM

SCHOOLCRAFT, 1832.
NICOLLET, 1836.

MARY LAKE

ELK LAKE

MARY VALLEY

THE TWIN LAKES

DANGER LAKE

MIDWAY RESERVOIR

CLARKE RESERVOIR

ARD LAKE

MISSISSIPPI SPRINGS FLOATING MOSS LAKE

JOSEPHINE LAKE

THE HAUTEUR DE TERRE.

Waters Flow North.
Waters Flow South.

WHIPPLE LAKE

ELK POOL

GROSEILLIERS LAKE

THE LESSER ULTIMATE RESERVOIR BOWL

N. E. CORNER OF BECKER CO.

TRIPLET LAKES

LITTLE ELK LAKE

MIKENNA LAKE

SIBILANT LAKE

THE PICARD LAKE

MORRISON LAKE

THE GREATER ULTIMATE RESERVOIR BOWL

HERNANDO DE SOTO LAKE

THE HAUTEURS DES TERRES

THE LITTLE MAN TRAP

REFERENCES.

ALTITUDE ABOVE THE SEA.

Lake Itasca, ... 1,470 Feet.

ALTITUDE ABOVE LAKE ITASCA.

Mary Lake,	35 Feet.
Josephine Lake,	59 "
Elk Lake,	1 Foot.
Nicollet's Lower Lake,	3 Feet.
" Middle Lake,	4 "
" Upper Lake,	20 "
Mississippi Springs,	78 "
Floating Moss Lake,	91 "
Whipple Lake,	94 "
North Triplet Lake (at low water),	99 "
Morrison and Hernando de Soto Lakes (at low water),	101 "
Summit of Hauteur de Terre, South of Hernando de Soto Lake,	200 "

DISTANCES FROM THE GULF OF MEXICO,
BY THE CHANNEL OF THE MISSISSIPPI RIVER.

To Outlet of Lake Itasca,	2,546.53 Miles.
" Elk Lake,	2,549.30 "
" Head of Boutwell Creek,	2,550.74 "
" Mary Lake,	2,551.50 "
" Head of Howard Creek,	2,552.02 "
" Extreme Limit, Lesser Ultimate Reservoir, beyond Surface Channel,	2,553.07 "
" Extreme Limit, Greater Ultimate Reservoir, beyond Surface Channel,	2,555.95 "

DISCOVERIES AT THE SOURCE.

Earliest Probable Occupants,	Prehistoric.
Earliest Known Occupants,	Aboriginal.
First Known of White Men,	William Morrison, 1805.
First Authentic Discovery, Lake Itasca,	H. R. Schoolcraft, 1832.
Second Authentic Discovery, Principal Stream,	J. N. Nicollet, 1836.
Third Authentic Discovery, Elk Lake,	Julius Chambers, 1872.
Fourth Authentic Discovery, United States Survey,	Edwin S. Hall, 1875.
Fifth Authentic Discovery, Special Survey,	Hopewell Clarke, 1886.

GEOGRAPHIC POSITION.

Schoolcraft Island,	North Latitude 47° 13' 10". Longitude West from G., 95° 12'.
Brower Island,	North Latitude 47° 9' 50". Longitude West from G., 95° 12' 48".

PIONEER PRESS, ST. PAUL, MINN.

CHAPTER 5

THE PRIME MERIDIAN OF A NEW COUNTRY

The Louisiana Purchase

President Thomas Jefferson's 1803 purchase of the French province of Louisiana more than doubled the size of the United States. No maps accompanied the cessation treaty, however, and while officials generally regarded the eastern and southern borders of Louisiana as the Mississippi River and the Gulf of Mexico, the treaty was purposely vague on the colony's northern and western boundaries. Shortly after its formal transfer to the United States, Congress enabled a bill that divided Louisiana into two territories and provided for its government. The areas south of the 33rd parallel became the Territory of Orleans, and the remainder of the province the Territory of Louisiana.

Although the borders of the Louisiana Purchase could only be guessed at on its early cartographic representations, the first map shown here soon became the leading depiction of the newly acquired land and its surroundings. Drawn in 1804 by the American cartographer and draftsman Samuel Lewis, it was boldly placed in a publication entitled *A New and Elegant General Atlas, comprising all the New Discoveries, to the Present Time*, which was a collaboration between Lewis and the English mapmaker Aaron Arrowsmith. This volume provided its readers with two distinct and competing conceptions of the Territory of Louisiana: Arrowsmith's *British Possessions in America and North America* and the Lewis chart.

Lewis's map is based on the work of the French engineer Antoine Soulard, who served the Spanish as surveyor-general of upper Louisiana from 1795 until its formal transfer to the United States in 1804. Given his knowledge of private land claims and his reputation as "an excellent draught man," the Americans also engaged Soulard as the surveyor-general of this region, now rechristened the Territory of Louisiana. While in the employ of the Spanish, Soulard drew a groundbreaking map of the upper Mississippi and

Title: Louisiana
Date Issued: 1804
Cartographer: Samuel Lewis
Published: *A New and Elegant General Atlas, comprising all the New Discoveries, to the Present Time* (Boston)
Copperplate engraving, 9.8 x 7.9 inches
The Historic Collection of New Orleans, Accession 1974.74.2

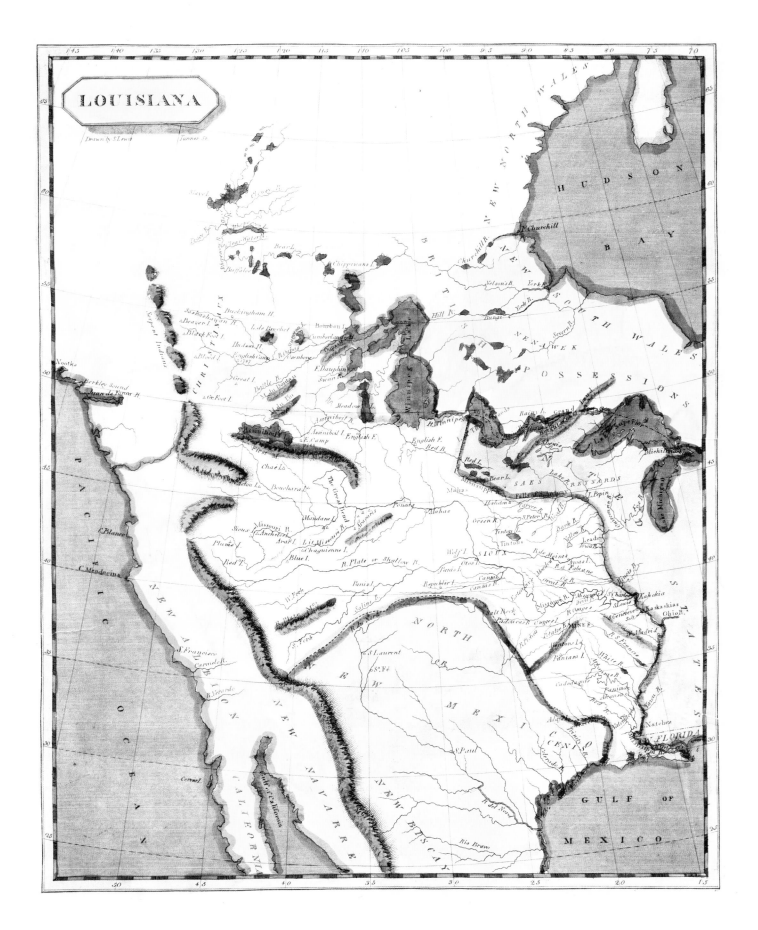

LOUISIANA

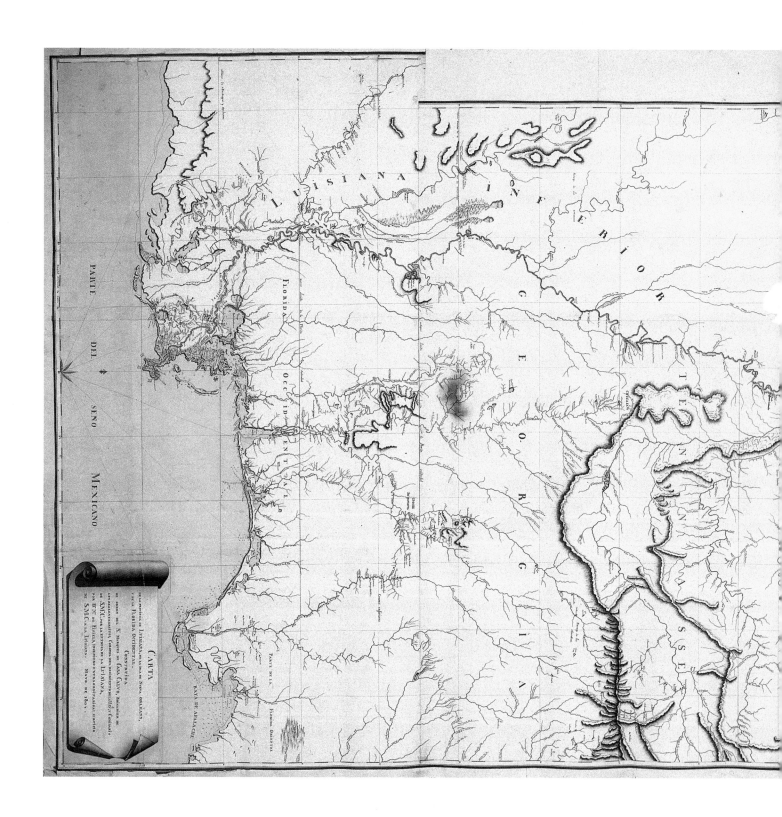

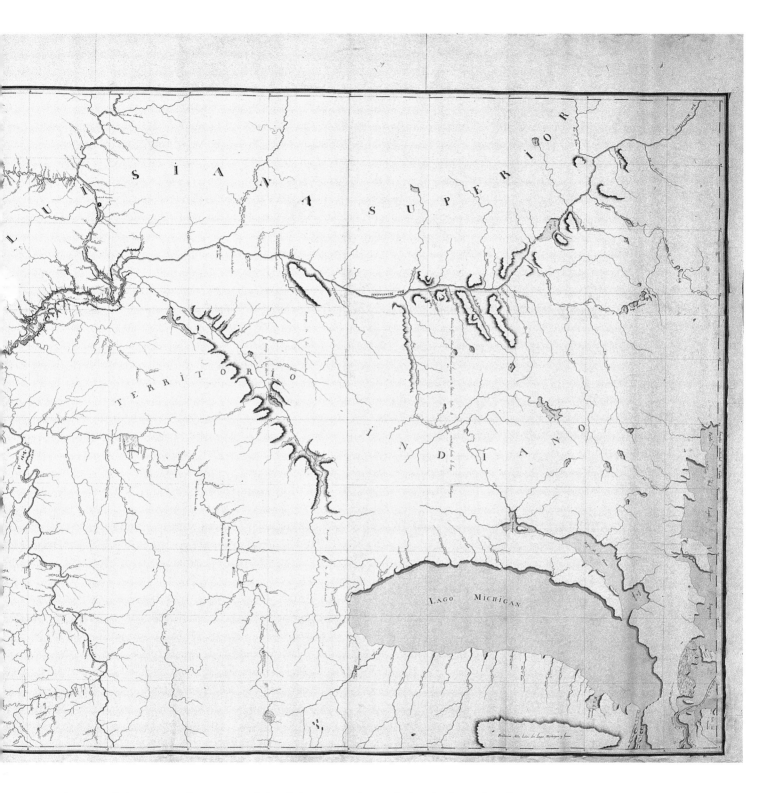

Title: *Carta de las Provincia de Lovisiana, de la Isla de Nueva Orléans, y de las Florida Occidental*

Date Issued: 1804

Cartographer: Nicolas de Finiels

Published: Manuscript

Pen and ink, 98.8 x 49.6 inches

Patrimonio Nacional, Biblioteca del Palacio Real, Rollo/51

Missouri rivers using information from the Spanish-sponsored expeditions of Jacques d'Eglise and Jean Baptiste Truteau. This map was widely distributed in both manuscript and printed form, and it was an English manuscript version that Lewis used to create *Louisiana* (this version was also used by Lewis and Clark in planning their expedition).

Lewis's map depicts the southern boundary of the Louisiana Territory in the form of a dotted line that extends from the "Mexican R." (Sabine River) westward to around the headwaters of the "R. del Nord" (Colorado and Rio Grande) to the southern Rocky Mountains. The region below this line is labeled "North of New Mexico," making this the first widely circulated printed map to depict the border between Louisiana and Mexico.

Nicolas de Finiels was another French engineer who served the Spanish in the Louisiana colony. He initially worked in St. Louis, where he prepared several maps of the region and of the course of the Mississippi River before moving to New Orleans in 1798. Following the Louisiana Purchase, Finiels continued his Spanish service in West Florida. In 1804 Finiels prepared the map shown here for Sebastián Calvo de la Puerta y O'Farrill, marqués de Casa Calvo, a former military governor of Spanish Louisiana who was representing Spanish interests in the transfer of Louisiana from Spain to France and then to the United States. This magnificent map, which is expertly crafted and richly detailed in the

French cartographic tradition, includes a well-defined demarcation of the border between the United States and Spanish West Florida.

These two maps, which represent early attempts to delimit the frontiers of the Louisiana Purchase, would soon be outdated as the United States worked over the next decade to push these borders to the west and the northwest, and to include West Florida within the purchase. A fact that would not change, which is illustrated very nicely by the juxtaposition of these maps, is that the United States now had complete control of a great waterway system—the Mississippi and its principal tributaries, the Missouri and Ohio. It was, of course, the ability of Americans to freely travel the Mississippi River that first prompted the diplomatic overtures that led to the Louisiana Purchase. As a result of the purchase, the Great River now afforded the middle section of the country access to the world's markets, which in turn fueled the rapid settlement of this region. These maps also served to remind the young country that its reaches west of the Mississippi River remained *terra incognito*; the term "the Great West" came to denote this vast territory, a wilderness that was waiting to be explored, surveyed, mapped, and eventually settled. This gave the Mississippi a new place in American geography and made the "Northwest Territory" an anachronism. For the Mississippi was no longer the western edge of the United States, but the westernmost point of the eastern half of the country—it had become, in effect, the *de facto* prime meridian of a new country.

The Territory of Orleans

Barthélémy Lafon was a French engineer and architect who emigrated from France to New Orleans in 1790. Talented and industrious, he is one of the more intriguing characters in the annals of Louisiana cartography. Shortly after arriving in New Orleans, Lafon opened an iron foundry on lower Canal Street; later he worked as the chief deputy surveyor for Orleans Parish, prepared the first New Orleans city directories, and served as an officer in the Second Regiment of the United States Militia of the Territory of Orleans. He designed several public buildings, including a bathhouse (that was never built), a lighthouse, and numerous plantation homes. Lafon also laid out the plan for the town of Donaldsonville, Louisiana, and drafted plans for an elaborate subdivision of what is now the Garden District of New Orleans. He surveyed and prepared plats for all the private land claims issued by France and Spain in the province of Louisiana and the island of New Orleans; he published an important map of the city of New Orleans and drew another of the country surrounding the city. During the War of 1812 Lafon served as a military engineer, sketching maps of southern Louisiana and creating fine watercolor plans of military fortifications (see Chapter 7). After losing his fortune shortly after the war, Lafon turned to privateering and spying for the Spanish. He spent the last three years of his life working in league with the band of pirates run by Jean and Pierre Lafitte, first at Barataria and later on Galveston Island, where he prepared a manuscript map of Galveston Bay.

Lafon created the large and magnificent map shown here in 1806. Based on surveys he conducted between the years 1797 and 1805, it was drawn at the request of the governor of the territory and members of the legislature; at the time it was the most comprehensive printed map of the Territory of Orleans. Reproduced at a large scale (one inch to ten miles), it also contains a marine scale and a thirty-two-point compass rose to aid mariners. The area depicted on the map ranges from the Sabine River on the west to Pensacola Bay on the east, and from the 33rd parallel on the north to the tip of Mississippi River Delta on the south. The longitudes and latitudes of various locations in the territory are recorded on a scroll toward the middle of the map, including seven points along the Mississippi River. The large cartouche in the southwest corner of the map covers an area that was unexplored and unmapped; this region stretched from the Red River to the coast, and was claimed by both the United States and Spain. According to a November 22, 1805, advertisement in the *National Intelligencer and Washington Advertiser*, this map shows "the counties of the territory according to the new plan of division, which [Lafon] has executed himself, by order of the legislature."

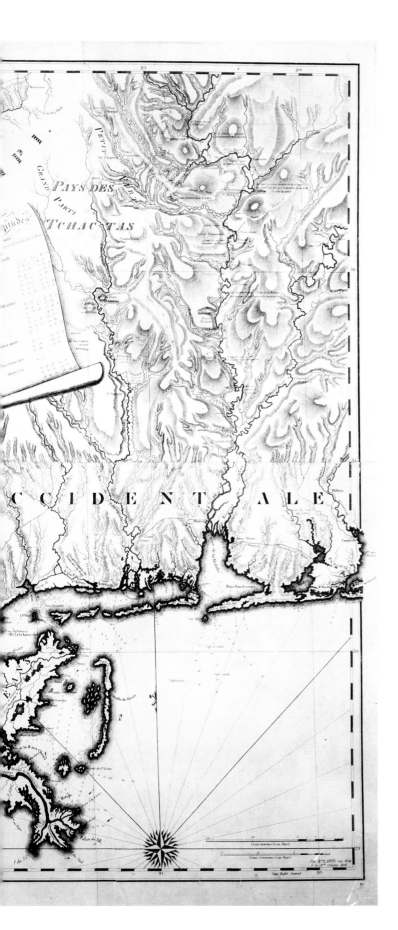

Title: *Carte Générale du Territoire d'Orléans Comprenant aussi la Floride Occidentale et une Portion du Territoire du Mississipi*

Date Issued: 1806

Cartographer: Barthélémy Lafon

Published: Separately

Copperplate engraving, 37.4 x 53.1 inches

The Historic New Orleans Collection, Accession 1971.52

The Lewis and Clark Expedition

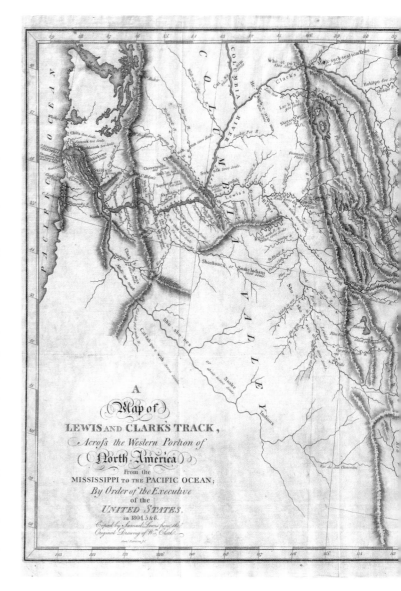

The Lewis and Clark expedition produced nearly two hundred maps, all but two drawn by William Clark. Most the maps Clark produced were large-scale compass traverse or route maps, but he also drew three composite maps that would greatly change the way the West was envisioned. The first of these was drawn at Fort Mandan in 1804–05, the second at Fort Clatsop in 1805–06, and the third in St. Louis in 1809–10. This last map also included information from other recent expeditions to the West, including additional explorations of the Yellowstone basin by Corps of Discovery members George Drouillard and John Colter, Zebulon Pike's treks to the southern Rockies and the headwaters of the Mississippi River, James Wilkinson's voyage on the Arkansas River, William Dunbar's observations of the Ouachita River, and Thomas Freeman's journey to the Red River.

This third map was faithfully copied and reduced for engraving by Samuel Lewis, and it was published in 1814 in Nicholas Biddle and Samuel Allen's *History of the Expedition under the Command of Captains Lewis and Clark, to the Sources of the Missouri*. As seen here, this map covers a large section of the trans-Mississippi west, covering a region from the Mississippi River to the Pacific Ocean and from the Canadian border to the Kansas River and St. Louis parallel. A dotted line labeled "Boundary of Louisiana" curves southwest from the Canadian prairies to the Rocky Mountains.

The publication of Clark's map revolutionized the American image of the Rocky Mountains and the Missouri River system. It replaced the pre-expedition view of the Rockies as a simple single ridge with a picture of a complex series of separate parallel ranges segregated by numerous rivers. And, it presented a remarkably accurate portrayal of the upper courses of the Missouri and Yellowstone rivers and their tributaries, which at the same time redefined the connections of the upper Missouri

with the Columbia River basin. In particular, Clark's map demonstrated that rivers greatly diminished in size from their mouths to their sources, a fact not clearly understood at the time. This, in turn, dashed Jefferson's hope for a "water communication across the continent for the purposes of commerce," which rested on the idea that the Missouri and Columbia rivers could be commercially navigated right to their sources, allowing for a short portage between the two.

Title: A Map of Lewis and Clark's Track across the Western Portion of North America from the Mississippi to the Pacific Ocean
Date Issued: 1814
Cartographer: William Clark
Published: *History of the Expedition under the Command of Captains Lewis and Clark, to the Sources of the Missouri, thence across the Rocky Mountains, and down the River Columbia to the Pacific Ocean, performed during the years 1804–5–6* (New York) Copperplate engraving, 9 x 5.5 inches
David Rumsey Collection,
Image No. 3493001

The First State West of the Mississippi

The population of the Territory of Orleans soared between the years 1803 and 1812 as thousands of immigrants—both free citizens and slaves—arrived from the Caribbean, Africa, Europe, and the United States. French citizens were particularly drawn to the region, where both the language and culture were familiar; others were attracted by the growing agricultural and commercial prosperity of the region. When the census of 1810 recorded the population of the territory at over seventy-six thousand, sixteen thousand more than was required for statehood, a convention was called to draft a constitution and form a state government.

Congress admitted the Territory of Louisiana to the Union on April 30, 1812, as the state of Louisiana, despite a movement in New Orleans to name the state after Jefferson. Almost nine years to the day after the Louisiana Purchase Treaty was signed, Louisiana became the first state to be carved out of the Purchase, as well as the first state west of the Mississippi River. Its original capital was New Orleans.

The earliest printed maps of Louisiana as a state were issued by Mathew Carey in his 1813 *American Pocket Atlas*. Enlarged versions of the two small folding maps in this atlas, which were drawn by Samuel Lewis and engraved by Henry Schenck Tanner, appeared the following year in *Carey's General Atlas… of Maps of the World and Quarters*. The first was a map of the trans-Mississippi west that portrayed the outlines of the new state of Louisiana (and is shown in the next section of this chapter); the second map, entitled *Louisiana*, was based primarily on Lafon's map of the Territory of Louisiana.

William Darby's *A Map of the State of Louisiana with Part of the Mississippi Territory, from Actual Survey* is shown here. Published by John Melish in 1816, this map was accompanied by Darby's book *A Geographical Description of the State of Louisiana*, in which he notes that he visited almost every section of Louisiana in the preparation of this map, traveling thousands of miles by foot or pirogue, often under the most difficult of conditions. He collected much of the data for this map during the years 1806 to 1811, when he worked as a United States deputy surveyor for the Western District of the Territory of New Orleans.

Darby's remarkable map advanced the cartography of Louisiana in many ways. He was the first to survey the Sabine and Calcasieu rivers of western Louisiana and the coastal wetlands extending from the Sabine to the Atchafalaya. "The state of Louisiana south of the Red River, and west of the meridian of Natchitoches," he triumphantly notes in his explanation of the map, "has never been surveyed except by myself." Louisiana's two largest lakes—Pontchartrain and Grand (Chetimaches)—are drawn more realistically than on earlier maps. So too, Darby based his depiction of the winding course of the Mississippi River, with its many bends, cutoff meanders, and oxbow lakes, on careful triangulation measurements and a modern understanding of river valley formation.

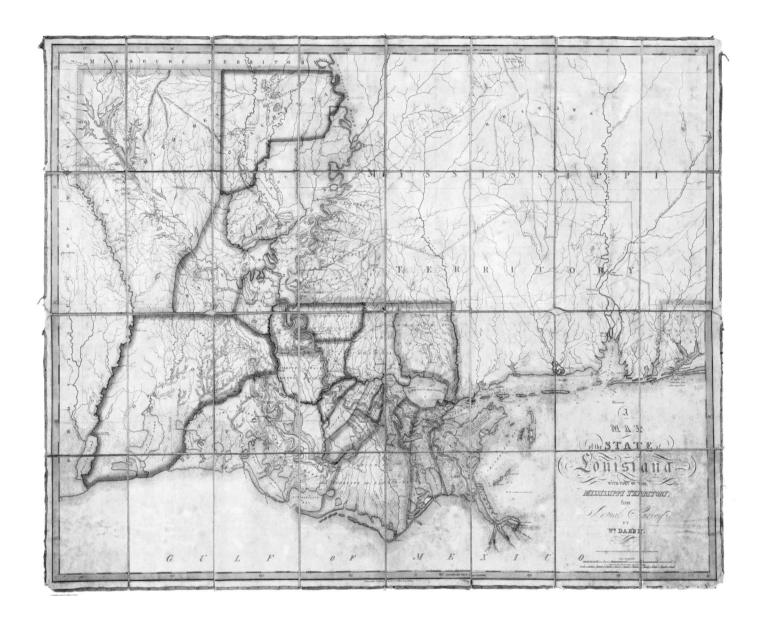

Title: A Map of the State of Louisiana with
Part of the Mississippi Territory
Date Issued: 1816
Cartographer: William Darby
Published: John Melish (Philadelphia)
Copperplate engraving, 31.5 x 44.9 inches
David Rumsey Collection, Image No. 2444000

The Missouri Territory

At the same time the state of Louisiana was admitted to the Union, the Territory of Louisiana received a new name — the Missouri Territory. This map of the *Missouri Territory formerly Louisiana* was drawn by Samuel Lewis and was one of the earliest commercially issued maps to incorporate data from the transcontinental expedition of Lewis and Clark. Marking longitude not only from Greenwich but also from Philadelphia, this map was also another attempt to delimit the boundaries of the Louisiana Purchase.

In the southeast corner of the map, the borders of the new state of Louisiana are recognizably demarcated. The "Probable North Boundary of the Missouri Territory," which meanders along a line from the Lake of the Woods on the east to the Olympic Peninsula on the Pacific Coast, clearly challenged British claims to the Pacific Northwest. Under the terms of the Anglo-American Convention of 1818, the United States and Great Britain agreed to set the 49th parallel from the Lake of the Woods (along the present border of Minnesota and Canada) to the continental divide of the Rocky Mountains as the northern boundary of the Louisiana Purchase, with the United States gaining territorial rights to the Pacific Coast. The "Probable Southern Boundary" of the territory works its way up the Colorado River from Matagorda Bay, angles northwest past the source of the Red River to a point near the "Source of the Rio del Norte" (Rio Grande), then snakes southwest to the Pacific just north of San Francisco. In the 1821 Adams-Onis Treaty the United States and Spain agreed to set this boundary starting along the Sabine and Red rivers that separate Texas and Louisiana, then north along the 100th meridian to the Arkansas River, which it followed westward to its source in the Rockies, then north to the 42nd parallel north, and on that line west to the Pacific Ocean. The Library of Congress has an undated edition of this map that has been amended by hand in watercolor to record some of these adjustments.

Title: Missouri Territory formerly Louisiana
Date Issued: 1812
Cartographer: Samuel Lewis
Published: *Carey's General Atlas, Improved and Enlarged; Being A Collection of Maps of the World and Quarters, Their Principal Empires, Kingdoms, etcetera . . .* (Philadelphia)
Copperplate engraving, 12.2 x 13.4 inches
Library of Congress, Geography & Map Division, G4050 1814 .C3 TIL

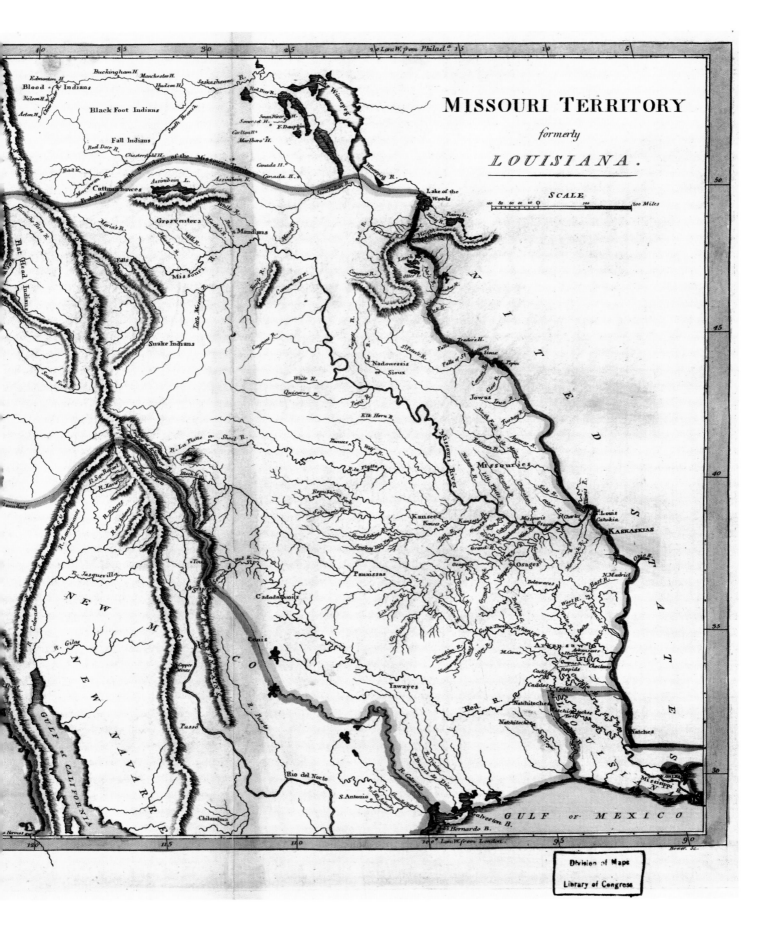

MISSOURI TERRITORY
formerly
LOUISIANA.

SCALE

Bower. sc.

131

Fort Snelling

Following the War of 1812 the federal government set out to secure the northwestern frontier and its fur trade by establishing a chain of forts between Lake Michigan and the Missouri River. These forts not only protected the territory from Canadian and British encroachment, the soldiers and government officials stationed at them administered government and protected commerce, negotiated treaties with neighboring American Indian nations, and built military roads. Fort personnel included soldiers and officers, a factor in charge of fur trading activities, and Indian agents charged with administering treaty provisions. These personnel would often provide social, legal, medical, and educational services to settlers living near the fort.

In 1819 the Fifth Regiment of Infantry arrived at the junction of the Mississippi and Minnesota rivers to build the northwest link in this chain of forts. The site of this fort, which had been acquired by Lieutenant Zebulon M. Pike from the Dakota in 1805, would allow the army to control traffic on these two major rivers. Originally called Fort Anthony, its name was changed to Fort Snelling in 1824 to honor Colonel Josiah Snelling, who commanded the regiment that built it, and oversaw its construction.

In its early years, settlers lived close to the fort along the confluence of the Mississippi and Minnesota rivers. However, when a whiskey trade began to flourish outside the fort, the military banned them from the lands it controlled. One of these squatters, a retired fur trader turned bootlegger named Pierre "Pig's Eye" Parrant, eventually relocated downriver to an area known as Lambert's Landing. The Mississippi River Valley in this vicinity is defined by a series of limestone bluffs that line both sides of the river north to Saint Anthony Falls, and Lambert's Landing was located at a natural break in the bluffs—one of the last places to unload boats coming upriver, some fourteen miles downstream from the falls. Parrant's whiskey business became so popular that rivermen and settlers began to refer to the area as "Pig's Eye Landing." Steamboats continued to bring new immigrants, and soon another settlement grew up around the "upper landing," another break in the bluffs just upriver from Pig's Eye, the "lower landing." These two settlements would coalesce into the community of Saint Paul, a name adopted in 1841 at the urging of Father Lucien Galtier, who had built a local chapel dedicated to the Christian apostle. Saint Paul was made the capital of Minnesota Territory in 1849 and continued to be the seat of government when Minnesota entered the Union in 1858.

In 1852 Hennepin County was created by the Minnesota Territorial Legislature, named after the Flemish friar who had traveled to New France with La Salle. In 1680 Hennepin had named the only waterfall on the Mississippi River "Saint Anthony

Falls" in honor of his patron saint, Saint Anthony of Padua. The county seat would be built on land just west of the falls, and by popular acclaim the planned town was named "Minnehapolis." This name was formed using a derivative of laughing waters, *Minnehaha*, and the Greek suffix for city, *polis*, and was intended to denote "city of the falls." The "h" was dropped early on, and the literal meaning of Minneapolis became "city of waters." The hydropower offered by Saint Anthony Falls facilitated the rapid development of Minneapolis, which soon led the nation in sawmilling, and later became one of the nation's leading flour producers, with a dozen mills operating at the falls.

A beautiful view of Fort Snelling is illustrated here. Painted by John C. Wild in 1844, it shows the fort located high on the bluffs overlooking the Mississippi near its confluence with the St. Peters (later Minnesota) River. Although an idealized view, Wild successfully captures the impressive monument of stone and timber that Colonel Snelling's Fifth Infantry built hundreds of miles beyond the fringe of the frontier.

NEXT PAGES
Title: Fort Snelling
Date Issued: 1844
Cartographer: John Caspar Wild
Published: Painting
Watercolor and gouache, 20 x 30 inches
Minnesota Historical Society, AV1988.45.348

Gateway to the West

It was from the St. Louis area that Lewis and Clark started on their trailblazing journey across the Louisiana Territory in May 1804, and it was their return in September 1806 that heralded St. Louis as the "Gateway to the West," as many adventurers, settlers, and trappers would soon follow their path into the new frontier. And yet, despite its importance as an outfitting center for these westward expeditions and as a home base for the fur trade, St. Louis remained a small village in the early nineteenth century.

It was the steamboat that spurred the development of St. Louis, and as steamboat traffic on the Mississippi grew, so did St. Louis. Indeed, its location on the river—just below the confluence of the Missouri and Illinois rivers, and 190 miles above the mouth of the Ohio—practically guaranteed its importance as a terminus for river traffic. The 1844 map shown here depicts the city just after a period of rapid growth, at a time when its population numbered over thirty thousand, and before the railways would bypass the city to the north.

Three illustrations decorate the map: the courthouse, the Planters' House Hotel, and a steamboat. The courthouse is the domed structure pictured on the left side of the map, soon to become famous as the site of the first Dred Scott decision. The Planters' House Hotel, which is shown on the right side of the map, was the largest hotel of its day in the West. Just to the right of the hotel is a Doric temple that housed the Unitarian church, founded by T. S. Eliot's grandfather. The steamboat depicted at the bottom of the map lies directly below three small lines inscribed in the river at Market Street; this was the ferry boat landing from Illinois. A bridge spanning the Mississippi at St. Louis would not be built until 1874.

A box on the upper left of the map details the explosive growth of St. Louis's population, and on the right is a legend that identifies the city's religious, civic, charitable, and commercial institutions. This map shows the 1841 city limits of St. Louis, as well as the city's six political wards, which are color-coded and marked on the city's grid. The large body of water in the center of the city is Chouteau's Pond, which was originally outside the village. By the 1840s the pond was no longer a place for country respite, but a dumping ground for factory and mill waste and sewage. It was drained in the 1850s, after a cholera epidemic was linked to the condition of the water supply.

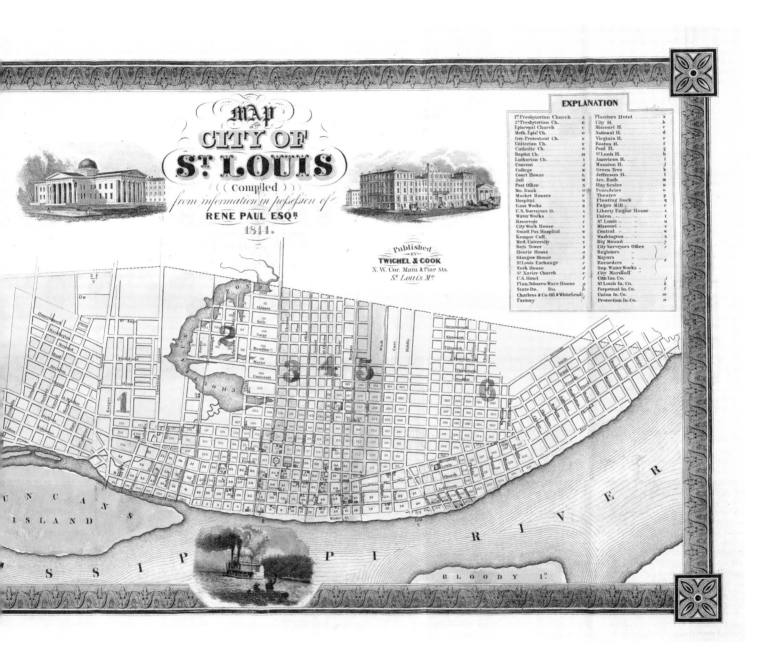

EXPLANATION

1st Presbyterian Church	A	Planters Hotel	a
2nd Presbyterian Ch.	B	City H.	b
Episcopal Church	C	Missouri H.	c
Meth. Epis! Ch.	D	National H.	d
Ger. Protestant Ch.	E	Virginia H.	e
Unitarian Ch.	F	Boston H.	f
Catholic Ch.	G	Paul H.	g
Baptist Ch.	H	St Louis H.	h
Lutharian Ch.	I	American H.	i
Convent	J	Mansion H.	j
College	K	Green Tree	k
Court House	L	Jefferson H.	l
Jail	M	Arc. Bath	m
Post Office	N	Hay Scales	n
Mo. Bank	O	Foundries	o
Market Houses	P	Theatre	p
Hospital	Q	Floating Dock	q
Gass Works	R	Pages Mill	r
U.S. Surveyors O.	S	Liberty Engine House	s
Water Works	T	Union	t
Reservoir	U	St Louis	u
City Work House	V	Missouri	v
Small Pox Hospital	W	Central	w
Kemper Coll.	X	Washington	x
Med. University	Y	Big Mound	y
Boys Tower	Z	City Surveyors Office	
Henrie House	a	Registers	
Glasgow House	b	Mayors	z
St Louis Exchange	c	Recorders	
York House	d	Sup. Water Works	
St Xavier Church	e	City Marshall	
U.S. Hotel	f	City Ins. Co.	
Plan.Tobacco Ware House	g	St Louis In. Co.	k
State Do. Do.	h	Perpetual In. Co.	l
Charless & Co. Oil & WhiteLead		Union In. Co.	m
Factory		Protection In. Co.	n

Title: Map of the City of St. Louis

Date Issued: 1844

Cartographer: René Paul

Published: *Map of the City of St. Louis,*

compiled from information in the possession of
Rene Paul Esqr., 1844 (St. Louis, Missouri)

Copperplate engraving, 5.1 x 3.1 inches

David Rumsey Collection, Image No. 4197001

CHAPTER 6

THE MISSISSIPPI IN TIME OF WAR

Colonial Conflicts on the River

From the time the French claimed the Mississippi in 1682 until the defeat of British forces at the Battle of New Orleans in 1815, the colonial powers that vied for North American sovereignty understood that the Great River was the key to control of the interior of the vast continent. La Salle envisioned a grand waterway that included the Mississippi, the Great Lakes, and the St. Lawrence River—secured by a string of forts and posts along the way—that would serve as the central axis of Louisiana. To rule this immense empire, which stretched from Canada to the Gulf of Mexico and from the Allegheny Mountains to the Rockies, the French thought it sufficient to control movement and communication along this route. This plan, which was based on a faulty understanding of the geography of the territory, was never really put to the test; for France was eliminated as a colonial power in North America in 1763.

By the Treaty of Paris, which ended the French and Indian War, Great Britain obtained Canada and Louisiana east of the Mississippi River from France, as well as Florida from Spain. The Isle of Orleans and all lands west of the Mississippi formerly under French dominion went to Spain. The Mississippi River thus became the border between the British and Spanish empires in North America. The British were given navigation rights on the Mississippi and managed to garrison several locations on the east bank of the river. New Orleans gave Spain a commanding position on the lower river, however, and for the most part, the British were never able to take control of the river. The British considered enlarging the Iberville River, so as to permit navigation to the Gulf of Mexico via a route that bypassed New Orleans, but their plans never came to fruition. Indeed, Great Britain was only able to hold eastern Louisiana for twenty years before being expelled by its own insubordinate colonies.

Military action along the Mississippi during the American Revolution began early in 1778, when James Willing led an American raid on pro-British settlements along the river. In July of the same year American troops led by George Rogers Clark captured the river posts at Kaskaskia and Cahokia, which effectively ended British control of the Illinois country. Although initially neutral in the war, Spain sent supplies from New Orleans up the Mississippi to help the American cause. Then, in June 1779, the Spanish declared war on Great Britain. The governor of Spanish Louisiana, Don Bernardo de Gálvez, immediately set out to drive the British from the lower Mississippi. Gálvez and his troops cunningly captured the British garrisons at Fort Bute at the junction of the Iberville and Mississippi rivers and at Fort New Richmond at Baton Rouge; shortly thereafter the British surrendered Fort Panmure at Natchez. Having secured the Great River, Gálvez went on to take Mobile and Pensacola, regaining the territory that Spain had ceded to Great Britain in 1763 and effectively consolidating Spanish rule in the lower Mississippi Valley.

Spain closed the Mississippi to non-Spanish traffic in July 1784 and employed gunboats in an attempt to govern traffic on the river and to halt illegal trade. A string of forts along the Mississippi from Tennessee to the river's mouth served as the first line of defense of Spanish territory to the west. It would not be long before the Spanish were embroiled in an undeclared economic war with the American inhabitants of the western interior, a conflict they were destined to lose; for although river boats from Kentucky and Ohio could be confiscated before they reached market, the Spanish could not stop the growing westward movement of the American population. Appeals to lift the prohibition on river traffic went unanswered

until 1795, when Spain granted the United States both the right to navigate the Mississippi River and an *entrepôt* at the port of New Orleans. Soon after, Louisiana and Florida would be abandoned to the Americans, allowing them in the course of a few years to either penetrate the region peacefully or take by force a portion of the defensive borderlands Spain had hoped to retain.

The reacquisition of Louisiana by France and its subsequent sale to the United States in 1803 placed the Mississippi in the heartland of the young nation. The Louisiana Purchase, which came to be defined by the western drainage basin of the Mississippi River, gave the United States complete control of the continent's main waterway system—the Mississippi-Missouri-Ohio rivers—and enabled Americans to send corn, cotton, indigo, and tobacco to the world market. The success of this American trade would soon rankle the dominant powers of Europe.

The War of 1812

On June 18, 1812, the United States declared war on Great Britain, for myriad reasons. Great Britain was at war with France at the time, and both countries had endeavored to block the United States from trading with the other. Frustrated by trade restraints that the United States considered a violation of international law, animosity toward the British grew as the Royal Navy impressed thousands of American sailors into service. The United States also blamed British intrigue for American Indian resistance to the encroachment of their tribal lands by settlers along the northwestern frontier (in what today are the states of Ohio, Michigan, and Illinois).

As a result, many American settlers believed that the elimination of the British from Canada would solve their problems with the Indians. Meanwhile, Canadians suspected that Americans were using Indian unrest as an excuse for a war of conquest and territorial expansion of the republic. Over two years of hostilities ensued, with neither side winning a decisive victory. A peace treaty signed at Ghent in December 1814 was based on status quo antebellum (the situation before the war), but before news of the signing reached Washington, one of the most critical victories in American history would take place—the defeat of the British in the Battle of New Orleans.

An attack on the Crescent City—the key to control of the Mississippi River and thus the interior of the continent—had not gone unanticipated. Brigadier General Thomas Flournoy, commander of the Seventh Military District, ordered Barthélémy Lafon to prepare plans "of all the points to be fortified for the general defense of Louisiana." Lafon, who served as the chief engineer for the American forces during the Gulf Campaign of the war, carried out this survey during the years 1813 and 1814, and packaged his work in a manuscript atlas entitled *Atlas of the 7th Military District exhibiting the General Map of the States of Tenessee Louisiana Mississipi Territory with the Fortifictions Formerly Built, Projected, or Built Since the Beginning of the War*, now housed in the Historic New Orleans Collection.

Many of Lafon's plans are of installations built by Spanish, French, and English engineers. One such example is shown here, that of Fort St. Philipp. Originally constructed in 1795 by Francisco Luis Hector, Baron de Carondelet, then the governor of Spanish Louisiana, this fort was located south of New Orleans on the east bank of the Mississippi River. Rebuilt by the Americans in 1808 Fort St. Philipp withstood nine days of bombardment by the British in January 1815, preventing five British vessels from reaching New Orleans. Lafon's drawing depicts Bayou "Mardy Gras," named by French explorers in 1699 on the first observance of the holiday in this region.

Title: Plan of the Fort of St. Philipp, Plaquemine
Date Issued: 1814
Cartographer: Barthélémy Lafon
Published: *Atlas of the 7th Military District exhibiting the General Map of the States of Tenessee Louisiana Mississipi Territory with the Fortifictions formerly Built, Projected, or Built Since the Beginning of the War* (Manuscript)
Pen and ink and watercolor, 10.6 x 18.1 inches
The Historic Collection of New Orleans, Accession 1970.2.6i, ii

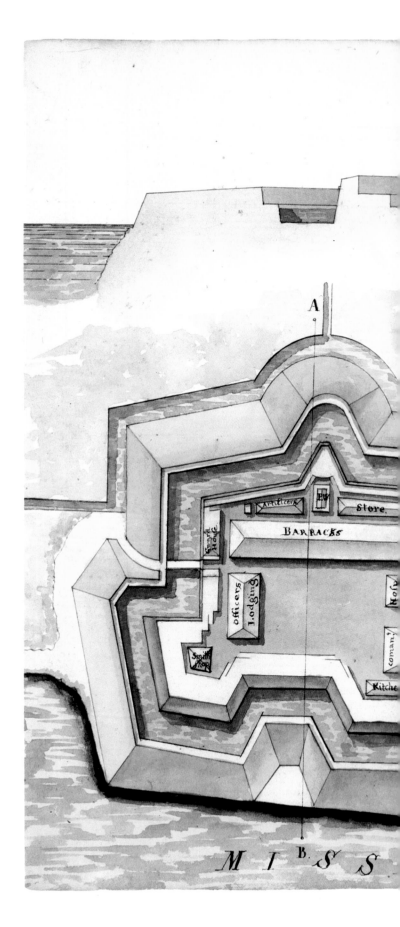

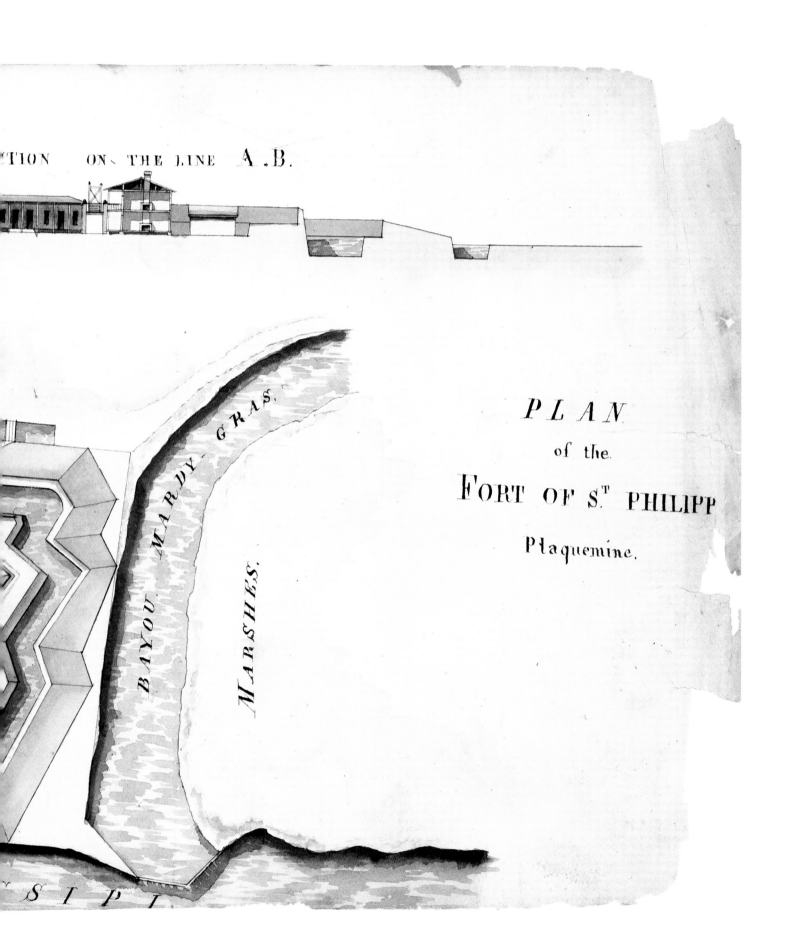

SECTION ON THE LINE A.B.

PLAN

of the

FORT OF St PHILIPP

Plaquemine.

BAYOU MARDY-GRAS.

MARSHES.

MISSISIPI

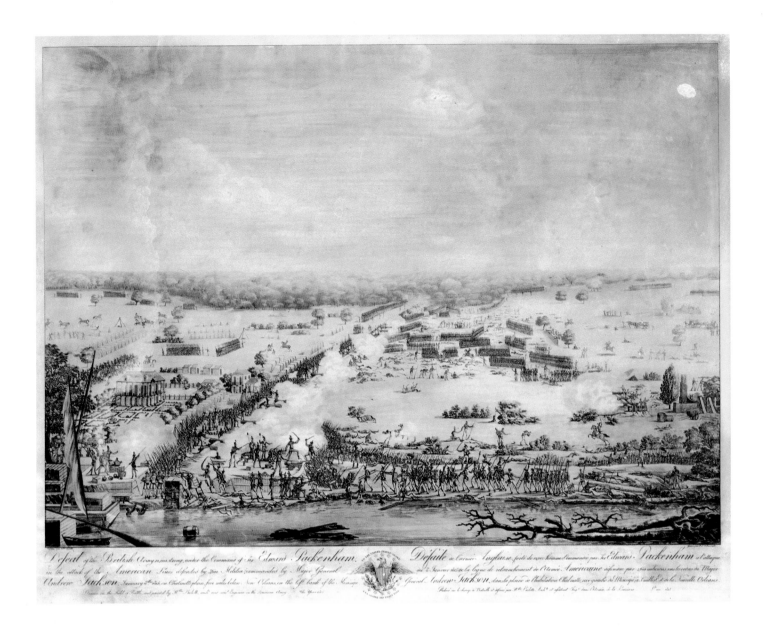

Defeat of the British Army, 12,000 strong, under the Command of Sir Edward Packenham. *Défaite de l'Armée Anglaise, forte de vingt mine hommes commandée par Sir Edward Packenham et attaquée* *in the attack of the American Lines defended by 3600 Militia commanded by Major General* *le 8. Janvier 1815 de la ligne de retranchement de l'Armée Américaine defendue par trois mille cinq cent cinquante Major* *Andrew Jackson January 8th 1815 on Chalmette plain five miles below New Orleans, on the left bank of the Mississippi* *General Andrew Jackson, dans la plaine de Chalmette Chalmette chalmette, avec quatre de Mississipi à vingt de Nouvelle Orléans*

General Andrew Jackson arrived in New Orleans late in 1814 to defend the city from British attack. Earlier in the year "Old Hickory" and a force of Tennessee militia, Cherokee warriors, and U.S. regulars had broken the Creek Nation, a powerful confederation of American Indian tribes in Georgia and Alabama supported by the British. Moving south, Jackson secured Pensacola on the Florida panhandle, and then cleared the British from Mobile. He now faced the advance of an army of over eleven thousand British Redcoats intent on sweeping up the Mississippi.

Jackson recruited anyone who would fight: the Tennessee militia was joined by a company of long rifles from Kentucky along with Mississippi and Louisiana militiamen; the pirate Jean Lafitte and nearly

Title: Defeat of the British Army, 12,000 strong, under the Command of Sir Edward Packenham, in the attack of the American Lines defended by 3,600 Militia . . . January 8th, 1815, on Chalmette plain . . .
Date Issued: 1817
Cartographer: Jean Hyacinthe Laclotte
Published: Separately (Paris)
Etched aquatint, 8.6 x 10.6 inches
The Historic Collection of New Orleans,
Accession 1944.5

a thousand of Lafitte's men enlisted; so did some six hundred free black soldiers; the ranks also included a group of Choctaw Indians and local townsmen of all ilks—even the mayor and governor signed on. Jackson managed to muster a hodgepodge force of roughly four thousand six hundred men.

Action started December 14, 1814, with the British overpowering American gunboats on Lake Borgne. After a night battle with the British on December 23, Jackson had his troops fall back to a defensive position six miles south of the city on the old Macarty plantation along the Rodriquez Canal, a twenty-foot-wide and four-foot-deep abandoned canal between the Mississippi and a cypress swamp. Jackson had the canal widened and deepened, and filled partly with water. His men built an earthen rampart strong enough to withstand a cannon shot and used cotton bales to form additional barricades. They looked out over a stubbled sugarcane field that would afford the American artillerymen a clear field of fire. The British were garrisoned on the Chalmette Plain two miles to the south.

Major General Edward Pakenham—a veteran of the Napoleonic wars and the Duke of Wellington's brother-in-law—was commander of the British invasion. Pakenham launched a full-scale attack against Jackson's forces on January 8, 1815, sending five thousand four hundred of his soldiers into battle. The Redcoats marched in ranks, bayonets fixed, for a quarter of a mile toward the earthen fortifications that protected Jackson's troops. The attack had begun under darkness and fog, but as the British neared the American lines, the fog lifted. The Americans were fine marksmen and mowed down wave after wave of the advancing British. General Samuel Gibb's brigade came under fire from Tennesseans holding the American left flank near the swamp. Gibbs was killed,

along with many other officers. General John Keane attempted to come to Gibbs aid and ordered the Ninety-Third Highlanders diagonally across the field of action. This exposed them to a raking fire, and the company sustained heavy casualties, including Keane himself. Pakenham rode into the fray in an attempt to rally his troops and was also shot and killed. With two generals killed and one severely wounded, many of the British troops fell back; their retreat broke morale and threw the British army into disarray.

The battle lasted barely a half an hour and the American force suffered only seventy-one casualties while inflicting more than two thousand. The overwhelming victory was followed by the British naval bombardment of Fort St. Philipp, to which the American garrison responded with cannon fire, slowly forcing a British retreat downriver. In the meantime, the British army had retreated through Lake Borgne and into the Gulf of Mexico.

Some have argued the Battle of New Orleans was pointless, coming as it did after the signing of the Treaty of Ghent signaled the end of the war. It certainly wasn't for Jackson, who soon became a national hero and in 1828 would ascend to the presidency. When Jackson left the White House in 1837, he was asked if the Battle of New Orleans had any historical significance. His response is noteworthy: "If General Pakenham and his ten thousand matchless veterans could have annihilated my little army . . . he would have captured New Orleans and sentried all the contiguous territory, though technically the war was over. . . . Great Britain would have immediately abrogated the Treaty of Ghent and would have ignored Jefferson's transaction with Napoleon."

The best cartographic summary of the Battle of New Orleans is Arsène Lacarrière Latour's 1815 *Map shewing the landing of the British Army, its several Encampments and*

Fortifications on the Mississippi. Shown here, it depicts the routes of the different British army corps in their advance on New Orleans, as well as the areas they held prior to their defeat. Latour was a Frenchman who served as Jackson's principal topographic officer during the Battle of New Orleans. After the war, he joined Lafon and Lafitte as secret Spanish agents, surveying and mapping the southwestern frontier for Spanish officials in Havana and Madrid. He also published his *Historical Memoir of the War in West Florida and Louisiana* (1816), which is still considered a primary source for the Battle of New Orleans. It was accompanied by an atlas of nine folding maps, including the one shown here.

A bird's-eye view of the battle is illustrated on page 142. Based on an 1815 painting by Jean Hyacinthe Laclotte, it depicts the battleground from a vantage point above the west bank of the Mississippi. The cypress swamp can be seen in the background, and the house and garden of Edmund Macarty's plantation to the left. Laclotte served as a volunteer engineer in the First Louisiana Militia and was an eyewitness to the combat. He had emigrated from France in 1804 and joined Latour in 1810 in establishing an architectural and engineering firm that designed many historic buildings in New Orleans, including the first Orleans Theater. He returned to France after 1815 to have his painting of the battle reproduced as an aquatint engraving and returned to New Orleans in 1817, where he sold the print in various bookstores.

Title: Map shewing the Landing of the British Army, its several Encampments and Fortifications on the Mississippi, and the Works they erected on their Retreat, also the Different Posts, Encampments, and Fortifications made by the several Corps of the American Army during the Whole Campaign
Date Issued: 1815
Cartographer: Arsène Lacarrière Latour
Published: Accompanying atlas to *Historical Memoir of the War in West Florida and Louisiana* (Philadelphia)
Lithograph, 18.5 x 23.6 inches
The Historic Collection of New Orleans

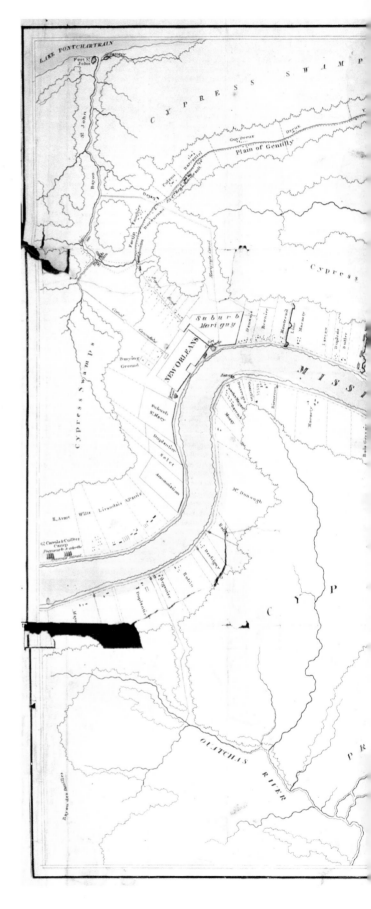

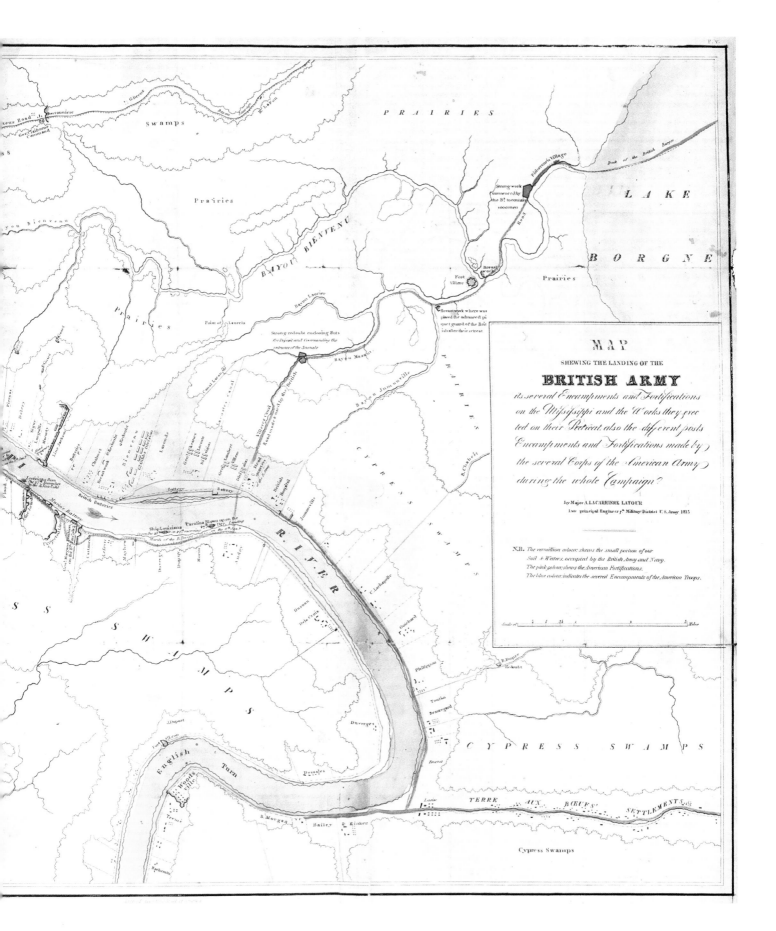

MAP

SHEWING THE LANDING OF THE

BRITISH ARMY

its several Encampments and Fortifications
on the Mississippi and the Works they erec
ted on their Retreat, also the different posts
Encampments and Fortifications made by
the several Corps of the American Army
during the whole Campaign

by Major A. LACARRIERE LATOUR
late principal Engineer 7th Military District U.S. Army 1815

N.B. The vermillion colour shews the small portion of our
Soil & Waters, occupied by the British Army and Navy.
The pink colour shews the American Fortifications.
The blue colour indicates the several Encampments of the American Troops.

Scale of   3 Miles

The War Between the States

Control of the Mississippi River was of inestimable importance to both sides of the Civil War. Its course meandered over one thousand miles between Cairo, Illinois, and the Gulf of Mexico and straight through the heart of the Confederacy. Northern control of the river would reopen the great commercial artery to New Orleans, which was the natural outlet to market for the agricultural and industrial products of the Northwest. It would allow the Union to move troops and their supplies through an area ill-provided with roads and railroads, and the numerous navigable streams tributary to the Mississippi would offer ready routes of invasion into the heart of the South. It would also slice the Confederacy in two, effectively isolating that half lying west of the river—Texas, Arkansas, and most of Louisiana—which was an important source of food, military supplies, and recruits for the Southern armies. The defense of the river was imperative to South's ability to survive, and command of the Mississippi the linchpin to Northern victory in the War Between the States.

The logistical importance of the Mississippi River is clearly illustrated by the first two maps seen here; both were released as the North and South were developing their war strategies. In 1861 Winfield Scott, commanding general of the Union army, devised a plan that would avoid an invasion of the South, a tactic he sagaciously foresaw as much too costly to both sides. He proposed a naval blockade of all Confederate Atlantic and Gulf ports, along with a major offensive movement to gain control of the Mississippi River. According to Scott, this strategy would "envelop the insurgent states and bring them to terms with less bloodshed than by any other plan." The Northern mindset at the time was that the rebellious South could quickly be overrun, and Scott's plan was rejected as too deliberate. The press came to derisively refer to it as the "Anaconda Plan," after the snake that kills by constriction. Ironically, as the war progressed, the implementation of Scott's plan would become the Union's winning strategy.

The second map is the work of John Bachman, a skilled New York artist and lithographer who between the years 1861 and 1862 produced a series of at least eight panoramic maps of likely theaters of the coming war. Panoramic or "bird's-eye views" were very popular during the second half of the nineteenth century and were more easily understood by a public unskilled in map reading. Shown here is a view of the Gulf Coast, which Bachman portrays as besieged by a flotilla of Union naval ships. Major ports such as Mobile and New Orleans would be the primary targets of such a blockade; Vicksburg is shown on the northern border of the map, soon to become the defiant objective of Union maneuvers on the Mississippi.

Late in 1861 the Union began a campaign to wrest control of the lower Mississippi River from the Confederacy. Early in September of that year, Confederate troops led by General Leonidas Polk had seized Columbus, Kentucky, which was located at a strategic point overlooking the Mississippi just south of its junction with the Ohio. This was the South's first line of defense of the lower Mississippi, and throughout the autumn and winter, over nineteen thousand soldiers worked to fortify the bastion: 145 heavy guns were positioned on the bluffs above the river; a floating battery was positioned on the Mississippi, including river steamers that were converted to gunboats; a huge chain of twenty-pound links supported by anchored barges was stretched across the river; and river mines— then called torpedoes—were placed in front of the chain. In addition, a large earthen fort named Fort DeRussy and two smaller detached forts on the bluff were surrounded by miles of infantry trenches and protected by abatis. Across the river, at Belmont, Missouri, a small observation camp and an artillery battery were installed.

On November 6, 1861, General Ulysses S. Grant left his headquarters at Cairo, Illinois, to make a demonstration against the Columbus fortress. The next morning, after learning that Confederate troops had crossed the Mississippi River from Columbus to Belmont, Grant attacked the camp on the western river bank. A back-and-forth battle ensued, but eventually the Confederates were forced to retreat, and Grant's troops routed the camp. As the Federals began to withdraw, they were attacked by Confederate reinforcements that had crossed the river; guns from the Rebel stronghold rained down on Grant's battalion. The Union gunboats returned fire as the Union soldiers successfully fought their way back to their transports.

The Battle of Belmont was General Grant's first real test in combat leadership, and provided him with valuable experience for future campaigns; it also made it clear that the Confederate citadel at Columbus could

not be taken by a direct river assault. Instead, Union troops outflanked Columbus after having captured weaker Confederate positions to the east (Forts Heiman, Henry, and Donelson). Although General Polk argued for standing a siege in the elaborate earthworks that had been constructed at Fort DeRussy, he was ordered to evacuate Columbus on March 2, 1862. As a detachment of the U.S. Navy converged on Columbus from Cairo, Confederate supplies, ammunition, heavy cannon, and gun crews were sent down the river to the Southern position on Island No. 10 just below the Kentucky border near New Madrid, Missouri. The following day Grant's forces occupied the Columbus area and set about reopening the Mississippi River.

Federal troops under the command of General John Pope were already making their way toward the Confederate line at New Madrid, which they reached on March 3, laying siege to the tiny hamlet. The Southern commanders had chosen to fortify this area for several reasons. New Madrid lay at the terminus of a road to St. Louis, and thus could serve to launch an invasion of that city 175 miles to north. As can be seen on the map here, the town itself was located at the top of the second of two horseshoe bends of the river, sweeping arcs that appear on the map like the letter "S" laid on its side. Slightly upriver from New Madrid was Island No. 10, situated in the middle of the river, which could be easily fortified to block Federal passage down the river. After ten days of siege, the Confederates decided to evacuate New Madrid and make their stand at Island No. 10.

A Union Navy armada, known as the "Western Flotilla," arrived March 15 and immediately began a bombardment of the island and the surrounding batteries, but to little effect. The island was protected

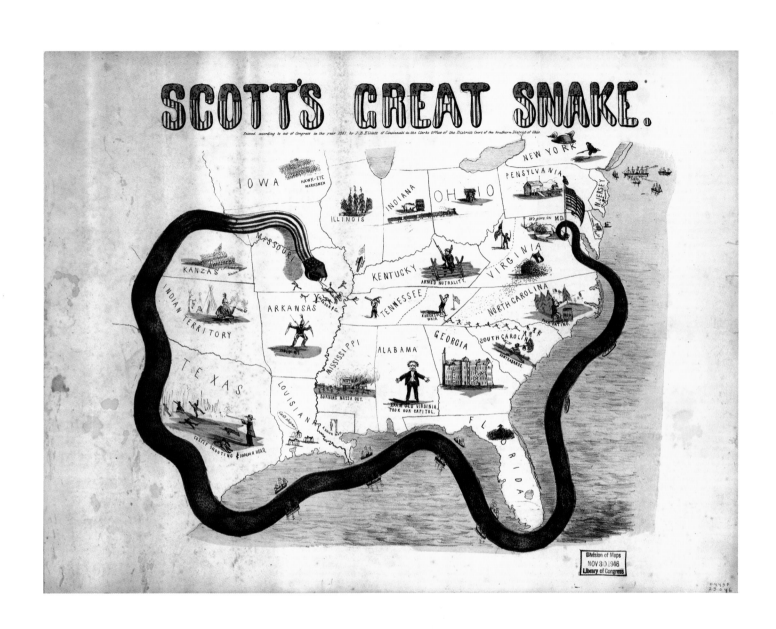

Title: Scott's Great Snake
Date Issued: 1861
Cartographer: J. B. Elliott
Published: Separately (Cincinnati, Ohio)
Lithograph, 13.8 x 17.3 inches
Library of Congress, Geography & Map Division,
G3701.S5 1861 .E4 CW 11

from an overland assault from the east by a combination of Reel Foot Lake and heavy flooding (see the areas marked as "Impassable for troops on account of high water" on the map); so, the only possible land approach was to march down the Tennessee peninsula (known as "Madrid Bend") along the east bank of the river, from which the island could be attacked from the south. This meant that Pope's troops would have to cross the river, but the logistics of this maneuver were problematic, for two reasons: Pope did not have transports to ferry his troops across the river—they were moored safely upriver from Island No. 10—and even if he did, the Confederate batteries along the banks of Madrid Bend made safe conveyance across the river impossible.

Pope solved the first problem by cutting the canal marked on the map across the Missouri peninsula. The area was already flooded, so this project really amounted to cutting a path through the bayous, which Union engineers accomplished by devising an ingenious method of cutting trees below the water line. Four small transports and six coal barges made their way through the canal to New Madrid, but the draft of the ironclad gunboats Pope needed was too great to get through the shallow water. The only choice left was for the gunboats to run the Confederate gauntlet at Island No. 10. On April 4 the ironclad *Carondelet* make its way past the island's batteries and quickly dislodged the Confederate batteries opposite New Madrid and Point Pleasant, demonstrating the superiority of the Federal gunboats against small land batteries. During the night of April 6 a second ironclad, the *Pittsburgh*, ran the gauntlet in time to cover Pope's morning crossing into Tennessee. The Union forces—numbering nearly twenty-five thousand—quickly overwhelmed the four thousand Confederate troops defending Island No. 10, whose escape was blocked at a point near Tiptonville (as marked on the map). The Rebels surrendered on April 8, and the Mississippi River was now open down to Fort Pillow, Tennessee.

Union forces wasted no time in targeting Fort Pillow, which stood high on the Chickasaw Bluffs overlooking the Mississippi River, about forty miles north of Memphis. An attack on the fort by Pope's army was called off, and the Western Flotilla was charged with its capture. Union mortar boats began daily bombardments of the fort on April 14, which proved to be ineffectual. The famous naval battle of Plum Point Bend occurred on May 10, 1862, within sight of Fort Pillow. It was a decisive victory for the Confederate River Defense Fleet, which rammed and sank the Union ironclad *Cincinnati* and badly damaged the *Mound City* before retreating to safe harbor under the guns of the fort. Fort Pillow was evacuated after the main Confederate army had been forced to retreat from Corinth, Mississippi, leaving the fort exposed to an attack from the rear. On the night of June 4, the Confederate garrison destroyed the fort and withdrew to Memphis.

On June 6 the Union's Western Flotilla, now reinforced by its own rams, fought and defeated the Confederate fleet at Memphis. The destruction of the Confederate River Defense Fleet forced the surrender of Memphis, which had served as a key Confederate supply depot and ship building center. The river was now open to Union ships all the way to Vicksburg, Mississippi.

While Union forces were fighting their way downriver, a major upriver offensive was launched far to the south. By late December 1861 a Union fleet was assembled in the Mississippi sound near Ship Island. Early the next year Commodore David Farragut arrived to lead the Union fleet, known as the West Gulf Blockading Squadron. Farragut planned to capture New Orleans, the biggest city in the Confederacy; from here Union forces could close off the Mississippi from Rebel ships. The Confederate defense of the river consisted of Forts Philipp and Jackson about seventy miles south of the city, a hastily laid barrier across the river that would allow only one ship to pass at a time, and a fleet of ships that included the ironclad ram *Manassas*, the unpowered ironclad *Louisiana*, and the unfinished ironclad *Mississippi*.

Farragut began bombarding the forts on April 19, 1862, and his gunboats were able to clear a way through the obstruction blocking the river several days later. After five days Farragut sent his ships past the forts in a daring and chaotic nighttime maneuver. New Orleans's line of defense had been breached, and the city was now in Union hands; cut off and surrounded by Union troops, the garrisons of the two forts surrendered on April 28.

The Rebel defenses of New Orleans and Farragut's April 24 attack are depicted by Robert Knox Sneden on the map shown on page 155. Sneden was a Union map-maker who had been captured in 1863 and suffered through internment at Andersonville. He devoted the rest of his life to memorializing the Civil War; drawing wonderfully detailed watercolor sketches

Title: Panorama of the Seat of War: Bird's-Eye View of Louisiana, Mississippi, Alabama, and part of Florida
Date Issued: 1861
Cartographer: J. Bachman
Published: Separately (New York)
Lithograph, 22 x 28.7 inches
Collection of Martayan Lan Augustyn, Inc.

BIRDS EYE VIEW

MISSISSIPPI, ALABAMA AND PART OF FLORIDA

John Bachmann, Publisher,
115 & 117 Nassau St. New York

Drawn from Nature and Lith by John Bachmann.

DISTANCES FROM

NEW ORLEANS TO SOUTH PASS LA	110 MILES
MOBILE AL	135
PENSACOLA FA	210
MONTGOMERY AL	310
COLUMBUS GA	375

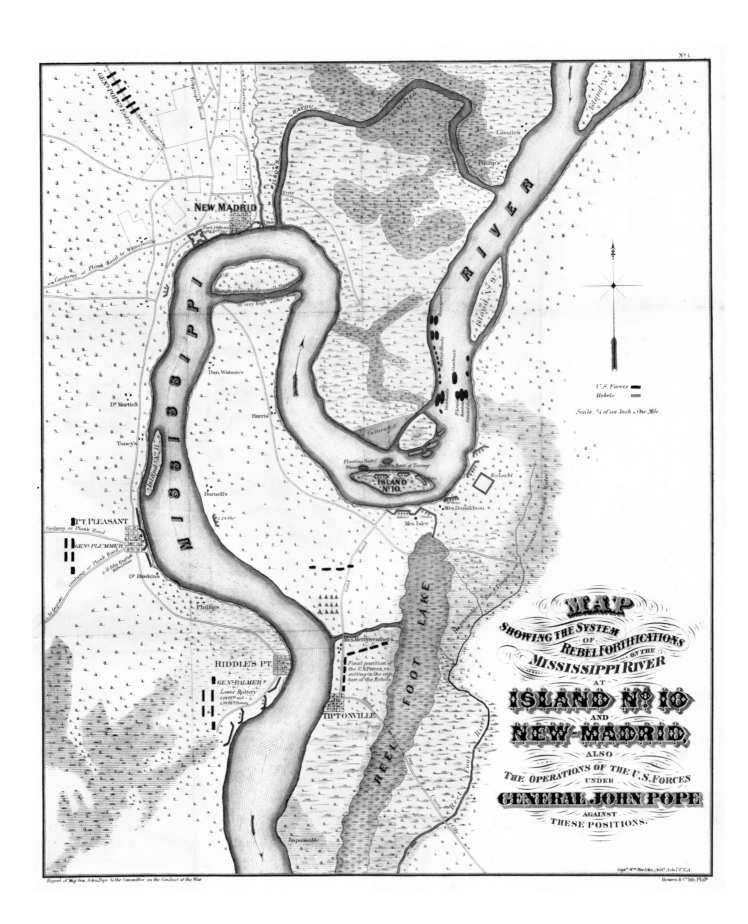

No. 1.

NEW MADRID

MAP
SHOWING THE SYSTEM
OF
REBEL FORTIFICATIONS
ON THE
MISSISSIPPI RIVER
AT
ISLAND Nº 10
AND
NEW-MADRID,
ALSO
THE OPERATIONS OF THE U.S. FORCES
UNDER
GENERAL JOHN POPE
AGAINST
THESE POSITIONS.

U.S. Forces
Rebels

Scale, ¾ of an Inch = One Mile.

PT. PLEASANT

RIDDLE'S PT.

TIPTONVILLE

REEL FOOT LAKE

ISLAND Nº 10

and intricate maps, including the one seen here. In all, Sneden's opus numbers nine hundred works, now housed in the Virginia Historical Society.

In August 1862 Confederate forces set out to regain control of Louisiana, beginning with the capture of Baton Rouge. A bird's-eye view of the August 5 Rebel attack on the city, drawn by H. S. Chandler, a member of the Ninth Regiment of the Connecticut Volunteers, is shown here. Chandler shows the ground fighting behind the city, as well as the bombardment of Confederate troops by Union batteries and gunboats in the river, including the ironclad *Essex*. Prominent city buildings are numbered and identified in a key below the image. The planned Confederate water assault failed when the Confederate ram *Arkansas* suffered mechanical failure and could not engage the Union fleet. This allowed Union troops to retreat to a line within an area of Union gunboat protection, and doomed the Confederate attempt to recapture the capital.

By December 1862 the only significant Confederate positions remaining on the river were at Port Hudson and Vicksburg. Situated on a bluff two hundred feet above the Mississippi and surrounded by deep ravines and swamplands, Vicksburg was a natural fortress. Earlier in the year Admiral Farragut's naval fleet had engaged Vicksburg's batteries, but failed

in two attempts to force the town to surrender. Shown here is a map and view of Vicksburg about the time of Farragut's second attack. Marked on the map is a canal (labeled "CUTOFF") that Union troops had begun to dig while Farragut was bombarding the town. This canal was intended to provide a channel for navigation that would bypass the Confederate batteries at Vicksburg; it was also hoped that the canal might catch enough of the river's current to cause it to change course, leaving Vicksburg high and dry and without military value. The canal was never fully completed.

A five-mile line of Rebel batteries along the river is depicted on the map, as are roads, levees, railroad lines, and landowners on the river. Ships from Farragut's fleet can be seen patrolling the river south of Vicksburg, while others—after having daringly run past Vicksburg's guns—rendezvous north of the town with the Western Flotilla, which had made its way downriver from Memphis. An even more courageous maneuver, by the Confederate ram *Arkansas*, is also depicted. On July 15, 1862, the *Arkansas* gallantly made its way down the Yazoo River, where it encountered the U.S. gunboats *Carondelet* and *Tyler* and the ram *Queen of the West*, leaving the first two badly damaged. As seen here, the *Arkansas* continued out into the Mississippi River, where it fought its way through the assembled Federal fleet to the safety of the Confederate fortress at Vicksburg. A week later, while at Vicksburg, the *Arkansas* was attacked by the *Queen of the West* and ironclad *Essex*, but was not severely damaged. Though badly in need of repairs, the *Arkansas* was ordered to steam down the river to assist Confederate forces in the attack on Baton Rouge.

In October 1862 General Grant was charged with the capture of Vicksburg. After repeated attempts

Title: Map showing the System of Rebel Fortifications of the Mississippi River at Island No. 10 and New-Madrid
Date Issued: 1866
Cartographer: William Hoelcke
Published: Separately (Philadelphia)
Lithograph, 20 x 17.3 inches
Rucker Agee Collection at the Birmingham Public Library,
Image No. CivilWar1866

to mount a direct assault, Grant reluctantly laid siege to the city on May 18, 1863. Confederate commander General John Pemberton held out for forty-seven days, waiting for reinforcements in the form of thirty thousand troops led by General Joseph Johnston. On the way to Vicksburg, however, Johnston determined that he had an insufficient force to break the siege, and retreated. With food supplies dwindling, illness and disease rampant, not to mention the constant shelling from Union batteries, it became increasingly clear to Pemberton that Johnston would not be coming; with the morale of his men beginning to break, Pemberton surrendered Vicksburg on July 4, 1863. The town no longer resembled the picturesque view seen on page 158.

The next map shows the Confederate fortifications of Port Hudson, which also had been surrounded by Union troops during the summer of 1863. This map was published in *Harper's Weekly*, the most popular newspaper during the Civil War. Despite its Northern editorial slant, the *Weekly* provided balanced reporting of the events, settings, and personages of the war. *Harper's Weekly* sent numerous artists and cartographers to the front to cover the action, and their work provides an invaluable pictorial record of the war. Although the Rebels garrisoned at Port Hudson could have held out much longer, the fall of Vicksburg rendered any further resistance pointless; five days after Vicksburg surrendered, so did Port Hudson. After two years of land and naval warfare, the Northern campaign to reopen the Mississippi River was complete, and Union merchant and military traffic had a safe avenue to the Gulf—prompting Lincoln to proclaim that "The Father of Waters again goes unvexed to the sea."

The last map seen here provides a panoramic view of the Mississippi River during wartime operations. The area between St. Louis and the Gulf of Mexico is shown on four panels that depict islands, tributaries, roads, railroads, towns, villages, cities, forts, churches, saw mills, occasional landowner or plantation names, steamboat provisioning and wooding stops, court houses, and individual stores along the river. Inset views of St. Louis, Memphis, Vicksburg, and New Orleans are included on the map, as is a table of distances to various points on the Mississippi from St. Louis to New Orleans. This map was sold to a public eager to learn the geography of the various seats of action during the war.

Title: Map showing the Defenses of the Mississippi below
New Orleans and Farragut's attack 24 April 1862
Date Issued: 1863
Cartographer: Robert Knox Sneden
Published: Manuscript
Pen and ink and watercolor, 5.9 x 4.3 inches
Virginia Historical Society, Mss5:1 Sn237:1 v. 6 p. 528

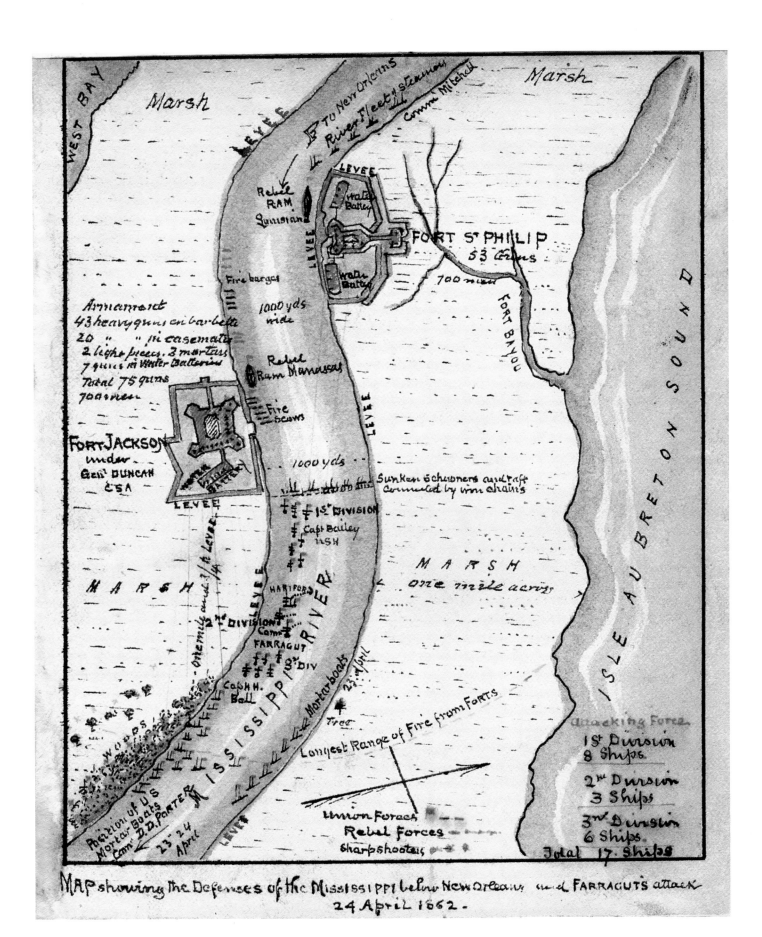

WEST BAY

Marsh

Marsh

LEVEE

To New Orleans
River Fleet & steamers

Comm Mitchell

Rebel
R.A.M.
Louisiana

LEVEE

Water
Battery

FORT St PHILIP
53 Guns

Water
Battery

Fire barges

1000 yds
wide

FORT BAYOU

700 men

Armament
43 heavy guns on barbette
20 " " in casemate
2 light pieces. 3 mortars
7 guns in Water Batteries
Total 75 guns
700 men

Rebel
Ram Manassas

Fire
Scows

FORT JACKSON
under
Genl DUNCAN
CSA

LEVEE

1000 yds

Sunken Schooners and raft
connected by iron chains

1st DIVISION
Capt Bailey
USN

ISLE AU BRETON SOUND

MARSH

MARSH
one mile across

Chain and 1/4 ft LEVEE

LEVEE

HARTFORD

2nd DIVISION
Comr
FARRAGUT
3d DIV

Capt H.H.
Bell

MISSISSIPPI RIVER

Mortarboats

23d April

Tree

Longest Range of Fire from Forts

WOODS

Position of US
Mortar boats
Comr D.D. PORTER

23. 24
April

Attacking Force
1st Division
8 Ships

2nd Division
3 Ships

3rd Division
6 Ships

Total 17 Ships

Union Forces
Rebel Forces
Sharpshooters

MAP showing the Defenses of the Mississippi below New Orleans and FARRAGUT'S attack
24 April 1862.

155

1 State Capitol of Louisiana. 2 Deaf Dumb & Blind Asylum. 3 U.S. Barraks. 4 Former Residens of President Taylor. 5 Iron clad Essex. 6 & 7 Gun Boa
12. Everitts Battery. 13 Nimms Battery 14 Camp of the 14 Main Regt. where

United States Forces commanded by Brig. Genl. THs. WILLIAMS, who lost his life in gallantly leading his men.

BATTLE OF BATON

AUGUST 5th. 1862.

PUBLISHED BY H.S. CHANDLER, BAND. 9 REGt.

Entered according to Act of Congress A 1863 by H.S CHANDLER, in the Clerks Office C

un of Connecticut.   Lith by Punderson & Prisand, New Haven, ct.

Sloop of War Mississippy   9 General Williams Quarters   10 Arsenal Buildings   11 Manning's Battery
        the Battle first commenced   15 State Prison   16 Position of Col. Cahills & Conm Regt.

GE. 9

nfederate Forces commanded by Genl. J. C. BRECKENRIDGE, of Kentuckey.

Title: Battle of Baton Rouge
Date Issued: 1862
Cartographer: H. S. Chandler
Published: Separately
(New Haven, Connecticut)
Lithograph, 12.2 x 18.1 inches
The Historic Collection of New Orleans,
Accession 1947.9

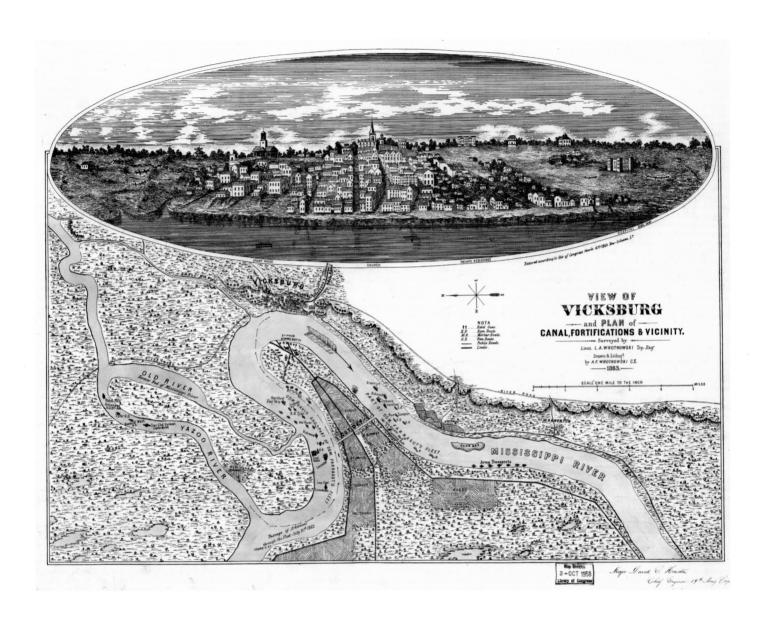

Title: View of Vicksburg and Plan of Canal,
Fortifications & Vicinity

Date Issued: 1863

Cartographer: A. F. Wrotnowski

Published: Separately (New Orleans)

Lithograph, 15.7 x 21.3 inches

Library of Congress, Geography & Map Division,
G3984.V8S5 1863 .W7 CW 294

RIGHT

Title: Survey of Mississippi Fortifications from
Port Hudson to Bayou Sara

Date Issued: 1863

Cartographer: J. Covington

Published: *Harper's Weekly* (New York)

Colored woodcut, 9 x 14.1 inches

Author's Collection

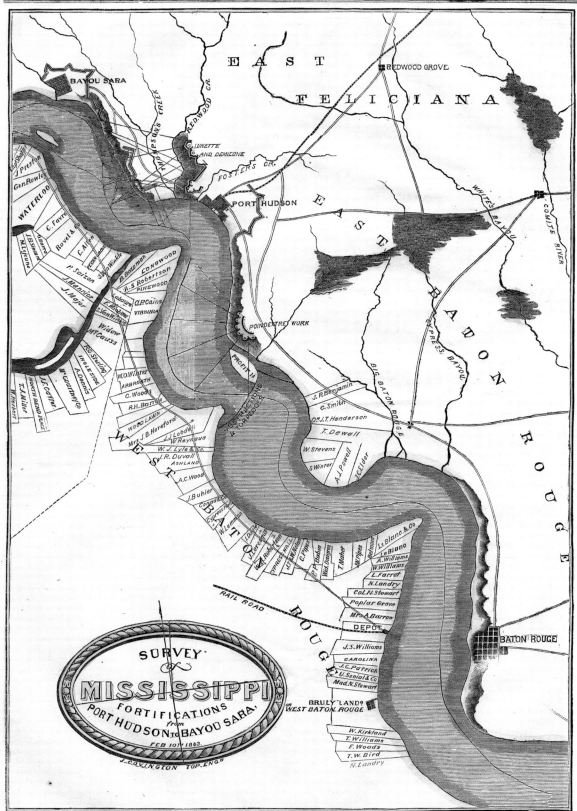

MAP OF THE COURSE OF THE MISSISSIPPI FROM BAYOU SARA TO BATON ROUGE.

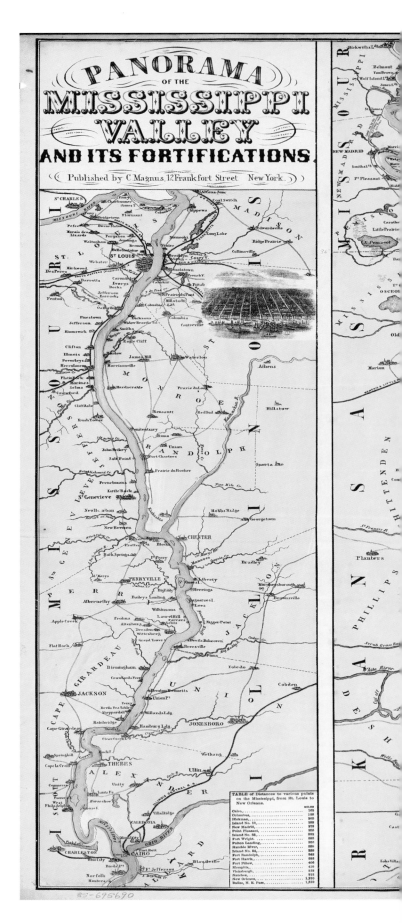

Title: Panorama of the Mississippi Valley
and its Fortifications
Date Issued: 1863
Cartographer: Charles Magnus
Published: Separately (New York)
Lithograph, 23.6 x 25.2 inches
The Historic Collection of New Orleans, Accession 1961.16

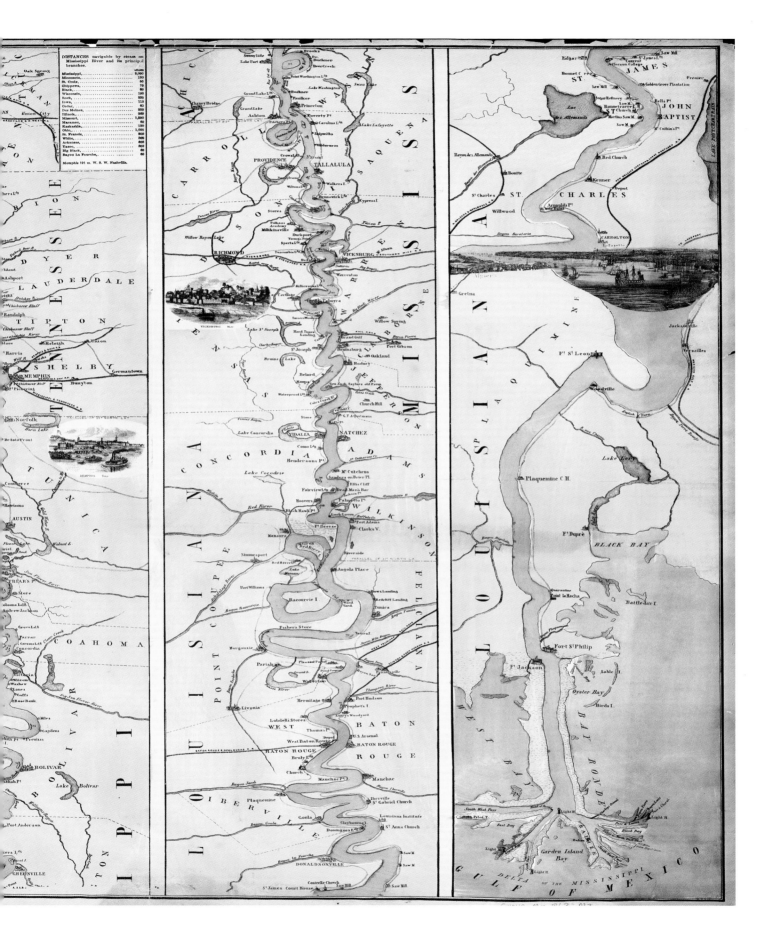

CHAPTER 7

COMMERCE ON THE RIVER

French Commercial Interests

Jacques Nicolas Bellin served as the first chief hydrographic engineer of the Dépôt des Cartes et Plans de la Marine (Maps and Plans of the Navy), was appointed the hydrographer to the French king, and was a member of the Royal Society in London. One of the most important and prolific French cartographers of the mid-eighteenth century, his maps and charts were expertly engraved and produced and set a high standard of accuracy. He provided many coastal and route maps for French shipping interests, including the first map seen here.

This beautiful and finely detailed map depicts the course of the Mississippi below the Iberville River, and the Gulf Coast from bayous Lafourche and Barataria to Mobile Bay. New Orleans is prominently located, as is the hermitage in Bayou Barataria and various American Indian villages along the Mississippi. Bellin identifies many coastal islands, provides soundings of coastal waters, and clearly marks English Turn ("Detour des Anglois") on the river. This map was included in Bellin's magnificent five-volume *Le Petit Atlas Maritime*.

The next map was drawn by the New Orleans merchant James Pitot and accompanied his journal *Observations sur la Colonie de Louisiana de 1796 à 1802*. Pitot had left St. Domingue after the revolts of 1791

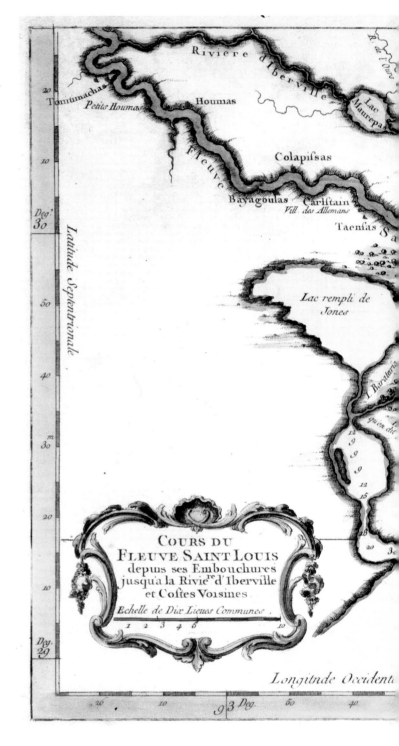

and, after a brief stay in Philadelphia, moved to New Orleans in 1796. In 1801 he began his memoir, which he took with him when he sailed for France in June 1802. Pitot intended to use his chronicle as a kind of publicity piece as he explored business opportunities

Title: *Cours du Fleuve St. Louis depuis ses Embouches jusqu'a a la Riviere d'Iberville et Costes Voisines*

Date Issued: 1763

Cartographer: Jacques Nicolas Bellin

Published: *Le Petit Atlas Maritime*, Volume 1 (Paris)

Copperplate engraving, 12.6 x 17.3 inches

The Historic Collection of New Orleans, Accession 1975.24

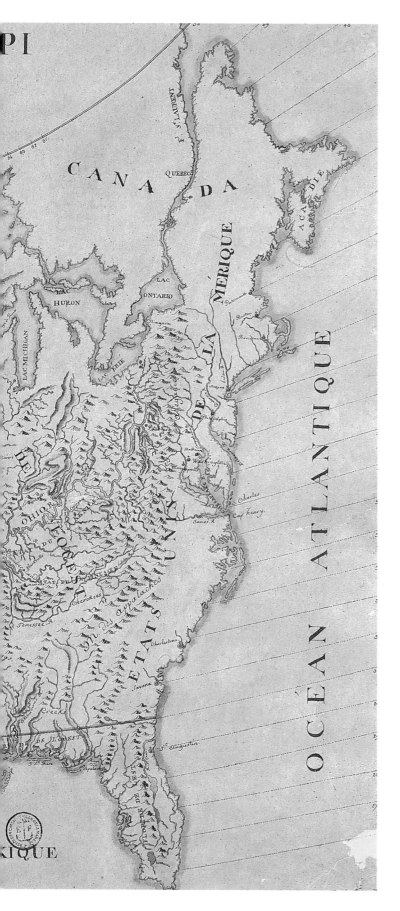

in the colony on the eve of its retrocession from Spain to France. Included in the final chapter of his book, entitled "Analytical Topography," Pitot boasted that this map "is, so far as the Mississippi is concerned, more perfect than any other that yet appeared." And indeed, his map is one of the best depictions of the upper Mississippi, the greater part of the Missouri, and the principal tributaries of those rivers just prior to the Louisiana Purchase.

Pitot based his map on his travels throughout the colony, and on reports of numerous hunters he sought out in the lower marshes of Louisiana. He also acknowledges the help of the New Orleans architect, engineer, and cartographer Barthélémy Lafon, "who worked steadfastly to secure the information that he gave to me." Of Lafon, Pitot also writes that "the map which I offer here is based on his sketches which were copied in my presence." Pitot was diligent in only including geographical details that he could verify; in the case of Lafon's contributions, he only accepted particulars about places he had not seen after confirming that particulars about places he knew "have appeared to me to be quite accurately presented." He omitted unreliable or conjectural information about areas "such as the outer boundaries of this map," where it was not possible to gather "sketches during my travels."

Title: *Carte du Mississipi et de ses Embranchemens*
Date Issued: 1802
Cartographer: James Pitot
Published: Manuscript
Pen and ink and watercolor, 21.3 x 28.7 inches
Service Historique de la Marine, Recueil 69, No. 9

River Guides

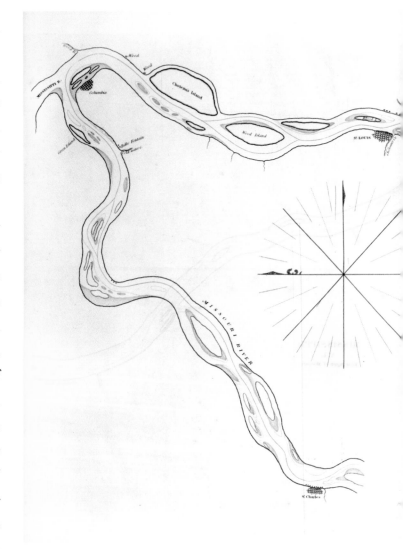

Before the coming of the railroads, rivers served as America's commercial highways, and the Mississippi was the country's main thoroughfare, moving lumber, wheat, corn, and meat from the Midwest, along with cotton and tobacco from its southern flanks, to the world market via New Orleans. River guides, or "navigators," were first published to meet the needs of farmers, immigrants, and others who floated down the rivers in clumsy flatboats and keelboats; later, they were used by steamboat pilots. These handbooks contained charts and directions for navigating rivers, along with details about various ports and other information deemed important to river travelers. One of the earliest and most famous guides was Zadok Cramer's *Navigator*, of which twelve editions were published in Pittsburgh from 1801 to 1824. Other guides soon followed, the most important of which were J. C. Gilleland's *The Ohio and Mississippi Pilot* (1820), Samuel Cumings' *Western Navigator* (1822), which was republished for thirty years under the title *The Western Pilot*, and George Conclin's *River Guide* (1848), also reissued between 1857 and 1871 as *James River Guide*.

Most of these river guides focused on the Ohio River proper and on the Mississippi south of Cairo or St. Louis. They varied widely in their detail and preciseness of directions, and in the quality of their charts. Cramer's *Navigator* included very brief and general directions and its charts were crude woodcuts on a scale of twelve miles to the inch. Gilleland's *Pilot*

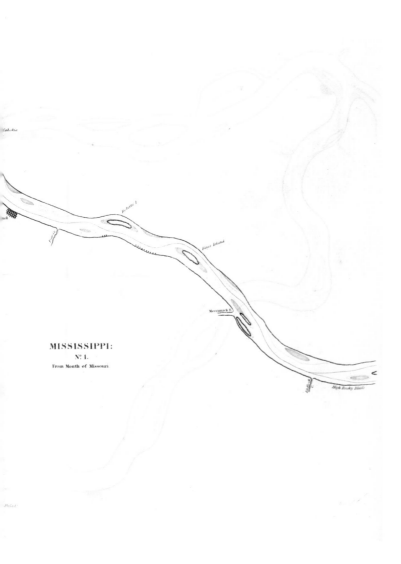

Title: Chart of the Mississippi Section 1
Date Issued: 1822
Cartographer: Samuel Cumings
Published: *Western Navigator, containing directions for navigating the Ohio and Mississippi, and such information concerning the towns, etcetera, on their banks, as will be most useful to travelers, accompanied by Charts of the Ohio River its whole extent and of the Mississippi River from the mouth of the Missouri to the Gulf of Mexico* (Philadelphia) Copperplate engraving, 16.5 x 16.5 inches
Newberry Library, Graf 947

was a better guide, and the first edition of Cumings was by far the finest. It consisted of two volumes: the first volume contained the charts and was larger than the second volume, which contained the directions. The *Western Navigator* was also unusual in that it covered a section of the Mississippi north of the Ohio to the mouth of the Missouri.

The charts of the Cumings guide, one of which is seen here, were finely engraved and depicted river sections on a large scale (two miles to the inch). These charts not only illustrated the main navigation channels and islands, but minor shoals, obstructions, and secondary channels as well. The chart illustrated here shows the junction of the Missouri with the Mississippi, and is accompanied by the following directions: "Boats descending the Missouri at a low stage of water, when near its mouth, must keep near the middle of the river, and when you have entered the Mississippi incline over to the left shore. At high water you may pass to the right of Willow islands, which is considerable of a cut-off."

Changes in river beds and channels would quickly make a river guide outdated, and their publishers rarely kept up with these alterations. Cumings' *Navigator*, for example, did not receive a thorough revision until 1836. As a result, these guides were rarely current enough to be of real value to riverboat pilots; after several decades of use, steamboat pilots began to use them principally to record channel changes and other navigational data.

Mining on the Upper River

The Driftless Area is a unique region of the upper Mississippi River basin that was bypassed by the last continental glacier, leaving the hills, valleys, and bluffs in this area intact, and making it one of the most scenic spots in the Midwest. It also left rich lead and zinc deposits readily accessible near the surface of the land.

The Ho-Chunk, Mesquakie (Fox), Sauk, and other indigenous peoples had been mining lead (which they used as a paint source) in the region for hundreds of years before reports of their mines reached the French. Nicholas Perrot visited the mines around 1690, and in 1700 Pierre-Charles Le Sueur took sample ore from the deposits along the Mississippi River. These mines were marked on early French maps of this territory, and in 1717 John Law emphasized their potential to promote investment in his Compagnie de la Louisiane.

When the French withdrew from the area in 1763, the local Indians guarded the mines carefully, revealing their sites only to favored traders such as Julien Dubuque (the first person of European descent to settle in the area of the Iowa city named after him). American settlement of the region remained slow until a series of treaties between 1804 and 1832 gradually ceded all American Indian lands south of the Wisconsin River to the United States.

There was a strong market for lead at this time, as it was widely used in the manufacture of pewter, pipes, weights, paint, and ammunition. This brought a steady stream of pioneers up the Mississippi and into southwestern Wisconsin looking for quick rewards: the tools and techniques involved in lead mining in these early years were relatively simple and inexpensive, allowing lucky miners to strike it rich with little personal expense. By 1829 ten thousand miners in this area produced thirteen million pounds of lead a year. Most of the miners who moved to the region in the 1820s and 1830s wasted little time in constructing shelters; some simply burrowed holes into hillsides, earning them the nickname "badgers." Communities quickly sprang up around the mines, and other industries and businesses were founded to serve both the residents of these towns and the mining operations near them. In the 1830s experienced miners began emigrating from Cornwall in southwestern England. The Cornish settled primarily in Mineral Point, Wisconsin, and constructed small limestone homes similar to those they had left in England.

Shown here is a map of southwestern Wisconsin and the corner of northeastern Illinois during the lead mining boom of the 1820s. The map depicts the location of all the major mines and the surrounding settlements. Also shown are smelting furnaces, roads, copper deposits, farms, many taverns, as well as the mounds of the region that stood several hundred feet over the surrounding countryside. Most of the lead that was smelted in this region went to Galena, Illinois, from where it was shipped to St. Louis and New Orleans. The text in the upper-right corner

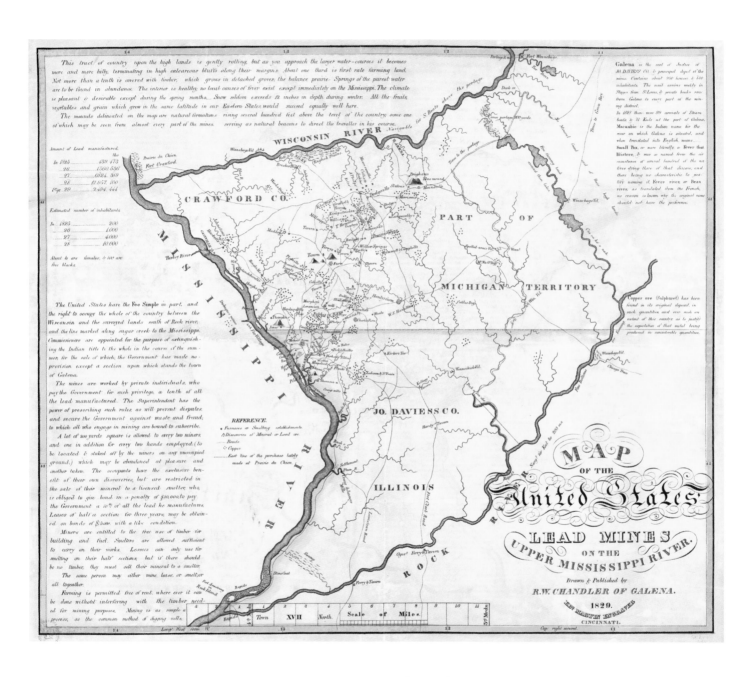

Title: Lead Mines on the Upper Mississippi River
Date Issued: 1829
Cartographer: R. W. Chandler
Published: Separately (Cincinnati)
Lithograph, 15 x 17.7 inches
Newberry Library, Graff 645 [map]

describes Galena and some of its business operations. The text on the upper-left side of the map describes the terrain of the region; below that are tables listing lead production and population by year starting in 1825. The lower-left corner details some of the legalities of the mining business. Portage, Wisconsin, and Fort Winnebago are shown at the extreme upper right of the map; the future site of Madison, the state capital of Wisconsin, is on the four lakes on the right; Prairie du Chien, Wisconsin, and Fort Crawford are seen at the upper left; and Rock Island, Illinois, and Fort Armstrong are at the lower left.

Wisconsin lead mining peaked in the 1840s, when the state produced more than half of the national output. By this time, the supply of easily obtainable ore in surface veins had been exhausted, which made mining more expensive and less appealing to investors looking for speedy profits. In 1844 a third of the region's residents left for copper and iron mines elsewhere, and the discovery of gold in California lured many others west in 1849. For those who remained, mining often became a part-time supplement to farming. By 1860 the former lead mining region of southwestern Wisconsin was recognized as one of the best agricultural areas in the state.

Louisiana Plantations

Marie Adrien Persac was a French-born Louisiana artist, and is best known as a chronicler of the antebellum plantation scene and the post–Civil War commercial architecture of New Orleans. He painted some two dozen gouaches (opaque watercolors) of plantations that depict rural life in the southern part of Louisiana along the Mississippi River and surrounding bayou country; his twenty exquisite miniature drawings of life along Canal Street show a post–Civil War view of a bustling New Orleans that was ready for business. Between 1859 and 1867, Persac produced over twenty-four transparent watercolors of properties to be sold at public auction.

The map shown here was drawn by Persac, engraved by J. H. Colton, and published by Benjamin Moore Norman (who also published *Norman's Plan of New Orleans and its Environs* in 1845). Persac beautifully portrays plantation properties along the river from Natchez to New Orleans: plantation names and owners are listed, and the primary crops grown (sugar, cotton, and indigo) are color designated. Vignettes framing the map include a cotton plantation (cotton is shown growing on trees, obviously drawn before Persac had seen a cotton plant), a sugar plantation (probably Belle Grove), a view of New Orleans looking upriver from near Elysian Fields Avenue, and port activity at Baton Rouge. This map was originally conceived as a series of three that would extend upriver to Memphis, Tennessee, but only the lower section was completed.

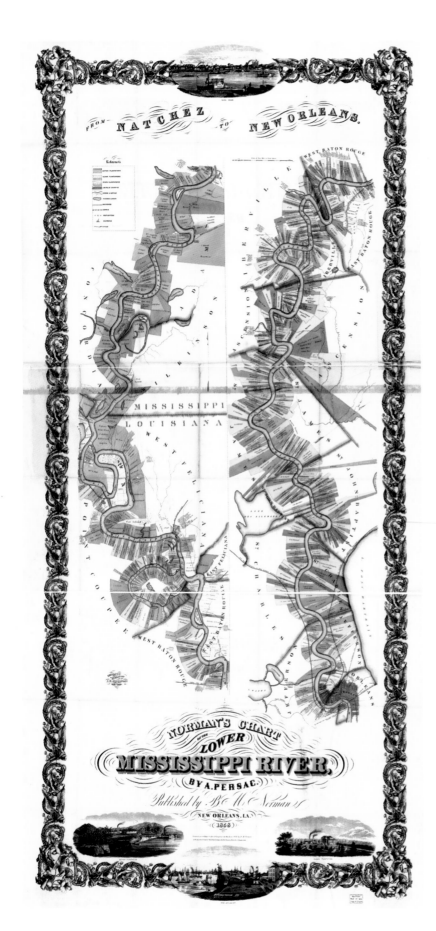

Title: Norman's Chart of the Lower Mississippi: From Natchez to New Orleans
Date Issued: 1858
Cartographer: Marie Adrien Persac
Published: Separately (New York)
Lithograph, 63 x 29.5 inches
Library of Congress, Geography & Map Division,
G4042.M5G46 1858 .P4

The Age of the Steamboat

The first steamboat to travel the Mississippi was the *New Orleans*, a 116-foot side-wheeler built in Pittsburgh in 1811. Its maiden voyage from the Ohio River to New Orleans coincided with a series of earthquakes centered in New Madrid, Missouri. The quakes caused widespread flooding, river waterfalls and obstructions, and the sudden relocation of sections of the Mississippi's main channel. The *New Orleans* persevered, however, and its journey marked the advent of the age of the steamboat—and the development of the Great River's basin.

Prior to the steamboat, the spread of goods and information on the river frontier had been primarily a one-way affair: settlers floated their products on flatboats and keelboats downriver and poled them upriver only at great expense. With the age of steam came a revolution in river commerce, as steamboats moved not only goods but also people both upstream and down. The result was an era of unprecedented prosperity, and town after town sprang up along the Mississippi's upper banks, each dependent on the regular arrival of packet boats bringing mail and passengers or freight boats that took on local produce and left off manufactured goods. On the lower river, plantations maintained their own landings so they could ship crops directly, while established riverside towns vied with each other to provide steamboat services such as fueling and warehousing. Along the levee at New Orleans, steamers were often moored in a double line mingled with oceangoing ships, as the Louisiana port became one of the busiest in the country.

The golden age of the paddle-wheeler has a special place in America's heritage, and it has been celebrated in artistic works ranging from the evocative lyrics of Oscar Hammerstein's *Old Man River* to those of its most famous chronicler, Samuel Clemens. Clemens grew up on the banks of the Mississippi in Hannibal, Missouri, and his *Life on the Mississippi*—recollections of his days as a cub-pilot—remains the outstanding classic of steamboat literature. Clemens was taken on as an apprentice in 1857 by Horace Bixby, pilot of the *Paul Jones*, in part due to a recommendation by the Bowen brothers, who helped produce the first map seen here. Bart and Will Bowen were Hannibal natives and childhood friends of Clemens, and Will is mentioned in many anecdotes of Clemens' youth. In fact, in his biography of Clemens, Albert Paine states that Tom Sawyer was a composite of Will Bowen and another friend of Clemens, John Briggs.

Published during the Civil War, this highly detailed map is scaled at five miles to one inch and depicts the course of the lower river from its junction with the Missouri to its mouth. Produced in five sheets, it shows forts, cities and towns, plantations and farms, riverboat landings, cut-offs, islands, bayous, river mileage, high-water and low-water channels, and the canal at Island No. 10. It was sold in various forms: in five sheets for one dollar; as a linen-backed pocket edition for two dollars; and varnished and mounted on rollers for two dollars and fifty cents. At the time of its publication, James Lloyd became involved in an acrimonious dispute with another

New York publisher, H. H. Lloyd and Company. On the second edition of this map (issued in 1863) James Lloyd cautioned the public "against another 'Lloyd' by which name he hopes to deceive the public with spurious 'Lloyd Maps.' This man's maps are engraved coarsely on wood and very erroneous. He follows us with an imitation of every map we issue."

The next map depicts the Mississippi River from the Gulf of Mexico to its source at "Lake Itaska," a distance—according to the map—of "2,600 miles." Known as a ribbon or strip map, it was published in St. Louis by Myron Coloney and Sidney B. Fairchild, who claim to have patented the design for this type of map in 1866 (the date the map was issued). It depicts the entire length of the river on a strip about three inches wide and eleven feet long that is backed on linen and rolls into a wooden cylinder that is fitted with a hand crank. This is the revised edition, which adds many islands, river towns, river landings, plantations, and other points of interest not shown on the first edition (the shape of Lake Pepin is also altered); the distance from the mouth of the river to important points along the river is given on both maps. Much of this additional material was provided by William Bowen, who at the time was the president of the Pilot's Association of St. Louis.

Although this map shows considerable detail, it was not meant to be a river guide for steamboat navigation. Rather, these ribbon maps were made for the tourist and other river travelers who could afford a souvenir of their trip. In particular, these maps gave the traveler a way to keep track of the boat's progress on a long trip and even marked a few points of interest along the way. An advertisement in the July 10, 1866 *Missouri Republican* might lead one to suspect that Captain Bowen had an ulterior motive in helping with this map's production: "To the traveler, it will be an exciting guide and companion, and will furnish him with more information at a glance than he can secure from a constant questioning of the officers of the boat . . . to say nothing of avoiding a short answer from, or an immensity of annoyance to, these monarchs of our Mississippi River palaces."

During the age of the steamboat, advances in technology led to the production of faster boats and to intense rivalries among them. The result was steamboat racing, which was not really a sport as much as a means to gain business. Thus, for example, in 1838 the Post Office Department offered a prize of five hundred dollars for any steamer that could make the trip from New Orleans to Louisville in less than six days. The *Diana* won the race, covering the distance in five days, twenty-three hours, and fifteen minutes; presumably, its owner was also awarded a contract to carry the mail on the river. Steamboat races were not only important to owners, but were immensely popular with the public, as Mark Twain recounts: "a race between two notoriously fleet steamers was an event of vast importance. The date was set for it several weeks in advance, and from that time forward, the whole Mississippi Valley was in a state of consuming excitement. Politics and the weather were dropped, and people talked only of the coming race. As the time approached, the two steamers "stripped" and got ready. Every encumbrance that added weight, or exposed a resisting surface to wind or water, was removed, if the boat could possibly do without it."

One of the river's most famous races pitted the *Natchez* and the *Robert E. Lee* against one another. The race commenced on June 30, 1870, and ran from New Orleans to St. Louis. The *Natchez* was considered the faster boat, but the captain of the *Lee* had stripped his boat of all unnecessary superstructure, a tactic the captain of the *Natchez* did not deem necessary. The *Lee* assured its victory by arranging to take on extra fuel supplies from tenders while steaming upriver at full speed. The *Natchez*, on the other hand, was forced to land and take a barge in tow, thereby losing valuable time that it could not make up. The progress of the race was telegraphed all over the country and even cabled to Europe. The final result: the *Lee* established a record of three days, eighteen hours, and fourteen minutes for the 1,210-mile trip; the *Natchez* arrived six hours and thirty-six minutes later.

The New York publishing firm of Currier and Ives published a number of splendid lithographic images of Mississippi steamboat races, including *The Great*

Title: Lloyd's Map of the Lower Mississippi River from St. Louis to the Gulf of Mexico: Compiled from government surveys in the Topographical Bureau, Washington, D.C., revised and corrected to the present time by Captains Bart and William Bowen, pilots of twenty years' experience on that River, exhibiting the sugar and cotton plantations, cities, towns, landings, sand bars, islands, bluffs, bayous, cut-offs, the steamboat channel, mileage, fortifications, railroads, etcetera, along the River.
Date Issued: 1862
Cartographer: James T. Lloyd and Barton and William Bowen
Published: Separately (New York)
Lithograph, 37 x 51.2 inches
David Rumsey Collection, Image No. 4842000

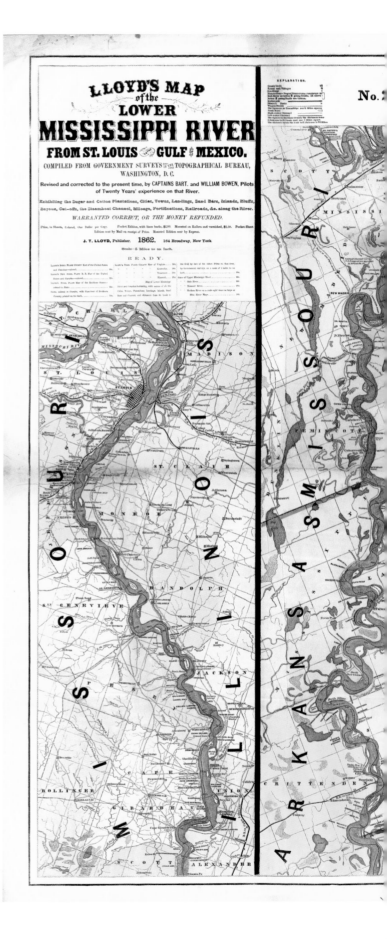

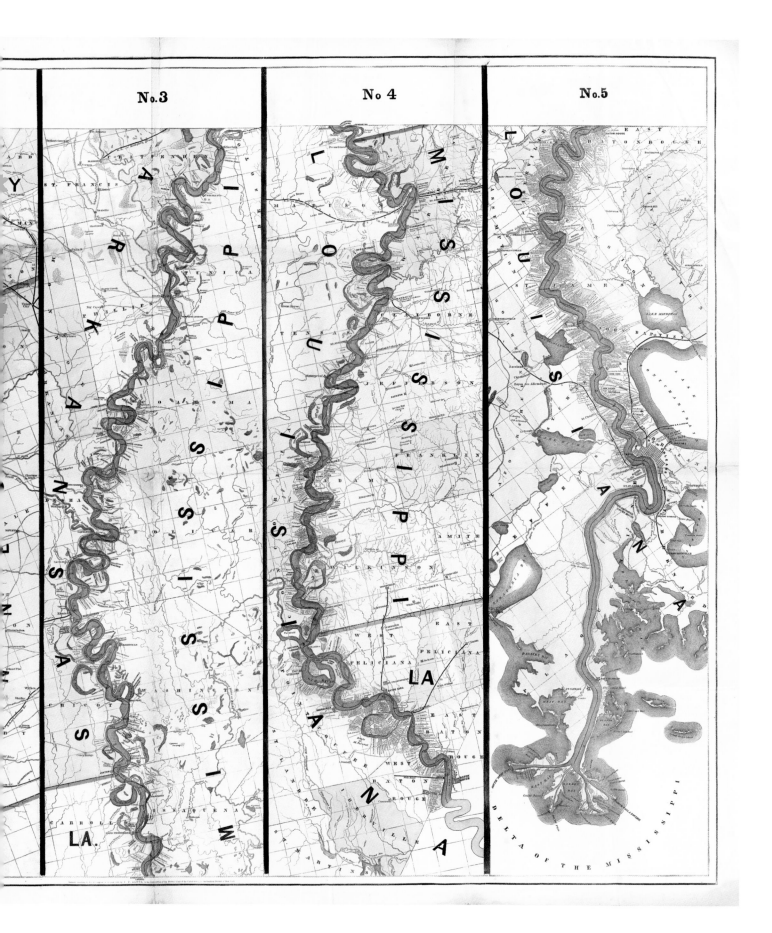

No.3 No.4 No.5

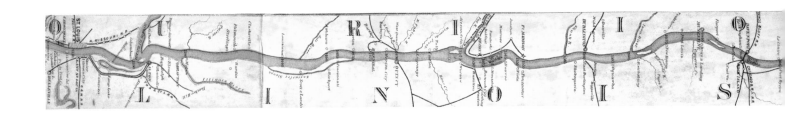

Title: Ribbon Map of the Father of Waters

Date Issued: 1866

Cartographer: Coloney, Fairchild & Co.

Published: Separately (St. Louis, Missouri)

Lithograph, 2.8 x 131.1 inches

David Rumsey Collection, Image No. 4995000

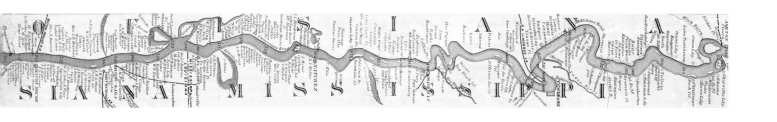

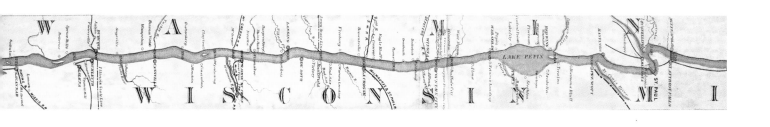

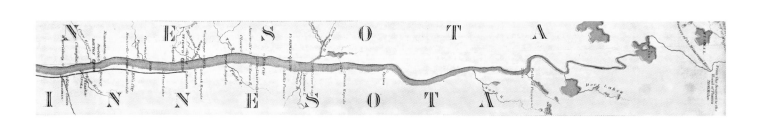

THE CHAMPIONS OF THE MIS
"A Race for the Buckhorns".

NEW YORK, PUBLISHED BY CURRIER & IVES, 152 NASSAU ST.

Race on the Mississippi that depicts the race between the *Natchez* and the *Robert E. Lee*. Other images of steamboat races published by Currier and Ives include: *A Midnight Race on the Mississippi*, which shows a race between the *Memphis* and *James Howard*; *A Race on the Mississippi* illustrates the competition between the *Diana* and the *Eagle* from New Orleans to Louisville, said to be the longest steamboat race of record; another version of *A Midnight Race on the Mississippi* portrays the *Natchez* leading the *Eclipse*, one of the longest and fastest steamboats of its time. Shown here is a very colorful night scene of several steamboats racing for the buckhorns, which the winner was entitled to mount and carry for a year between its stacks.

After its interruption by the Civil War, the age of the steamboat had a brief but glorious renaissance. By the 1870s, however, the railroad had become a more efficient mode of transportation, and the days of the steamboat became numbered. Indeed, the same westward expansion that had brought development to the river frontier now passed it over, and river towns that had once sought to become steamboat ports competed to become crossing points for railroads. Commercial steamboat traffic quickly dwindled, and the grand luxury paddle wheelers gave way to somber, more prosaic towboats with blocks of barges.

Title: The Champions of the Mississippi:
A Race for the Buckhorns
Date Issued: 1866
Cartographer: Fanny F. Palmer (Currier & Ives)
Published: Separately (New York)
Lithograph, 18.3 x 27.8 inches
Collection of the Old Print Shop, Inc.

CHAPTER 8

TAMING THE GREAT RIVER

The Mississippi River drains an area that stretches from Canada to the Gulf of Mexico and from the Appalachians to the Rocky Mountains—a watershed that makes up 41 percent of the continental United States, and includes all or part of thirty-one states and two Canadian provinces. This drainage basin is twice as large as the Yangtze River of China, three times that of India's Ganges, and sixteen times that of Europe's Rhine; only the Amazon and, just barely, the Congo have larger basins. If measured from the head of its major tributary, the Missouri—a point that could easily have been labeled the Great River's source—the Mississippi is the third longest river in the world. To control such a stream is a Herculean task, but with the development of the Mississippi's valley came political demands to protect commerce and capital investment from being ravaged by the river.

The federal government first responded to this pressure by seeking to safeguard navigation on the river. In 1824 Congress authorized the removal of snags (submerged logs and trees that had become embedded in the bottom of the river) and other obstructions that posed a persistent danger to steamboats. In 1837 a young lieutenant from the Corps of Engineers was dispatched to the Mississippi

to seek improvements to navigation on the upper river, and to restore the harbor at St. Louis. The lieutenant's name was Robert E. Lee.

The sole obstructions to steamboat traffic on the upper river were two sets of rapids: the Des Moines Rapids, an eleven-mile section of the Mississippi just above its confluence with the Des Moines River near the town of Keokuk, Iowa; and the Rock River Rapids, a treacherous fifteen-mile stretch of the river above the mouth of the Rock River near the present-day Quad Cities of Moline and Rock Island, Illinois, and Bettendorf and Davenport, Iowa. Accordingly, Lee's first task—improving navigation on the upper Mississippi—amounted to finding a way to render these rapids navigable at all stages of the river. After surveying both rapids, he began the work of blasting a channel through the Des Moines Rapids, but neither obstacle would be adequately addressed until some years later.

His second charge was to preserve the port of St. Louis, which was being threatened by the river's action on sandbars that had grown into tree-covered islands. To the north, almost in the middle of the river, was Bloody Island (so named because of the many duels that had been fought there), and to the south near the Missouri shore was Duncan's Island. The river's current was scouring Bloody Island and depositing silt and sand on the north end of Duncan's Island, causing an impediment to steamboat traffic into St. Louis Harbor. If allowed to continue unabated, this accretion would soon seal off the docks of St. Louis from the main channel of the river.

Lee devised a plan to direct the current of the river away from its preferred channel on the eastern side of Bloody Island toward the Missouri side of the river. The hope was that by directing the full force of the current down the western channel, the sandbar that was Duncan's Island would eventually be washed away. As detailed on the first map shown here, Lee proposed to implement this plan by first building a dam from the head of Bloody Island to the Illinois shore, which would divert the river to the western side of the island. Next, a dike was to be constructed at the foot of Bloody Island directly downstream for at least three thousand feet in order to throw the full force of the altered current against the head of Duncan's Island and against the shoals that were forming just upriver of the island. Finally, Lee would shield the western face of Bloody Island from its head to its center by a stone revetment, so that it would not be washed away by the force of the current.

Lee's project, which much to the delight of the citizens of St. Louis proved to be a success, would mark the beginning of the Corps of Engineers' attempt to wrestle the Mississippi into submission—a battle that continues today. Flooding has been the major impetus for river control, particularly along the river below St. Louis, an area that averages a flood every three years. Another problem for landowners along the lower river is the tendency for the Mississippi to meander. River meandering is a complex and incompletely understood phenomena whereby rivers shift course by depositing sediment on the inside of bends while simultaneously eroding the outer banks of their meander bends. As a river changes course, waterfront property can suddenly become landlocked hundreds of yards or even miles inland, and property that once was some distance from the river can just as quickly become waterfront acreage.

This unpredictable behavior had played havoc with property values along the Mississippi and with the ability of landowners to manage their farms and plantations. A good appreciation of the problem can be gleaned from the next chart, which depicts meanders made by the Mississippi in the last several hundred years. The sequence of migrations during this period was reconstructed from aerial photography and is beautifully represented in contrasting colors. This is one sheet of fifteen that shows the Mississippi meander belt from Cape Girardeau, Missouri, to Donaldsonville, Louisiana; it was included with Harold Fisk's 1944 report on the alluvial valley of the lower Mississippi River. This sheet focuses on the Mississippi Delta just south of Memphis (Tunica and Coahoma counties) and Lee and Phillips counties across the river in Arkansas. This region, which was created by regular flooding over thousands of years, is remarkably flat and contains some of the most fertile soil in the world.

Prior to the Civil War, state and local governments waged the war against flooding. In 1849, in response to demands of the increasingly populated Mississippi Valley, Congress ceded millions of acres of federally owned "swamp and overflowed lands" to the states along the lower river. The states were to sell this land and use the proceeds for flood control. Their principal weapon was the levee system, which had

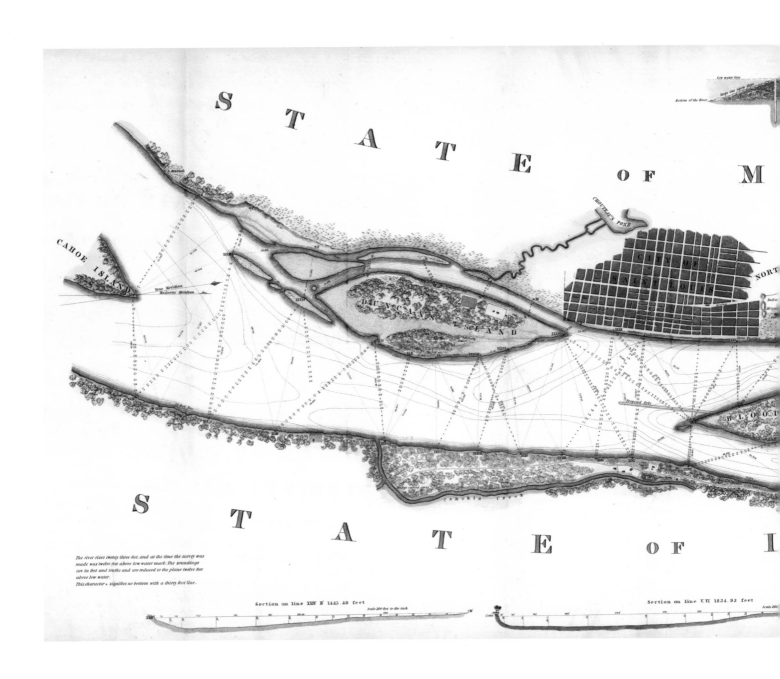

Title: No. 3 Map of the Harbor of St. Louis, Mississippi River, Oct. 1837

Date Issued: 1837

Cartographer: Robert E. Lee and Montgomery C. Meigs

Published: U.S. Army Corps of Engineers (Washington, D.C.)

Lithograph, 17.7 x 45.3 inches

Birmingham Public Library, Rucker Agee Collection, Image No. MississippiRiver1837a

No. 3.

MAP OF THE

HARBOR OF ST. LOUIS,

MISSISSIPPI RIVER.

OCT. 1837.

Surveyed by Lt. R.E. Lee Corps of Engineers
Assisted by Lt. M.C. Meigs do. do.
J.S. Morehead and H. Kayser
Drawn by Lt. Meigs Corps of Engineers

SCALE 5 INCHES TO 1 MILE

Respectfully submitted
to the Chief Engineer
R.E. Lee Lt. Eng.rs

Copied from the original by M.C.Ewing Civ. Engineer

NEXT PAGES

Title: Mississippi Meander Belt (Sheet 6 of 15)

Date Issued: 1944

Cartographer: Harold N. Fisk

Published: *Geological Investigation of the Alluvial Valley of the Lower Mississippi River* (Vicksburg, Mississippi)

Printed map, 28.7 x 1.2 inches

U.S. Army Corps of Engineers, Lower and Middle Mississippi Engineering and Geology Mapping Program

been used to hold back the river since Bienville founded New Orleans. By the late 1850s, more than one thousand miles of levees had been constructed on both sides of the river. Although this construction was done without any comprehensive overall plan or standards of engineering (Louisiana, Mississippi, and Arkansas, for example, all maintained different standards on levee size and composition), those along the river felt confident this forty-million-dollar investment would hold back the waters of the Great River. They were proved wrong by the flood of 1858–59, the largest flood yet recorded, as levees cracked and fell by the dozens. The pressure on Washington to address flooding problems on the Mississippi continued to build.

Congress had, in fact, already authorized a survey with the "aim to discover the laws governing the Mississippi River and how to tame it." After intense debate between the War Department and supporters of the civilian engineering profession in Congress, the money appropriated for the survey was split between Andrew Atkinson Humphreys, a captain in the Corps of Engineers, and Charles Ellet, Jr., a French-educated civilian engineer who had just finished a survey of the Ohio River and the construction of a suspension bridge (then, the longest in the world) across the Ohio at Wheeling, West Virginia.

In 1851 Ellet submitted a report to Congress that attributed the increase in Mississippi River flooding to several recent developments, the first and foremost being the extension of levees along the river's banks and those of its tributaries and outlets. He noted that the effect of these levees was to force water that was once allowed to spread over many thousands of miles of lowlands into a confined channel, which in turn compelled it to "to rise higher and flow faster,

until, under the increased power of the current, it may have time to excavate a wider and deeper trench to give vent to the increased volume which it conveys." He also pointed to increased cultivation, manmade cutoffs and shortcuts, and the lengthening of the delta as additional factors that increased the probability and magnitude of floods.

According to Ellet, "each of these causes is likely to be progressive," and he warned that "future floods throughout the length and breadth of the delta, and along the great streams tributary to the Mississippi, are destined to rise higher and higher, as society spreads over the upper States, as population adjacent to the river increases, and the inundated low lands appreciate in value." He proposed a comprehensive solution to the problem of flooding that included improving levees, enlarging the river's natural outlets, and adding artificial outlets and reservoirs. Although time would prove Ellet's report to be a prescient document, his recommendations were not carried out. First came the Civil War (in which Ellet lost his life) and then a political war over control of the Mississippi.

Humphreys had begun his study at the same time as Ellet, but suffered a nervous breakdown that delayed its completion until 1861. He credited his assistant, Lieutenant Henry Abbot, as coauthor of the work, which had a ninety-word title that began *Report upon the Physics and Hydraulics of the Mississippi River.* Humphreys considered the report to be the work of his life, and indeed, it would become the single most influential composition ever written about the Mississippi. It records observations of riverbanks, levees, sandbars, currents, the riverbed, and a wealth of other hydrological information on the Mississippi, and includes drawings, charts, graphs, and critical

PLATE 22
SHEET 6

GEOLOGICAL INVESTIGATION
MISSISSIPPI RIVER ALLUVIAL VALLEY
ANCIENT COURSES
MISSISSIPPI RIVER MEANDER BELT
CAPE GIRARDEAU, MO.-DONALDSONVILLE, LA.

IN 15 SHEETS   SCALE IN MILES   SHEET 6

OFFICE OF THE PRESIDENT, MISSISSIPPI RIVER COMMISSION
VICKSBURG, MISS.   1944

TO ACCOMPANY REPORT OF HAROLD N. FISK, PH.D. CONSULTANT
LOUISIANA STATE UNIVERSITY, BATON ROUGE, LA. DATED 1 DEC. 1944

R. H. S. - H. N. F.   FILE NO. MRC/2588 SH 33-F

BANKLINE SYMBOLS

Traceable prehistoric final bankline positions of
meanders and mapped historic banklines.

Arbitrarily selected traceable prehistoric bankline
positions marking stages of meander growth.

Indefinite prehistoric bankline positions.

CUT OFF SYMBOLS

Neck cut off following indicated stage.

Chute cut off following indicated stage.

Fault

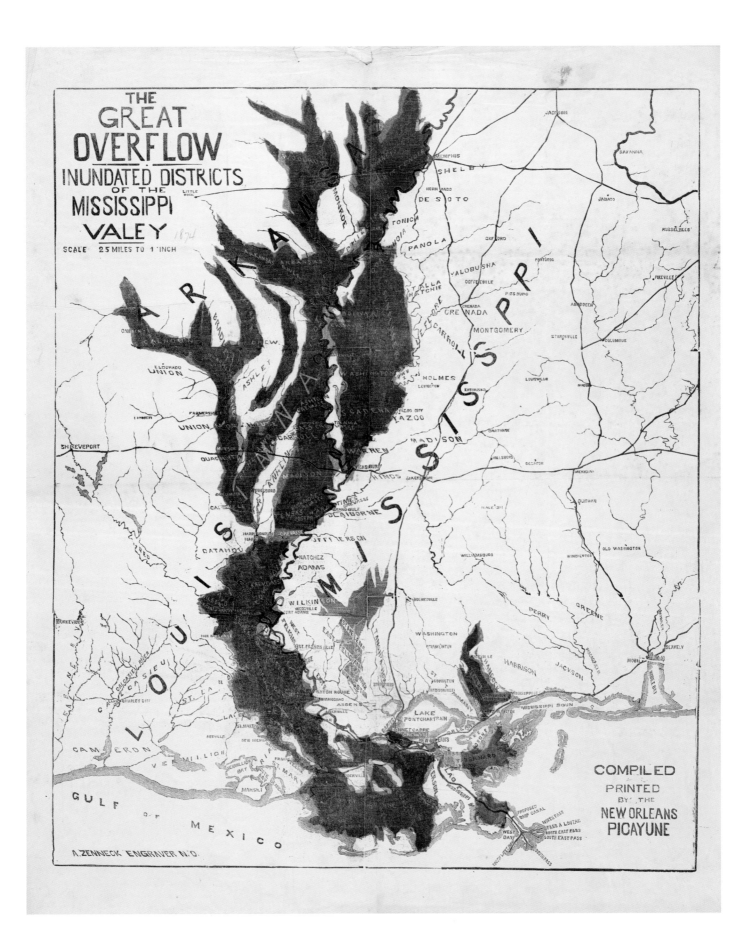

analyses of several centuries of scientific literature. And, much to Humphreys' chagrin, much of this data seemed to corroborate Ellet's intuitive conclusions.

Humphreys would have none of it, for his masterpiece could not simply confirm another's findings. As John Barry in *Rising Tide* notes, Humphreys "would not be second. Instead, he would become corrupt. The corruption did not infect his data—even today his data are considered reliable and instructive—but it did infect his reasoning and his recommendations." What Humphreys did was to find a way to advocate a levees-only approach to flood control, in spite of his rejection of the engineering hypothesis that underlay this strategy and the fact that his own data seemed to favor outlets as well. Against the latter, he argued that outlets risked creating a new main channel for the river (a conclusion the assistant who provided the data for the analysis had already called "groundless"), and that creating outlets would cost too much for the benefits gained (a conclusion that ignored any further development of land along the river). So it was that Humphreys rejected outlets and Ellet with them.

The success of his report was enough to make Humphreys the chief of engineers of the U.S. Army, a position that he assumed in 1866. It was the same year that St. Louis admitted it needed a railroad

Title: The Great Overflow Inundated Districts of the Mississippi Valey
Date Issued: 1874
Cartographer: A. Zenneck (Engraver)
Published: *Daily Picayune* (New Orleans)
Lithograph, 19.7 x 15.4 inches
Library of Congress, Geography & Map Division,
G4042.M5 1874 .Z4

bridge across the Mississippi and the city turned to James Buchanan Eads to build it. Eads was a self-educated man who had made a fortune salvaging wrecked vessels from the river, and had supplied the Union army with ironclads during the war. He knew the river perhaps better than any man alive, having invented a diving bell that allowed him to walk the shifting river bottom and guide his salvage boats to their targets. He had political and financial connections and would soon meet Humphreys in battle for control over the Mississippi.

The two had already skirmished when Humphreys had Eads' bridge—the world's first steel bridge—labeled an obstruction to river traffic and ordered it torn down. Eads made a personal appeal to President Grant, who ordered the Secretary of War to stop the harassment by the Corps of Engineers. In spite of Humphreys, the bridge opened on July 4, 1874. Humphreys and Eads would next clash over how to best keep the mouth of the Mississippi open to oceangoing traffic, where sandbars were choking commerce. The Corps of Engineers had been trying for forty years to solve the problem, but with little success. Now they planned to dig a canal from the river to the Gulf, in effect outflanking the sandbars, which they pronounced were permanent, immovable barriers. Eads had what he thought was a better idea.

As a child he had watched Robert E. Lee use a jetty to force the river current to wash away the sandbar known as Duncan's Island, and he now proposed to use the same principle to eliminate the sandbars at the river's mouth. Forced by Humphreys' machinations to work in the smaller and shallower South Pass, Eads would spend the next four years building his jetties into the Gulf. Moreover, he built

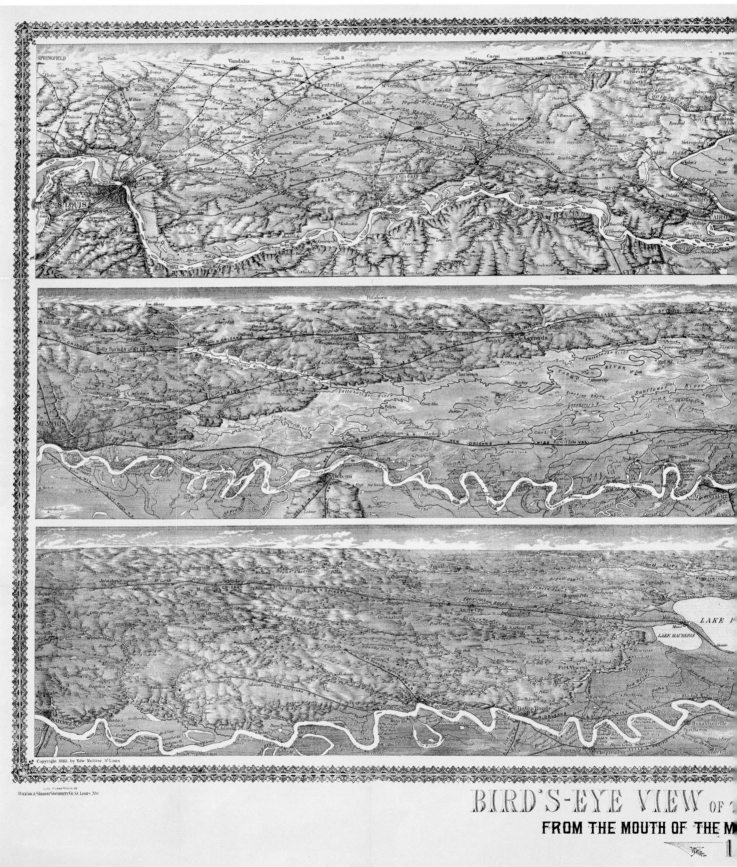

BIRD'S-EYE VIEW OF 1

FROM THE MOUTH OF THE M

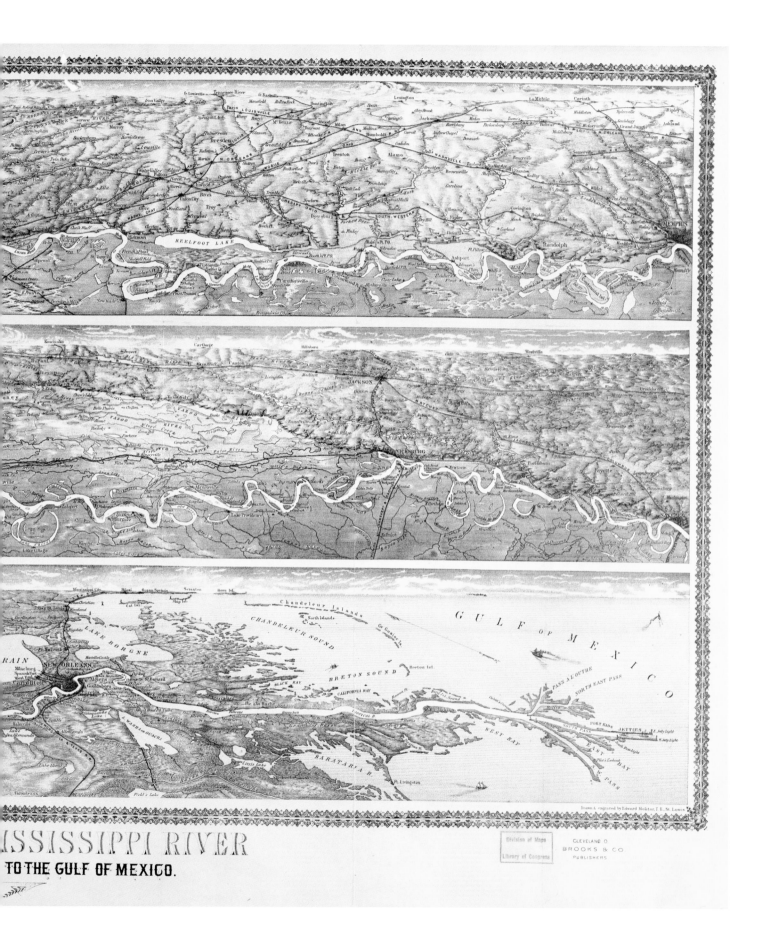

MISSISSIPPI RIVER
TO THE GULF OF MEXICO.

CLEVELAND. O.
BROOKS & CO
PUBLISHERS

Drawn & engraved by Edward Molitor, T.K. St. Louis

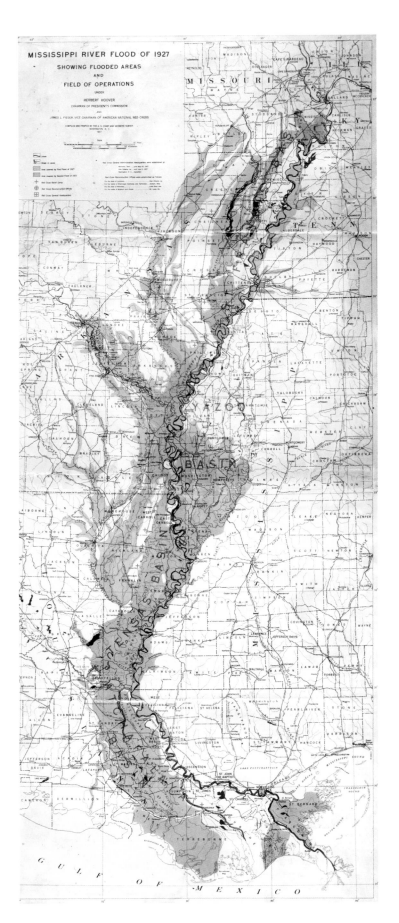

PREVIOUS PAGES
Title: Bird's-Eye View of the Mississippi River from the
Mouth of the Missouri to the Gulf of Mexico
Date Issued: 1884
Cartographer: Edward Molitor
Published: Separately (Cleveland)
Lithograph, 13.8 x 30.3 inches
Library of Congress, Geography & Map Division,
G4042.M5 1884 .M6

Title: Mississippi River Flood of 1927 showing
Flooded Areas and Field of Operations
Date Issued: 1927
Cartographer: U.S Coast & Geodetic Survey
Published: *Monthly Weather Review*, Supplement 29
(Washington, D.C.)
Lithograph, 40.5 x 20 inches
Louisiana State Museum, Accession No. 10786

them at his own expense and his own risk, agreeing that the government would only pay for them if they worked. They worked just as Eads had predicted, forcing the river to dig its own channel by speeding the flow of water and thereby digging out the sandbars, which were dispersed at sea.

Humphreys, who had staked his reputation on the failure of Eads' plan, fought back with increasing hostility, claiming that new sandbars were forming beyond the jetties. Exasperated, Eads published an article that brutalized Humphreys' original report, and he called for an independent civilian commission to govern the Mississippi. On June 28, 1879, Congress attempted to heal the burgeoning schism between the military and civilian engineering communities by creating the Mississippi River Commission, a mix of army and civilian engineers that included Eads, to control the Great River. Two days later Humphreys resigned his post and retired from the Army.

The next two maps document how dire the situation in the lower Mississippi Valley was becoming, and both were used to make the case to elected officials that immediate action was needed in the flood-prone region. The overflow of 1874 is depicted on a newspaper map clearly intended to deliver a political message. Edward Molitor's bird's-eye view of the lower river was drawn the year after a series of crevasses (breaks in the levees) had resulted in the worst flooding in the nineteenth century. This map was designed to educate the public about the geography and topography of the region, and it shows the considerable agricultural development along the river. Rendered in three horizontal strips, it also features the extensive railway links between towns; Eads' jetties are visible in the last strip.

Eads was never able to dominate the Mississippi River Commission, and he resigned in 1882 to protest what he saw as a bureaucratic—as opposed to a scientific—enterprise. Indeed, the commission that was supposed to combine the ideas of both civilian and military engineers was in practice controlled entirely by the Corps of Engineers. In 1885 the Mississippi River Commission adopted a levees-only policy of controlling the river. This policy was astonishing, given that it was based on a supposition that Ellet, Humphreys, and Eads all had vehemently rejected—that is, the idea by containing the river with levees, the force of the high water would scour out the floor of the river, deepening the channel sufficiently to carry any flood water straight out to the sea. The commission also repeatedly rejected the use of manmade reservoirs and outlets to capture run-off (as Ellet had urged), and the building of cut-offs to shorten the river and reduce flood heights (as Eads had proposed). For the next forty years the commission adhered to its policy, refusing not only to build any manmade outlets for flood waters, but also actively sealing up the river from many of its natural outlets.

The folly behind this myopic program was exposed in 1927, when a swollen and rampaging Mississippi overwhelmed the levee system designed to contain it. As illustrated on the map shown here, the flood inundated an area of twenty-seven thousand square miles in the lower Mississippi Valley with as much as thirty feet of water. It made refugees of over nine-hundred thousand people and at least two hundred fifty people lost their lives. By July 1, even as the flood waters began to recede, over one-and-one-half million acres were still under water and the river was seventy miles wide. The flood destroyed or damaged over 137 buildings, and financial losses were

Title: Upper Mississippi River System — Navigation Pool 11

Date Issued: 2000

Cartographer: National Mapping Division, United States Geological Survey

Published: Upper Midwest Environmental Sciences Center (La Crosse, Wisconsin) Digital Orthophoto Quadrangle

Upper Midwest Environmental Sciences Center Data Library

estimated at $347 million (over $4 billion in 2006 dollars). Then Secretary of Commerce (and later President) Herbert Hoover called it "the greatest disaster of peace times in our history."

In the aftermath of the flood, the Corps of Engineers abandoned its levees-only policy. In 1928 Congress passed the Flood Control Act that compelled the Corps to employ more comprehensive flood control measures, including many that had been proposed seventy-five years earlier. Today the Mississippi River Commission oversees the largest flood control project in the world, one that employs levees, floodways, outlet channels, channel stabilization measures (dikes, cutoffs, revetment, and dredging), and tributary basins. By far the most serious engineering problem the Corps of Engineers faces today is keeping the main channel of the Mississippi from diverting entirely into the Atchafalaya River, which provides a substantially shorter and steeper route to the Gulf than the Mississippi's existing route and delta. Although such a change in course is a natural process that has happened time and again throughout the millennia of the Great River's existence, it would have a devastating effect on development along the river: New Orleans and Baton Rouge, for example, would be left on little more than a tidal estuary, and the petrochemical and shipping industries that line the river between these cities would instantly collapse.

Prior to the twentieth century, the Corps of Engineers did not describe any of its work on the Mississippi as "flood control"; rather, federal projects concerning the river were invariably termed "navigational improvements"—no doubt an attempt to boost public confidence in the flood-prone regions of the lower river. Safeguarding navigation continues to be an important task for the Corps of Engineers today, as the river floats nearly five hundred million tons of waterborne commerce a year. The largest tonnage item moved is grain, followed by petroleum products and coal; other products shipped on the river include fertilizers, sulfur, cement, machinery, and sugar. The river is also used by an increasing number of recreational boaters.

The Corps maintains the main navigation channel of the river by a number of structural engineering inventions, including cut-offs to shorten the river and reduce flood heights, revetments to stop the river's meandering and maintain channel alignment, dikes to direct the river's current and deepen its channel, and dredging to realign the channel or maintain depth and consistency of the water. On the upper river the Corps has built a series of locks and dams that maintain a nine-foot channel from St. Louis to Minneapolis. A section of the river that has been dammed forms what is called a "navigation pool"; these pools are connected by a series of locks that allow vessels to step up or down from one pool to another. There are currently twenty-nine locks on the upper Mississippi that literally form a stairway of water from Minneapolis to St. Louis, bridging a change in elevation of over four hundred feet.

Shown here is a digital orthophoto quadrangle of the Upper Mississippi River System Pool 11—that is, the region of the upper Mississippi impounded by Lock and Dam 11, an area that extends from Lock and Dam 11 located near Dubuque, Iowa, upstream to Lock and Dam 10 located near Guttenberg, Iowa. An orthophoto is an aerial photograph that has been modified to remove the distorting effects caused by the tilting of the camera and by the relief (topography) of the terrain being photographed. This gives an orthophoto a uniform scale, making it possible to measure directly on it like a map. An orthophoto may thus serve as a base map upon which other geographic information may be overlaid, as is the case here.

The Mississippi has yet to be tamed, as it demonstrated in the Great Flood of 1993. After months of unusually heavy rains fell on midwestern soils already saturated by a rainy autumn and above average snowfall, the swollen river overwhelmed its elaborate system of dikes and other water control structures, resulting in the greatest flood ever recorded on the Upper Mississippi. Over 80 percent of the levees along the upper Mississippi were destroyed, and the flooded area covered over seventeen thousand square miles. The states of Minnesota, Iowa, Illinois, and Missouri suffered the most damage as the flood destroyed over fifty thousand homes, and displaced over seventy-four thousand people. Fifty-two flood-related deaths were recorded. The river height at St. Louis, Missouri, remained above flood stage from April to October and was fifty feet above flood stage for over one hundred days. The costliest flood in U.S. history, the Great Flood's final damage estimate had been calculated at somewhere between fifteen and twenty billion dollars.

A pair of images taken from the Landsat-5 Thematic Mapper shows the region near St. Louis before (August 1991) and during the flood (August 1993). The three rivers seen in this image are, from top to bottom, the Illinois, the Mississippi, and the Missouri. St. Louis is just south of the Missouri River in the center of this image. The 1993 image was captured slightly after the peak water levels in this part of the Mississippi River when flood waters had started to recede, but remained well above normal. (The pink areas near the flooded regions show the scoured land from which the flood waters have receded.) These images may be evidence that Twain was right when he declared that "ten thousand River Commissions, with the mines of the world at their back, cannot tame that lawless stream, cannot curb it or confine it, cannot say to it, Go here, or Go there, and make it obey. . . ."

NEXT PAGES
Title: Landsat-5 Images Before and During the Great Mississippi Flood of 1993
Date Issued: 2006
Cartographer: National Aeronautics and Space Administration
Published: NASA Scientific Visualization Studio Image ServerLandsat Thematic Mapper Images
NASA—Goddard Space Flight Center Scientific Visualization Studio

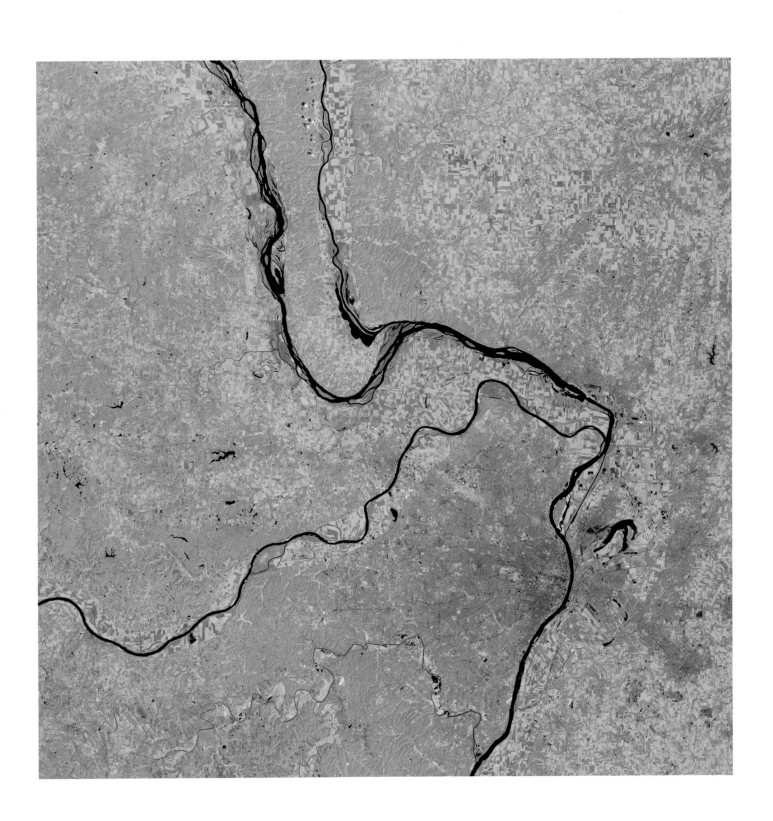

CHAPTER 9

RIVER VIEWS

By the middle of the nineteenth century the Mississippi River had become urbanized and its banks were lined with scores of cities and towns. Most of this development was along the upper river, from the mouth of the Ohio to as far north as St. Cloud, Minnesota—a frontier that had only recently been tamed by the steamboat. The meandering banks of the lower river afforded fewer opportunities for settlement, due to a lack of suitable topography and to the existence of numerous plantations along the river. This stretch of the river included such cities as New Orleans, Baton Rouge, Natchez, Vicksburg, and Memphis, along with numerous towns and hamlets clustered around steamboat landings.

This development of the Great River was recorded by dozens of itinerant artists seeking fame and fortune. Indeed, this was a time when Americans hungered for information about the growth of their country, and these artists fed this hunger with images produced in numerous forms. Copper, wood, and steel engravings found their way into reports, magazines, newspapers, and books. Lithographed images were also used in books or atlases, but more often than not were sold as separately issued prints.

Most of the artists of these separately issued prints adopted a high-level panoramic view of a city or town. Also known as bird's-eye views, these representations portrayed a town from above at an angle that allowed the artist to show street patterns, individual buildings, and major landscape features in perspective. In the case of towns and cities along the Mississippi, this vantage point was typically from a point across the river. Although generally not drawn to scale, accuracy and detail helped to sell bird's-eye views, which often were displayed on walls of parlors, offices, and public buildings such as hotels, banks, and government buildings.

The owners of urban views generally regarded them with a sense of civic pride, for they were evidence of the prosperity, growth, and importance of their city or town. The following images lead up the course of the river, from an abandoned village near its mouth to the northern conurbation known as the Twin Cities.

Title: *Die Belize an der Mündung des Missisippi*
Date Issued: 1828
Cartographer: Paul Wilhelm, Duke of Württemberg
Published: Separately (Anstalt, Germany)
Lithograph, 11.8 x 16.6 inches
New York Public Library, Stokes P.1822-F-34

The Belize

The Belize was a squalid settlement of river pilots, boatmen, and fisherman at the head of Belize Bayou on the southeast pass of the mouth of the river. Also known as Pilot's Town, the Belize "branch pilots," as they were called, guided ships across the bar, up Southeast Pass, and into Pass à l'Outre to the mainstream of the Mississippi. Basil Hall, an English traveler who visited the area around the time this view was drawn, described the community as follows: "We went down the South-east Pass to the dreary abode of the Pilots, called the Belize — from the Spanish word *Valiza*, a beacon. . . . From this wretched place — planted in the midst of a boundless swamp or morass — no firm land is in sight, or within fifty or sixty miles of it. There are about twenty buildings in all, six of which are dwelling houses. The intercourse between them is carried on exclusively along paths made of planks and trunks of trees laid over the slime and water. It is impossible, indeed, to walk ten yards in any direction, without sinking up to the neck in a mud-hole or a quicksand; so that, for all the usual purpose of location, the inhabitants might just as well be at sea."

Die Belize an der Mündung des Mississippi.

New Orleans

John Bachman was one of the finest city view artists to work in America during the nineteenth century. Prior to this view of New Orleans, he had published skillfully drawn and beautifully lithographed views of New York, Boston, and Philadelphia. Here he depicts New Orleans from a vantage point high above and opposite the Garden District. Note the fanlike system of streets that lead to the river as well as the cross streets that follow the bend of the river that was responsible for the name, the "Crescent City." The spire of the cathedral on Jackson Square is visible to the right of the view, marking the center of the French Quarter. The dark diagonal street just to the left is Canal Street. On the river Bachman drew steamboats, ferries, and sailing ships, including steamboats docked along the levee with their sterns angled upriver, something the river's current would never have allowed (giving credence to the idea that these features may have been added by a lithographer in the publishing office).

Title: Bird's-Eye View of New-Orleans
Date Issued: 1851
Cartographer: John Bachman
Published: Separately (New York)
Lithograph, 24.3 x 31.5 inches
New York Public Library, Stokes 1851-G-13

BIRDS' EYE VIEW OF

NEW-ORLEANS

PUBLISHED BY THE VOIGTS & GUERBER & CIE. BROADWAY N.W. YORK

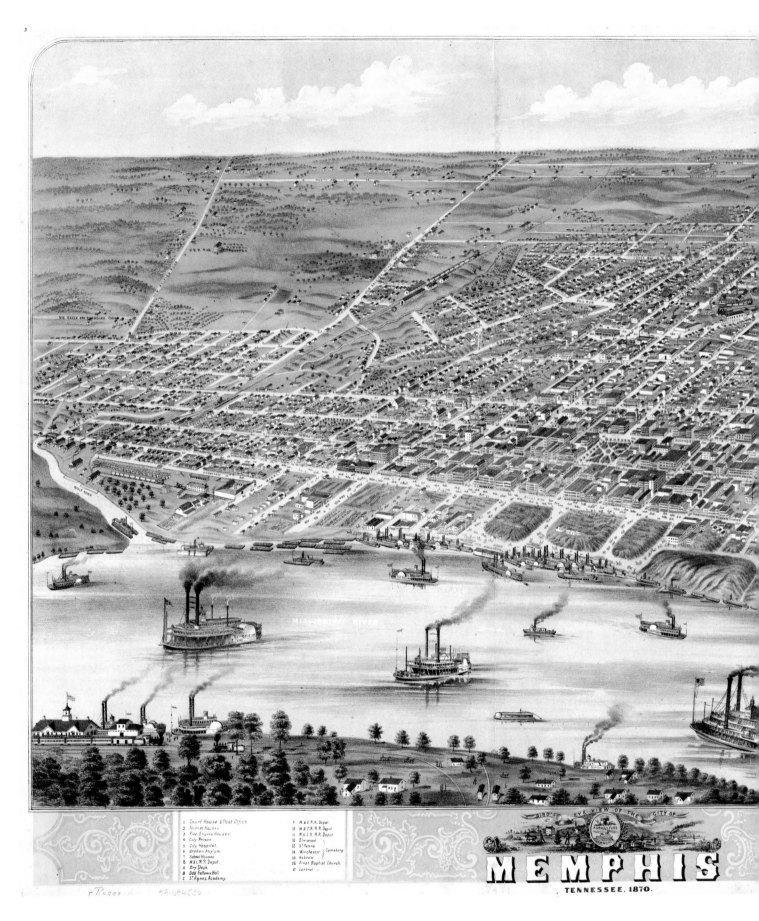

1	Court House & Post Office.	9	M. & C. R.R. Depot.	
2	Market Houses.	10	M. & T. R. R.R. Depot.	
3	Fire Engine Houses.	11	M. & L.R. R.R. Depot.	
4	City Prison.	12	Elmwood	
5	City Hospital.	13	S! Peters	Cemetery
6	Orphan Asylum.	14	Winchester	
7	School Houses.	15	Hebrew	
8	M.& L. R.R. Depot.	16	First Baptist Church.	
A	Dry Dock	D	Central	
B	Odd Fellows Hall			
C	S! Agnes Academy.			

BIRD'S EYE VIEW OF THE CITY OF

MEMPHIS

TENNESSEE, 1870.

Memphis

Albert Ruger was the most prolific viewmaker in the Mississippi Valley during the decade following the Civil War. Beginning in 1867, he worked for four years and produced eighteen city panoramas, principally of towns that did not have previously published views. In 1879 he created a second drawing of the rapidly growing city of Minneapolis. The only town south of Cairo that Ruger depicted was Memphis, which was undergoing a building boom at the time of his visit. Memphis had suffered no devastation during the war, and as a result, its cotton trade quickly rebounded. By 1870 no less than eleven steamboat lines and four railroads served the city. Ruger included two of the most famous steamboats on the Mississippi in this view, the *Natchez* (second from the right) and the *Robert E. Lee* (the larger of the two vessels on the left). Their race from New Orleans to St. Louis in July 1870 had caused great excitement along the lower river. Ruger took artistic license in depicting the two boats together, since the *Lee* had unloaded, refueled, and departed before the *Natchez* reached Memphis a little over an hour later.

Title: Bird's-Eye View of Memphis, Tennessee
Date Issued: 1870
Cartographer: Albert Ruger
Published: Separately
Lithograph, 22 x 34.3 inches
Library of Congress, Geography & Map Division,
G3964.M5A3 1870 .R8 Rug 178

Cairo

Cairo was founded in 1837 by the Cairo City and Canal Company, and was to serve as the southern terminus of the Illinois Central Railroad. Situated at the junction of the Ohio and Mississippi rivers, it was incorporated as a city in 1858. Cairo was an important steamboat port in the nineteenth century and even had its own customs house. The impressive lithographic portrayal of Cairo seen here was produced to help win the approval of London bankers to underwrite an issue of Cairo City bonds. The city would never resemble this "prospective view," which, as one English visitor in 1845 remarked, shows "domes, spires, and cupolas, hotels, warehouses, and lines of steamboats along both rivers. How fair—how magnificent it all looked on the India paper." Instead of finding this vision, this visitor found that "Cairo is a swamp, overflowed by every rise of either river. The large hotel, one of the two buildings erected, is slowly sinking from the surface. The heaps of railroad iron sent out from England for the great central road to Chicago, of which this was to be the depot, are many feet beneath the surface. . . . The business of the place, consisting of selling supplies to steamboats, and transferring passengers from the down to the upriver boats, is done on floating store boats, made fast to the shore."

Title: Prospective View of the City of Cairo at the Junction of the Ohio with the Mississippi River, Illinois

Date Issued: 1838

Cartographer: William Strickland

Published: Separately (Philadelphia)

Lithograph, 10.2 x 19.4 inches

Knox College Library, Preston Player Collection

Wᵐ Strickland, Archᵗ del.

PROS

P.S.Duval, Lithog? Phil?   Drawn on Stone by A.Hoffy.

IVE VIEW OF THE CITY OF CAIRO,

tion of the Ohio with the Mississippi River, *Illinois.*

St. Louis

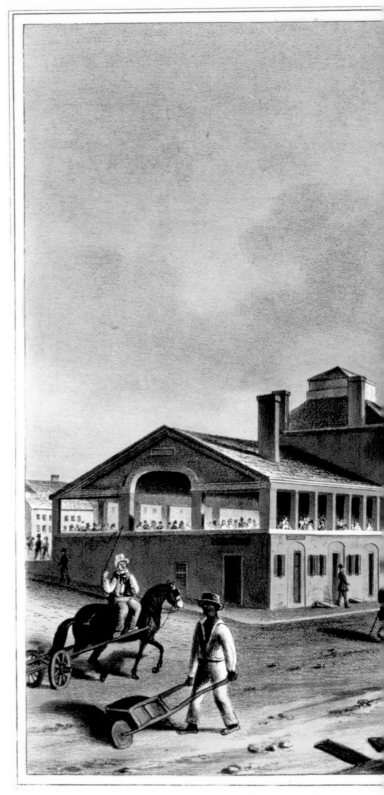

John Caspar Wild was a Swiss-born artist and lithographer who immigrated to the United States to seek his fortune creating urban and landscape views. He first worked in Philadelphia and Cincinnati before leaving for the West in 1838. By 1839 he was working in St. Louis, where he produced a superb set of eight views of the city, including the waterfront scene shown here. At the time of this drawing—the age of the steamboat—St. Louis was rapidly developing into a bustling center of river commerce. Here is the business hub of the city, Front Street along the Mississippi. Stores and places of business line one side of the street, the other side being open to the river. Docked along the levee are a line of steamboats as far as the eye can see.

Title: View of Front St. looking North from Walnut
Date Issued: 1840
Cartographer: John Caspar Wild
Published: Separately (St. Louis, Missouri)
Lithograph, 9.7 x 15 inches
Missouri Historical Society, J. C. Wild Prints Collection
St. Louis and Vicinity. 1840.

1. Court House.
2. County Jail.
3. Public School.
4. Hannibal Institute.
5. H. & St Jos. R.R. Depot.
6. H. & St Jos R.R. Machine Shops.
7. H. & Naples R.R. Depot.

8. Gas Works.
9. Rowe & Tull. Lumber Dealer.
10. John J. Cruikshank Jr Lumber Yard.
11. Dulany & McVeich Lumber Dealers.
12. Uriah Dorman. Lumber Yard.
13. Price & McKnight. Lumber Dealers.
14. W.J. Quialys Machine Works.
15. Eagle Mill.

16. Nagr
17. Four
18. Cong
19. Chri
20. Bapt
21. Epis
22. Luth
23. Metho

BIRD'S EYE VIEW OF THE CITY OF

HANNIBAL

MARION CO. MISSOURI
1869

Drawn by A. Ruger

Hannibal

One of the most attractive of Albert Ruger's river views is that of the town of Samuel Clemens' youth, Hannibal, Missouri. Clemens, the chronicler of life on the Mississippi, lived on Hill Street just two blocks from the river and the steamboat landing. Holiday's Hill, rising from the end of Main Street on the right, was memorialized as Cardiff Hill in *Tom Sawyer* and *Huckleberry Finn*. Near the center of the square is the school that both Clemens and the fictional Tom attended. The island at the left of the image may have been the setting for several of the adventures in these two books. Ruger's depiction of life along the river includes horse-drawn carriages awaiting passengers who have disembarked from the train at the waterside station of Hannibal and Naples Railroad on the east bank of the river; a steam ferry from Hannibal is also docked at the station. On the Hannibal side of the river is the station of the Hannibal and St. Joseph Railroad, one of several rail lines that would feed the Union Pacific-Central Pacific transcontinental route that was completed the year Ruger published this view.

Title: Bird's-Eye View of the City of Hannibal, Marion County, Missouri
Date Issued: 1869
Cartographer: Albert Ruger
Published: Separately
Lithograph, 20.2 x 25.7 inches
Library of Congress, Geography & Map Division, G4164.H2A3 1869 .R8 Rug 127

Muscatine

Alfred T. Andreas published atlases of Minnesota, Iowa, Indiana, and Dakota; he also published histories of Chicago, Milwaukee, northern Wisconsin, Nebraska, Kansas, and Cook County, Illinois. This view of Muscatine is from his Iowa state atlas. (Although it is unsigned, it may have been drawn by William Wallace Elliott.) The parallel horizontal lines in the water and the similar diagonal lines in the sky, the streets, and the buildings of the town reveal that it was produced using a mechanical ruling device. The bird's-eye perspective allows one to see into every block of the town, and the numbered legend below identifies eighteen of the public buildings, churches, and major industrial structures.

Title: Bird's-Eye View of Muscatine City, Muscatine County, Iowa
Date Issued: 1874
Cartographer: Anonymous
Published: *Atlas of the State of Iowa* (Chicago)
Lithograph, 9 x 12 inches
Muscatine Art Center

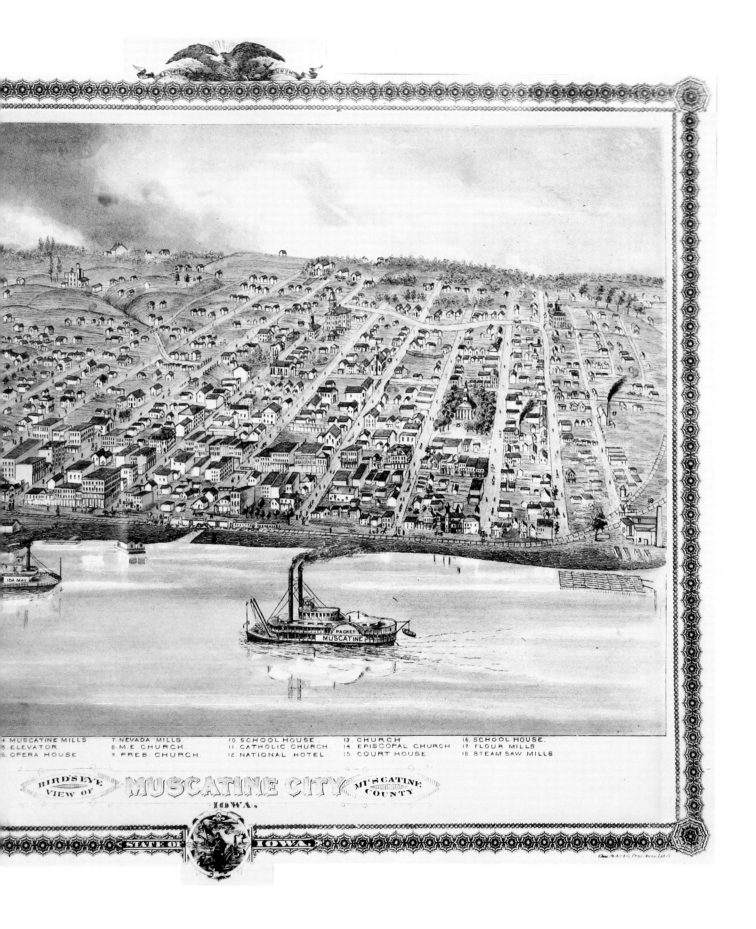

4. MUSCATINE MILLS	7. NEVADA MILLS	10. SCHOOL HOUSE.	13. CHURCH.	16. SCHOOL HOUSE.
5. ELEVATOR.	8. M.E. CHURCH.	11. CATHOLIC CHURCH.	14. EPISCOPAL CHURCH	17. FLOUR MILLS
6. OPERA HOUSE.	9. PRES. CHURCH.	12. NATIONAL HOTEL	15. COURT HOUSE	18. STEAM SAW MILLS

BIRD'S EYE VIEW OF MUSCATINE CITY MUSCATINE COUNTY IOWA.

STATE OF IOWA.

Dubuque

This view of Dubuque by John Caspar Wild was the first printed view of that town, and was one of the last works Wild produced before his death in 1846. It is a beautiful river view, but from the distant perspective it is hard to determine much about the town itself. It does, however, serve to illustrate these remarks by Mark Twain:

> It is strange how little has been written about the Upper Mississippi. The river below St. Louis has been described time and again, and it is the least interesting part. One can sit on the pilot-house for a few hours and watch the low shores, the ungainly trees and the democratic buzzards, and then one might as well go to bed. One has seen everything there is to see. Along the Upper Mississippi every hour brings something new. There are crowds of odd islands, bluffs, prairies, hills, woods, and village—everything one could desire to amuse the children. Few people ever think of going there, however. Dickens, Corbett, Mother Trollope, and the other discriminating English people who "wrote up" the country before 1842 had hardly an idea that such a stretch of river scenery existed. Their successors have followed in their footsteps, and as we form our opinions of our country from what other people say of us, of course we ignore the finest part of the Mississippi.

Certainly Wild and many other panoramic artists of the day shared Twain's sentiment.

Title: Dubuque, Iowa
Date Issued: 1844
Cartographer: John Caspar Wild
Published: Separately (Dubuque, Iowa)
Lithograph, 21.7 x 30.7 inches
Putnam Museum of History & Natural Science

DUBUQUE, IOWA.

Prairie du Chien

Henry Lewis was an English-born landscape artist who immigrated to the United States in 1819 as a ten-year-old boy. He moved to St. Louis in 1836, where he found work as a cabinetmaker, but by the mid-1840s he had gained some reputation as a landscape artist. About this time he conceived the idea of painting a one-thousand-foot-long panorama of the entire Mississippi River that would be moved through a huge frame while a speaker described to the audience what they were seeing. Such an idea was not unprecedented, as other moving panoramas of the river had been produced by John Banvard (1841), John Rowson Smith (1848), Samuel B. Stockwell (1848), and Leon Pomarede (1849). None of these exhibited both the upper and lower Mississippi, however, and Lewis deemed that such a project would not only enhance his reputation but would be quite profitable as well. In 1848 he began systematically sketching the river from Minnesota to St. Louis, and commissioned Charles Rogers to sketch the river below St. Louis.

Lewis also bought a number of sketches from the talented soldier-artist Seth Eastman, whom he acknowledged as the source for some of his views. Lewis toured the major cities of the United States and Canada with the painting and in 1851 began a tour of Europe. By 1853 Lewis had settled at Düsseldorf, where he decided to use his extensive collection of river sketches by himself, Eastman, and Rogers in an illustrated book about the Mississippi (*The Valley of the Mississippi Illustrated*), and which includes the view of Prairie du Chien seen here. Located on a beautiful prairie along the Mississippi near its confluence with the Wisconsin River, the city's name originated with early French explorers of the area, who met a group of Fox Indians there led by a chief that went by the name "The Dog." As a result, the explorers named the location "Prairie du Chien," or "Prairie of the Dog." Lewis depicts Fort Crawford, which was constructed in 1816, in the foreground; outside the fort, early nineteenth-century life was still dominated by the fur trade.

PRAIRIE DU CHIEN, WISCONSIN
in 1830

H. Lewis pinx.

Lith. Inst. Arnz & Cᵒ. Düsseldorf.

Title: Prairie du Chien in 1830
Date Issued: 1854–57
Cartographer: Henry Lewis
Published: *Das Illustrirte Mississippithal* (Düsseldorf, Germany)
Lithograph, 6.1 x 7.7 inches
New York Public Library, Stokes 1846-47-F75 and F-77

Title: View of St. Paul, Minnesota

Date Issued: 1874

Cartographer: George Ellsbury

Published: *Illustrated Historical Atlas of the State of Minnesota* (Chicago)

Lithograph, 16.1 x 31.5 inches

Library of Congress, Geography & Map Division, G4144.S4A35 1874 .E5

St. Paul

This stunning view of St. Paul was published both separately and in A. T. Andreas's *Illustrated Historical Atlas of the State of Minnesota*. It was drawn by George Ellsbury, who most likely also drew the only other lithographic city views found in the atlas—one that depicts Minneapolis and another of Winona. These two views were also published separately, but it is not known whether the separately issued versions or those in the atlas were the first to appear. It may be the case that the atlas versions had priority, since in August 1874 Ellsbury and his co-publisher, Vernon Green, were still trying to secure enough orders of the view of St. Paul to justify having it printed. A newspaper notice at the time notes that the view was to be "lithographed in six colors, making a very handsome picture, at the very low price of $1.50." Prominent in this view are the city's numerous churches, the U.S. Customs House, the new grain elevator along the river, and the Wabasha Street Bridge. The bridge was a wooden Howe truss, a state-of-the-art design that opened in 1859 and was officially named the Saint Paul Bridge. It connected St. Paul to the "west side," which actually was south of the city due to a bend in the river. This area was incorporated by St. Paul in 1874, for two reasons: "to aid law enforcement—criminals could escape St. Paul authorities by crossing to the West Side and Dakota County—and to eliminate the Wabasha Street Bridge tolls which were inhibiting development on the West Side." A bridge crossing was described by a writer in 1869: "We approach St. Paul from the south. . . . We ride over a long wooden bridge, one end of which rests on the low land by the railroad station, and the other on the high northern bluff, so that the structure is inclined at an angle of about twenty degrees, like the driveway to a New England barn where the floor is nearly up to the high beams."

Minneapolis

This panorama of Minneapolis appeared on a single-page "Report of the Leading Business Houses of Minneapolis, Minna.," published by Augustus Hageboeck in 1886. The image appeared at the center of the report and was bordered by no less than forty-five advertisements for local businesses. Hageboeck depicts the city from a perspective that looks directly upriver with the Tenth Avenue Bridge in the immediate foreground. A train is shown crossing the river on the Stone Arch Bridge that was built in 1882–83 by James J. Hill's Minneapolis Union Railway Company. It served as a railroad bridge until 1978, and is now a pedestrian and bike bridge on the St. Anthony Falls Heritage Trail. On the right side of the Mississippi is the former town of St. Anthony, which merged with Minneapolis in 1872. Flour mills line the banks of both sides of the river, and a great, albeit unidentifiable, turreted and domed structure—complete with what may be a bell tower or carillon—appears at the right of the picture. This view captures better than any other the reason for the founding of Minneapolis—the great resources of hydropower afforded by the only waterfall on the Mississippi River, St. Anthony Falls.

Title: View of Minneapolis, Minn.
Date Issued: 1886
Cartographer: Augustus Hageboeck
Published: Separately (Minneapolis, Minnesota)
Line engraving, 11.2 x 16.6 inches
Library of Congress Prints and Photographs Division, PGA - Hageboeck - View of Minneapolis … (B size)

Ent. according to act of Congress in the year 1886 by A. Hageboeck in the office of the Librarian of Congress at Washington, D.C.

EW OF MINNEAPOLIS, MINN.

ENGRAVED, PRINTED AND PUBLISHED BY A. HAGEBOECK, MINNEAPOLIS, MINN.

SELECTED BIBLIOGRAPHY

Barry, John M. *Rising Tide: The Great Mississippi Flood of 1927 and How It Changed America*. New York: Simon & Schuster, 1997.

Beckwith, H. W. *Documents, papers, materials and publications relating to the Northwest and the state of Illinois*. Springfield, Ill.: H. W. Rokker, 1903.

Bosse, David. "Dartmouth on the Mississippi: Speculators and Surveyors in British North America in the Eighteenth Century." *Imago Mundi 41* (1989): 9-18.

Bragg, Marion. *Historic Names and Places on the Lower Mississippi River*. Vicksburg: Mississippi River Commission, 1977.

Brower, J. W. *The Mississippi River and Its Source*. Minneapolis: Harrison & Smith, 1893.

Brown, Douglas S. "The Iberville Canal Project: Its Relation to Anglo-French Commercial Rivalry in the Mississippi Valley, 1763-1775." *The Mississippi Valley Historical Review 32* (1946): 491-516.

Buisseret, David. *Mapping of the French Empire in North America*. Chicago: Newberry Library Exhibition Catalog, 1991.

___. "Spanish and French Mapping of the Gulf." In *The Mapping of the American Southwest*, Dennis Reinhartz and Charles C. Colley, eds. College Station: Texas A&M University Press, 1987.

Burden, Philip D. *The Mapping of North America II*. Rickmansworth, Herts, England: Raleigh, 2007.

Carswell, John. *The South Sea Bubble*. London: Cresset Press, 1960.

Cohen, Paul. *Mapping the West*. New York: Rizzoli, 2002.

Colin G. Calloway. *The Scratch of a Pen: 1763 and the Transformation of North America*. Oxford: Oxford University Press, 2006.

Cowdrey, Albert. *A History of The New Orleans District, U.S. Army Corps of Engineers, and its Life Long Battle with the Lower Mississippi and other Rivers Wending their Way to the Sea*. New Orleans: U.S. Army Corps of Engineers, 1977.

W. P. Cuming, R. A. Skelton, and D. B. Quinn. *The Discovery of North America*. New York: American Heritage Press, 1971.

Delanglez, Jean. "The 1674 Account of the Discovery of the Mississippi." *Mid-America 26* (1944): 301-24.

___. "The discovery of the Mississippi." *Mid-America 27* (1945): 219–31; *Mid-America 28* (1946): 2–22.

___. *El Río del Espíritu Santo: An Essay on the Cartography of the Gulf Coast . . . During the Sixteenth and Seventeenth Centuries*. New York: United States Catholic Historical Society, 1945.

___. "Franquelin: Mapmaker." *Mid-America 25* (1943): 29-74.

___. "The Joliet Lost Map of the Mississippi." *Mid-America 28* (1946): 67-144.

___. "Marquette's Autograph Map of the Mississippi River." *Mid-America 27* (1945): 30-53.

___. "The Sources of the Delisle Map of America, 1703." *Mid-America 25* (1943): 275-98.

___. "The Voyages of Tonti in North America, 1678-1704." *Mid-America 26*, (1944): 255-97.

Eads, James Buchannan. *Review of Humphreys and Abbot Report*. Pamphlet. Washington, D. C.: 1878.

Ellet, Charles, Jr. *The Mississippi and Ohio rivers: containing plans for the protection of the delta from inundation; and investigations of the practicability and cost of improving the navigation of the Ohio and other rivers by means of reservoirs, with an appendix, on the bars at the mouths of the Mississippi*. Philadelphia: Lippincott, 1853.

Ehrenberg, Ralph E. "'Forming a General Geographical Idea of a County': Mapping Louisiana from 1803 to 1820." In *Charting Louisiana*, Lemmon *et al*.

Freeman, Douglas S. *R. E. Lee: A Biography*. New York: C. Scribner's Sons, 1934-35.

Galloway, Patricia K., ed. *La Salle and His Legacy: Frenchmen and Indians in the Lower Mississippi Valley*. Jackson, Miss.: University Press of Mississippi, 1982.

Giraud, Marcel. *A History of French Louisiana*. Volume One: The Reign of Louis XIV, 1698-1715, trans. Joseph C. Lambert. Baton Rouge: Louisiana State University Press, 1974.

___. *A History of French Louisiana*. Volume Two: Years of Transition, 1715-1717, trans. Brian Pearce. Baton Rouge: Louisiana State University Press, 1993.

___. *A History of French Louisiana*. Volume Five: The Company of the Indies, 1723-1731, trans. Brian Pearce. Baton Rouge: Louisiana State University Press, 1991.

Hoffman, Paul E. "Discovery and Early Cartography of the North Gulf Coast." In *Charting Louisiana*, Lemmon *et al*.

___. *History of Louisiana before 1815*. Baton Rouge: Louisiana State University Bookstore, 1996.

Humphreys, Andrew Atkinson and Henry Abbot. *Report upon the Physics and Hydraulics of the Mississippi River*. Philadelphia: Lippincott, 1862.

Hunter, Louis C. *Steamboats on the Western Rivers: An Economic and*

Technological History. Cambridge: Harvard University Press, 1949.

Jackson, Jack. *Flags along the Coast: Charting the Gulf of Mexico, 1519-1759: A Reappraisal*. Austin: Book Club of Texas, 1995.

___. "The Soupart Map if 1716 and its Influence on Gulf Cartography." *Mapline 80-81* (Winter 1996-97): 6-15.

Klein, Michael. *Louisiana: European Explorations and the Louisiana Purchase*. Washington, D.C.: Library of Congress, American Memory Website, 2007. http://memory.loc.gov/ammem/collections/maps/lapurchase/essay1.html.

Lemmon, Alfred E. "La Louisane / La Luisiana: A Bourbon Colony. In *Charting Louisiana*, Lemmon *et al*.

Lemmon, Alfred E., John T. Magill, and Jason R. Wiese, eds. *Charting Louisiana: Five Hundred Years of Maps*. New Orleans: The Historic New Orleans Collection, 2003.

Mairson, Alan. "The Great Flood of '93." *National Geographic Magazine 185, No. 1* (1994): 42-81.

Mathur, Anuradha and Dilip da Cunha. *Mississippi Floods: Designing a Shifting Landscape*. New Haven: Yale University Press, 1991.

Merritt, Raymond H. *The Corps, the Environment, and the Upper Mississippi River Basin*. Washington, D. C.: Historical Division Office of Administrative Services Office of the Chief of Engineers, 1981.

National Park Service. *Draft Heritage Study and Environmental Assessment – Lower Mississippi Delta Region*. Memphis: Lower Mississippi Delta Development Commission, 1998.

Pittman, Captain Phillip. *The Present State of the European Settlements on the Mississippi with a geographical description of that river*. London: J. Nourse, 1770.

Reps. John W. *Cities of the Mississippi*. Columbia: University of Missouri Press, 1994.

Paine, Albert Bigelow. *Mark Twain: A Biography: the personal and literary life of Samuel Langhorne Clemens*. New York: Harper, 1912.

Parkman, Francis. *The Discovery of the Great West*. Boston: Little & Brown, 1869.

Peterson, William J. *Steamboating on the Upper Mississippi*. Iowa City: State Historical Society of Iowa, 1968.

Reed, Susan Martha. "British Cartography of the Mississippi Valley in the Eighteenth Century." *The Mississippi Valley Historical Review* 2 (1915): 213-224.

Robinson, Michael C. *Lower Mississippi Valley History, Hydrology, Floods, and Flood Control*. Vicksburg: U. S. Army Corps of Engineers, 1995.

Saucier, Roger T. *Geomorphology and Quarternary Geologic History of the Lower Mississippi Valley. Volume I*. Vicksburg: U.S. Army Corps of Engineers, 1994.

Schoolcraft, Henry R. *Summary Narrative of an Exploratory Expedition to the Sources of the Mississippi River, in 1820*. Philadelphia: Lippincott, 1855.

Schubert, Frank N. *Vanguard of expansion: Army Engineers in the trans-Mississippi West, 1819-1879*. Washington, D.C.: U.S. Army Corps of Engineers, 1980.

Schwartz, Seymour I., and Ralph E. Ehrenberg. *The Mapping of America*. New York: Harry N. Abrams, 1980.

Severin, Timothy. *Explorers of the Mississippi*. London: Routledge & K. Paul, 1967.

Shea, John Gilmary. *Discovery and Exploration of the Mississippi Valley*. Clinton Hall, N.Y.: Redfield, 1852.

Richard W. Stephenson. *Civil War Maps: An Annotated List of Maps and Atlases in the Library of Congress*. Washington. D. C.: Library of Congress, 1989.

Thomas, Emory. *Robert E. Lee: A Biography*. New York: Norton, 1995.

Twain, Mark. Interview in *Chicago Tribune*, July 9, 1886.

Twain, Mark. *Life on the Mississippi*. New York: Harper, 1903.

Upper Mississippi River Conservation Committee. *A River that Works and a Working River*. Rock Island, Ill.: Upper Mississippi River Conservation Committee, 2000.

Weddle, Robert S., Mary Christine Morkovsky, and Patricia Galloway, eds. *La Salle, the Mississippi, and the Gulf: Three Primary Documents*. College Station: Texas A&M University Press, 1987.

Weddle, Robert S. *Spanish Sea: The Gulf of Mexico in North American Discovery, 1500-1685*. College Station: Texas A&M University Press, 1985.

Carl I. Wheat. *Mapping the Transmississippi West, 1540-1861*. San Francisco: The Institute of Historical Cartography, 1957-63.

Wood, Peter H. "La Salle: Discovery of a Lost Explorer." *American Historical Review* 89 (1984): 294-323.\

INDEX